* The *
Modern Jewish Girl's
Guide to Guilt

* *The* *

Modern Jewish Girl's

Guide to

GUILT

Edited by

Ruth Andrew Ellenson

DUTTON

DUTTON
Published by Penguin Group (USA) Inc.
375 Hudson Street, New York, New York 10014, U.S.A.
Penguin Group (Canada), 90 Eglinton Avenue East, Suite 700, Toronto, Ontario,
Canada M4P 2YE (a division of Pearson Penguin Canada Inc.); Penguin Books Ltd, 80 Strand,
London WC2R 0RL, England; Penguin Ireland, 25 St Stephen's Green, Dublin 2, Ireland
(a division of Penguin Books Ltd); Penguin Group (Australia), 250 Camberwell Road,
Camberwell, Victoria 3124, Australia (a division of Pearson Australia Group Pty Ltd); Penguin
Books India Pvt Ltd, 11 Community Centre, Panchsheel Park, New Delhi - 110 017, India;
Penguin Group (NZ), cnr Airborne and Rosedale Roads, Albany, Auckland 1310, New
Zealand (a division of Pearson New Zealand Ltd); Penguin Books (South Africa) (Pty) Ltd,
24 Sturdee Avenue, Rosebank, Johannesburg 2196, South Africa

Penguin Books Ltd, Registered Offices: 80 Strand, London WC2R 0RL, England

Published by Dutton, a member of Penguin Group (USA) Inc.

First printing, August 2005
10   9   8   7   6   5   4   3   2   1

REGISTERED TRADEMARK—MARCA REGISTRADA

Library of Congress Cataloging-in-Publication Data
The modern Jewish girl's guide to guilt / edited by Ruth Andrew Ellenson.
p.   cm.
ISBN 0-525-94884-8 (alk. paper)
1. Jewish women—United States—Anecdotes.   2. Jews—United States—Humor.
3. Guilt—Humor.   4. Jewish wit and humor.   I. Ellenson, Ruth Andrew.
HQ1172.M64   2005
305.48'696'0973—dc22   2005002538

Printed in the United States of America
Set in Adobe Garamond
Designed by Eve L. Kirch

Names and details have been changed throughout this work to protect the privacy of individuals.

For my wonderful grandmother, Lillian Douglas Andrew,
who is neither Jewish nor guilty, but was excited
to read this book anyway.

And in memory of my grandmother, Rosalind Stern Ellenson,
whose life was a shining example of *tikkun olam*.

Louis: Rabbi, I'm afraid of the crimes I may commit.

Rabbi Isidor Chemelwitz: Please mister. I'm a sick old rabbi facing a long drive home to the Bronx. You want to confess, better you should find a priest.

Louis: But I'm not a Catholic, I'm a Jew.

Rabbi Isidor Chemelwitz: Worse luck for you, *bubbalah*. Catholics believe in forgiveness. Jews believe in Guilt.

—Tony Kushner, *Angels in America*

Contents

II. Our *Bubbes*, Ourselves:
Trying to Please the Family

I told them that Tenzin is the Dalai Lama's name and that I couldn't think of anyone more inspiring to be named after. And then my step-mother said, "Isn't there anyone in the family you could name him af-ter?" And my father said, "Yeah Rebec, what about Samuel? David? Moishe?" I felt like Judas.

III. Babes in Goyland: Love, Sex, and Self-Image in an Unkosher World

"It's so typical," my friend said, sipping on her cappuccino, glaring at the newspaper. "Jewish women are such givers. They give and give and give. Even when there's no hope of receiving." "You know, I'm not sure the Starr report is a testament to the Jewish womans' generosity," I said, shuffling the Times to a different section.

In college, a boyfriend casually asked if I ever felt self-conscious about my nose. "What nose?" I wondered, before making a mad dash to the nearest mirror. . . . Then I thought again, and flushed with shame: It had probably been sitting on my face, like a bump on a kosher pickle, for years. How had it eluded all those hours of adolescent self-scrutiny?

I've laid down the law. I will date only Jewish men. I've laid down the law many, many times. . . . So then why is it so hard? One soft look from almond-shaped eyes, or a tender whisper in a Cuban accent, and bam! I'm an outlaw.

Faced with the prospect of the double threat of one gay daughter and another who only dated non-Jewish men, my mother became desperate. She told my younger sister Shana and me that she and Dad put a con-

Introduction

*

RUTH ANDREW ELLENSON

ETWEEN the ideal of who you should be, and the reality of who you are, lies guilt. And when you're Jewish, there's no shortage of people who are willing to point out just how guilty you should feel. Families, rabbis, and communities happily, but perhaps not so helpfully, are all too eager to bring it to your attention, or you can even agonize over it yourself. For me, it often takes the form of the following internal reprimand:

"Jews have barely managed to survive for thousands of years, and you, you little *pisher*, are going to make one bad decision and screw it up for everybody."

As soon as I hear that word, the guilt works its way down into my chest and hooks my heart. It happens every time I'm faced with a decision that questions my Jewish loyalties, or whenever I've flat-out failed to live up to the prodigious expectations of my people. Whether it was enjoying pepperoni pizza on Passover, failing to move to Israel despite summers spent at Zionist youth camp, or dating boys who provoked the following reaction from my father, a rabbi: "I know you're going to marry a non-Jew and I want you to know it breaks my heart," I have heard the siren's call of Jewish guilt throughout my life. I have tried rejecting the voice, laughing at it, and sometimes even accepting it with a heavy heart—but I always stop when I hear it speak.

The voice spoke up particularly loud and clear one day as I sat in the front pew of a church in Virginia, watching my grandmother sing in the choir about her Lord and Savior. She wasn't talking about Moses either.

While I am a rabbi's daughter, I am also the child of a convert. My mother had converted to Judaism upon marrying, and when my parents divorced, I was raised in an observant home with my father and step-mother, who is also a rabbi. Still, I grew up knowing that a church dating back to the Civil War was just as much a part of my history as a *shtetl* in Russia.

So there I sat, a rabbi's daughter in the church of her forefathers, bathed in the ruby light of stained-glass windows depicting Jesus. And paralyzed by guilt. What in the name of Maimonides was I doing here? Not only was I violating some Talmudic edict about not being in a foreign house of worship (see, all that expensive Jewish education paid off after all), I was sure my Jewishness was obvious (okay, maybe not horns-on-my-head obvious, but still—obvious) to all the good Christians around me. I desperately wanted to leave. Then my grandmother caught my eye and smiled, clearly delighted by my presence. Was it worse to betray my Judaism by sitting in front of a giant cross, or to disrespect my beloved grandmother by bolting? Oy.

While the choir continued I closed my eyes and began to sing "Hear O Israel" under my breath and wondered: If my Jewish friends could see me now, what would they think? Would they understand that I was trying to bridge a gap for which I had no clear road map, or would it simply confirm for them that I was someone in need of lots of therapy, pronto?

Returning home after the visit with Grandma I felt as if I'd been in a boxing match with my Judaism that left a black-and-blue psyche on the mat. Think you're entitled to life, liberty, and the pursuit of happiness? Silly American! A constant sense of obligation and connection to family, community, and Torah is for Jews.

Talking to other Jewish women at home, I found that many of them had the same emotional experience, even if it was under very different circumstances. Some found all the pressure unbearable and simply re-belled. One woman I know secretly fantasized about marrying a Muslim just so her parents would shut up about her being single, while another spent the month of December seeking out Christian friends whose trees she could decorate, pleading her case as a victim of Madison Avenue and Hallmark commercials about keepsake ornaments. Another friend publicly flared up in anger when her non-Jewish spouse was spurned by her family, and she herself was treated as a traitor to the tribe, but alone at night she secretly worried that her parents might be right. One woman who lived a more religiously observant life struggled to reconcile feminism and Orthodoxy, while another tried to figure out how to be a Jewish mother without becoming *her* Jewish mother. A historian who had just completed her PhD was shocked to find that her parents still wondered when she'd finally grow up and start having kids. When would her accomplishments ever be enough?

For Jewish women today there is a fundamental struggle: Where do we end and where do our people begin? Even more confusing, when our needs are pitted against those of the community, who's right? Sure, Jewish guilt is a stereotype, but when it's raining down on your *keppe* that doesn't make it any less powerful. To be Jewish is to be part of a community, and to live within that community is to be both embraced and judged by it. We are loved because we belong, but when we break away we are met with cries condemning our selfishness. Don't we know what's good for the Jews (or that Aunt Esther waited all night for us to call)? And so the guilt begins.

In my early twenties, when I was still dating the aforementioned *shaygetz* who provoked the impassioned remarks from my father, my parents mentioned in a deceptively casual tone that Rachel Moscowitz from my Hebrew school class had married her boyfriend from Camp Shalom, had just given her parents their first grandchild, and was now working as a secretary at the same Hebrew school we'd attended. (Oh, and did I know she lived a mile away from her parents?) In my more articulate—and adolescent—moments my response to this pressure was the always-eloquent "bite me." How could I ever be true to myself and sufficiently Jewish for them: bring a Beastie Boy home to Seder so I could be hip and please my parents at the same time?

As much as I'd like to blame others for my modern martyrdom, I've often heard the voice of Jewish guilt all on my own. Reading articles warning that Jews would intermarry themselves out of existence, listening to sermons about how Holocaust deniers would rewrite the history books, and worrying about Israel's situation, I couldn't help but feel a nagging guilt that our people's future was all up to me; and I had better not screw up. When I unsuccessfully defended Israel at a dinner party of Europeans, or skipped second day Rosh Hashanah services in favor of a movie, I outwardly laughed but inwardly cringed. Was I contributing to the erosion of my culture? Let's face it: I was—and I wasn't alone.

Opportunities for Jewish women to feel guilty today are compounded, ironically, because we now have choices our *bubbes* never dreamed of. According to family legend, my *bubbe* used to come dangerously close to falling out of the women's balcony at shul in her longing to be part of the men's service below. I, on the other hand, am free to lead an entire Torah service if I choose to, but shamefully I'd probably rather fall off a balcony.

Today, thanks to the enormous strides of feminism and liberal thought, for many Jewish women (though certainly not all) the world is our non-kosher oyster. We can become rabbis or have no more connection to Judaism than a passing thought on Yom Kippur that maybe we should skip lunch. We can go study Talmud at a yeshiva in Jerusalem or walk around wearing a T-shirt that says YO SEMITE without fear of being hauled off by either a *beit din* or a roving white supremacist.

Although the opportunities for Jewish women to express ourselves have increased exponentially, so have the ways to feel guilty. Our *bubbes* may have worried that as immigrants to the new country they were "too Jewish" to fit in. Now, over one hundred years later, we worry if we're Jewish *enough*.

If the guilt of our parents was the guilt of Philip Roth's *Portnoy's Complaint*, brought on by a desperate need to fit in with a society that wouldn't really accept Jews, then the women I know are Portnoy's daughters—struggling with the guilt that springs from finally being accepted. Much like Irish, Polish, and other turn-of-the-century immigrants to America who were once marginalized, most of us are simply white folks now. But is this a good thing? Just how assimilated do we really want to be?

Has Judaism survived pogroms, the Holocaust, and countless other calamities only to be lost as we give in to temptation and eat a bacon cheeseburger or substitute *davening* with sessions on a shrink's couch? Are we really free to live and love as we see fit? After all, I find myself asking like the Wicked Child in the Haggadah, am I not an individual? Why should the future of Judaism rest entirely on my shoulders? Just because I might stray, doesn't mean Judaism will cease to exist outside a few fanatical sects in Brooklyn and Jerusalem. Or does it? How much do we owe to our heritage, and how much should we follow our hearts?

It would be easier to rebel against the constant sense of obligation if there weren't so much to love about being Jewish. It is an unparalleled source of warmth, comfort, intellectual richness, and spiritual meaning for me as I navigate the world. As a kid I found myself bizarrely eager to share with my friends that I called my father *"Abba,"* not out of homage to a Swedish pop group, but because it meant "father" in Hebrew. I felt profound love sitting around tables on holidays and sharing meals with people who were engaged morally and intellectually with the world, comfort in knowing that most Jews would get my jokes, and a real fascination with the amazing course of Jewish history and the stories of the Torah and Talmud. When I visited Israel, the strange thrill I felt when I saw graffiti in Hebrew in the alleyways of Jerusalem was equally powerful as the sense of awe I felt when I recited prayers that Jews had chanted for thousands of years. When you are part of a line of Jewish women stretching back to Sarah, laughing at an angel who told her she would bear Abraham's child in her old age, it can be pretty tough to tell the whole deal, *"kish mir in tuchis."*

Many of my peers seemed to have two responses to this dilemma: sanctimonious observance (the kids who paid attention in Hebrew school), or total obliviousness (the kids who beat up the kids who paid attention in Hebrew school). I wasn't comfortable with either response. I knew Judaism was not the only attribute that defined me, but I was certain that it formed the core of my self. Besides, since when is religion about personal fulfillment on your terms? This was God we were talking about, not therapy. It wasn't supposed to be easy. It was supposed to be biblical. And so as I searched for a way out of my guilty haze I found myself again and again in the strangest position for any Jew: outside of a community and alone.

As I offered my thoughts on Jewish guilt to women I knew—from those who were raised in the Hasidic world, to women whose only connection to Judaism was having one Jewish parent who couldn't care less about it—the answers I got were fascinating. Every time the topic came up my fellow Jewesses would be bursting with stories of their own—full of pent-up feelings and strangely hilarious tales about how their individual freedom and sense of duty had duked it out. The answers made me laugh, surprised me, and made me think.

At last, a community of Jews I felt I truly belonged to. And so this book was born.

This anthology is not called *The Modern Jewish Girl's Guide to Being Good and Nice* for a reason. Some of the voices you will find here are funny, some are angry, and some are perplexed. This book examines what is complicated about being Jewish and female today. It is focused on Jewish women, because, let's face it: Jewish male angst is such a cultural commodity that it is practically an industry unto itself, from sitcoms to novels, and it often features Jewish women as the butt of the joke. Stereotypes of Jewish mothers with magical guilt-inducing powers, nagging wives, and vapid Jewish American Princesses armed with Daddy's credit card abound, but those hackneyed images do not reflect the Jewish women I know nor the guilt they experience.

The stakes are also higher for women. Judaism is matrilineal (despite its deeply patriarchal theology) and Jewish women are the ones who give life to the next generation of Jews. More often than not we are the ones who maintain the connection to community and family. Even if we choose to reject every societal expectation Judaism foists upon us, women still feel guilty that our choices affect not only us, but future generations of the tribe.

In this collection of essays you will witness one woman's guilt over getting a pedicure on Yom Kippur, follow another as she worries about worrying enough, and find out what happens when a Jewish girl marries a German boy. As different as the essays are, they're all ultimately about women who, like me, and perhaps you, are trying to find a balance between our heritage and our modern life. These forces are both essential parts of our selves, but like Israelis and Palestinians, they can't always coexist peacefully.

The book begins with "*Chai* Anxiety," a guide to worrying in the twenty-first century. (Because really, we need more help with that, don't we?) The next section, "Our *Bubbes*, Ourselves," addresses the most guilt-inducing relationship of all: the *mishpocha*, the family. "Babes in Goy-land," the third section of the book, deals with sex and self-image and the gap between living in the modern world and living up to the expectations of being a nice Jewish girl. And as you'll see in "Guiltily Ever After," once you get married it doesn't get any easier (even though you finally own that lovely KitchenAid mixer). The collection ends with "Feeling *Treyfy*"—an exploration of what happens when we break down and actually bite into the forbidden fruit, and find that maybe, *oy vey,* we like it. After all, what's guilt without guilty pleasure? And what's the fun of guilt without a little public kvetching?

As I sat in church that day watching my grandmother, I wish I'd known I wasn't the first—or the last—Jewish woman to feel that my loyalties were as divided as Solomon's baby. In fact, I'm surrounded by women who are struggling to define themselves and be true to Judaism at the same time.

I hope that in these pages you'll find a voice that resonates with you, and offers a new perspective on whatever guilt you face. Guilt can make you laugh at its absurdity, break your heart, or in choosing which guilt you accept or reject, help you come to a clearer understanding of who you are. My hope is that the essays in this book will do all three.

Chai Anxiety:
What, Me Worry?

House of Love and Bragging

*

AIMEE BENDER

HERE is the scene. Something good just happened. I am happy about it. Maybe it was a good writing day, or I am in a good relationship, or I have helped someone, or I feel a sense of self in a true, deep way. I am walking to the market, to buy myself a peach and fizzy water. It's a beautiful blue day. Or, it's not, but my mood is so high that it doesn't matter. I myself am a beautiful blue day.

Little do I know that the piano shipment in the freight airplane high above me has had a mishap. The baby grand piano, which was right at the bottom of the aircraft, has come loose. Someone didn't lock that airplane door, at the bottom. He was drunk. He was in a bad mood. The piano wasn't tied properly. It has been hanging there, by three legs—by two legs—by one leg—and now it has tumbled out of the airplane. I am still walking to the store. Whistle, whistle. I do a little skip.

Miles above me, whirring through the air, is this giant black piano, gaining speed as it goes. Free-falling. I am thinking about the good thing that has happened today, thinking about it. How nice I feel. How glad I am today. You'd think I would look up at the whirring sound, and maybe the cars honk at me to look up, but I am oblivious, content, and proud. I step right into the path, and the piano flattens me into a pancake.

Better keep my eyes up. Better be vigilant, particularly on those good days. Any good day not marked by worry and vigilance will be met with tragedy. It exhausts me even to write it.

Secular me? Ha.

WHEN I unpack this worry of mine, a few layers emerge. First up, of course, is the guilt. I feel guilty for having a good day, so I should be punished. But what this image also assumes is that someone—someone powerful—is watching. Not only is someone watching, but he/she really, really cares about my good day, my small little good day, and this someone finds my small good day so threatening that he/she will engineer a piano drop to destroy it, flattening my hubris, creating an easy narrative of punishment that will be a warning to all others who hear about it on the nightly news, alerting them that their good day, too, should be paired with caution and much craning of the neck.

If I were better at physics, I could probably create an equation for this: It is not so much the piano falling; it is the constant potential that the piano will fall. It is an imagined piano, endlessly falling, waiting to take shape the minute I stop looking for it. As soon as I relax, it will form out of the air molecules. I am guilty of the happiness that comes from feeling good, from not craning my neck. That loose space, the space unwatched, the life lived.

I am not, in general, so God-fearing. I consider myself a highly assimilated Jew. At Jewish summer camp, in the big Shabbat sing-along, we all joyfully screamed, "Nutter Butter Peanut Butter" in between verses of Debbie Friedman's "Not by Might, Not by Power." My parents are assimilated, too. My mother freely confesses to eyeing the crosses around her classmates' necks as a girl, and wanting one for herself. Every year, my parents host a Seder, and everyone enjoys it, but it lasts ten minutes. Maybe twenty, including opening the door for Elijah and a plucky round of *Dayenu*.

And I am fine with this version of Judaism, with a pick-and-choose method of incorporating the religion into my daily life. It's a giant buffet here in America; in my yoga class, the guy in front of me has the Shema tattooed all over his back, so I sing "Hear O Israel" to myself while stepping into Warrior One. It's kind of nice.

But all that said, sometimes my unconscious seems much more religious and superstitious than my day-to-day self. I don't believe in a figure who is out there watching us; I don't think that the Nazis are going to return and take over Los Angeles. But I am still haunted by this fear of punishment when things are going well.

Now. Is this kind of guilt Jewish? Is it a Jewish trait? Even for the highly assimilated Jew? It's certainly a universal trait, because I know many people of varying belief systems and genetic backgrounds who have this similar fear, of getting run over by a bus on the day they plan that trip to Brazil. It's certainly all over movies and TV, because it makes for such simple dramatic irony—how many TV dramas have you seen where the lovers have a tender kiss on a bridge and you can practically hear the shattering glass and bent chrome of the upcoming car crash?

But I am certain, too, about the prevalence of this guilt among us Jews. There's even a phrase for it: *Kenna hora*—or *kein ayin hora*—which translates as "may the evil eye stay away." In Jewish superstition, to keep away this evil eye, you're supposed to spit three times when somebody compliments your baby. Aren't babies meant to be complimented? What's so harmful about a good thing? But then again, when you look to history, why not? When century after century, people strive to murder you to get you out of the way; it creates a strange, unsettled feeling of power. Terror, helplessness, rage, and also power. Because whew, we must be really threatening to have around if everyone wants to kill us. If they feel they *must* kill us in order to restore a sense of authority to their culture.

Anti-Semites have tended to view Jews as two ends of the spectrum: subhuman, and a giant threat. This dichotomy is one that Jews have experienced over dozens of centuries, in dozens of countries, and it's confusing. Are we that bad? Are we that amazing? What are we? I mean, of course, ideally, we understand that it's all an invention, but we have suffered the unbelievable consequences of these delusions, and so, even against our will, even generations later, it is hard not to soak up the message. We suck, we rule. We are worthless, we are superior.

It can be a bit of a mind switch to think that various persecuted groups—women, gays, blacks, Jews, Palestinians, minorities of all kinds—who have been victimized and made helpless at the hands of aggressors, are suffering, largely, for the *power*—real or imagined—that they hold over the persecutor.

But see, even as I write that, I feel a flicker of pride! Really! We Jews are threatening, I think. We really scared those Nazi bastards! But the feeling of power is an illusion, too. Perhaps one of the grandest challenges in being a part of any group like this, aside from processing the greatness of the pain, is also understanding that we are just regular. Regular people, regular desires. Regular. Even Jews! Even us!

It seems unbearably sad that we don't get to be superpowerful-fantastic, as our one compensation for all the horrors that have occurred. But grandiosity—that mutation of guilt—comes at a cost. Once the violence has cleared, and the generations are in a safer place, it means you can't enjoy the good days, because your eyes are always glued to the sky, waiting for that piano to fall on your head, because somebody is that invested in your downfall.

M y Jewish guilt is inevitably paired with surviving. There has been a lot to survive, and by the luck of the draw, some of us are plugging along, writing essays for anthologies because our grandparents happened to escape the pogroms and catch a boat to America in 1904. I am lucky, about those grandparents. I have known that since I was small.

But it doesn't do anyone any good to feel guilty all the time. In fact, it's annoying. It's self-absorbed. So several years ago, in an attempt to get over myself, I sat down on the floor, pulled out paper and a thick black marker, and made a sign for my apartment. I wrote one word on each piece of printer paper, until it said HOUSE OF LOVE AND BRAGGING in thick blocky letters. Then I took some tape and put the papers above the living-room window. As soon as you walked in the door, boom. It was impossible to miss.

I decided to put my sign up because I'd found out, after the fact—months after the fact!—that one friend had gotten a poem published, that another had met a great guy, that good things were happening, and they were happening underground. I wanted to be told. Friends knew their bad news would be welcomed and comforted, but why weren't they telling me when things were moving forward? Wasn't there space for that, too? Were they also scared of the falling piano? Certainly sharing *another* person's good news was encouraged, and Jews are no strangers to bragging about kin. There's a word for that, too: taking pride in others, *nachas*.

But what about sharing when good things happen to yourself? I knew that at times I kept good news private, because I honestly thought I should protect my friends, in case they couldn't handle hearing it and somehow would drop a piano on my head. Which is really condescending and annoying. When I put the sign up, it was because, for me, bragging would be a modest change. Not bragging was the most immodest of all.

The result was wonderful. People began calling with their good news. My answering machine revealed secrets untold: an art piece completed, a good moment in graduate school, a fun date, a sense of purpose. One friend shared an utter interior confidence that he couldn't reveal in groups: "I am going to be okay," he whispered, "I can feel it." I felt buoyed by their vulnerability, in sharing something they were proud of. No evil eye descended upon us. Everyone could handle it just fine.

I, in turn, told more people when things were going well in my own life, which had the unexpected result of a greater closeness.

ONE afternoon, I was having a conversation with my friend Miranda, who has a gift for stating things clearly. Under the mandate of the House of Love and Bragging, I was telling her about an upcoming trip to Italy for a reading, after my second book came out. She was excited to hear about the trip. I was excited, too, but also very anxious.

"I'm so scared the plane will crash!" I confessed to her on the phone. "Because I have a book out!"

"Well," she said, slowly, "you know, the plane might crash. But it won't be because you have a book out."

Okay then. Okay. Cut me down to size. It was the most relaxing thing she could've told me.

Letting go of grandiosity seems to mean that a person can really push herself, really do all she can, because the grandiose part has shrunken to regular size. So much of psychology deals in paradoxes. Only in letting go of my larger-than-life fear—that someone's-going-to-drop-a-piano-on-my-head self-importance—would I be able to make my actual self larger, in the actual world.

Only one friend, a Protestant Midwesterner (a double whammy of modesty), took offense at my word choice when he saw the sign on the wall. "Does it have to be '*bragging*'?" he asked. "Others won't understand, unless they know you. They'll think it's really obnoxious."

But you can't call it "House of Love and Support." That's just boring-sounding.

M Y mother eyed those crosses around her classmates' necks, but she never wanted to wear a Star of David. Perhaps it felt too vulnerable to her, to announce her Jewishness so loudly. Perhaps a cross felt, in a way, like a place to hide, a protection against a piano drop, whereas a Star of David would be an exposing indication of pride in her identity. She did not feel connected to her synagogue growing up, but, with hope, sent me and my sisters to Sunday School anyway.

I remember one instance in particular, where my mother seemed unusually compelled by the temple. It was my Confirmation, at Leo Baeck Temple in Los Angeles. For the big day, the rabbis let me and my classmates write a play. *The Breakfast Club* was a big hit movie then, and we each took on a different character archetype and gave speeches at the podium. I played the Molly Ringwald figure, and went on and on about how my dad said I could have a BMW if I got confirmed.

Even more scandalous was Joey Wagner, who, when channeling the Judd Nelson character, shook his fist in the air and did a monologue about how he wanted to grab the Torah off the bimah and roll it down the aisle to see how far it would go. Blasphemous! We were all so gleeful about our rebellion, our teenage Jewish edginess.

The rabbis could've reined us in, but they didn't. We did the play. People laughed. Afterward, two of the girls in my class strolled up to me, angry that I'd made fun of them. They were the popular, bitchy Hebrew School girls. "What do you mean?" I asked. I'd never spoken to them before. "It was a private deal, between me and my Dad," said one, jingling her new car keychain.

Later that evening, walking to the car, my mother kept shaking her head. "I can't believe they let you put on that play," she said. She paused at the car door. "They never told you to tone it down?"

"No," I said. "Can you believe anyone would buy their fifteen-year-old daughter a BMW?" She fingered her necklace, a plain gold chain. "I give the rabbis a lot of credit for that," she said, as we settled into the car. "You were not reverent to the temple."

I think of that play now with gratitude. We weren't reverent, no. What the rabbis did is they let us push against the religion. They were not worried. They let us be regular-size teenagers, and they knew that Judaism could handle our mini-rebellions, no problem. They were not so grandiose that we could not mock them. I wish I could've absorbed that lesson more at the time: Allowing people to have questions and desires, even pride, doesn't mean the structure will fall apart.

In this way, I think they took away some of the guilt and fear. "You're not such a big deal," was the message. The authority figures can handle it. Think away. Have your good day. Have your bad day. Have your questions. Think and question. Stay engaged. Don't get all caught up in the worries. Don't worry about that piano dropping. Do things in the world, people. Go do things you can brag about.

Tell Me About Your Mother

*

MOLLY JONG-FAST

I am sexually repressed. Or at least that's true according to every shrink I've had, which at the ripe old age of twenty-six is ten. According to them, as the daughter of the woman who coined the term "zipless fuck," I had no other choice. Let's face it: I am every therapist's wet dream. My mother wrote a book called *Fear of Flying*, and I in fact have a fear of flying. You don't need to be Freud to have a field day with my psyche.

Where to start when it comes to my relationship with the practitioners of the talking cure? I guess I should give you a little family history. We are Jews. We suffer from the two great inheritances of the Jewish people: irritable bowel syndrome and guilt. Irritable bowel syndrome can be solved by frequent trips to the gastroenterologist. But guilt—well, that's a little more complicated.

Every single one of my grandparents was born into backbreaking poverty, and every single one of them was a first-generation American. My family went from poor and crazy, like Dostoevsky's Raskolnikov, to rich and crazy, like Howard Hughes. And with money comes certain inalienable rights—the ability to employ many lawyers and accountants, knowledge of the geography of the first floor of Bergdorf's, and most importantly, a permanent position on the shrink's couch.

Not all of my grandparents' psychoanalyses stemmed from narcissism. My mother's mother legitimately needed a shrink, or at least some Prozac. Grandma Eda spent her life painting flowers on all the toilet seats, pulling her clothing off on the crosstown bus, and screaming at her children. She was always telling this endless (and to her 1930s mentality, titillating) story about how after meeting my grandfather Seymour in the Catskills and drinking out of a flask, my grandpa had asked her to paint his drum. What this meant to the bohemians of the 1930s is lost to me, but I suspect it meant they had sex before they were married.

When I knew her, grandma had stopped taking off her clothes on the crosstown bus and had evolved into a crazy alcoholic, obsessed with painting demonic portraits of her grandchildren. There is a particularly fetching one of me with hoofed feet and hair made of snakes that hung in her hallway for years. My father didn't mind, because he grew up with artistic parents on Fifth Avenue, back when Fifth Avenue was filled with rich old people pretending not to be Jewish (oh wait, it still is).

Affluence covered my family like a blanket of carbon monoxide. Money made people like my grandparents, who were already plagued by garden-variety Jewish guilt, even more guilty, because now they really had something to feel bad about. They were rich, and they weren't sure if they deserved the comfort of maids and luxury apartments when their ancestors had barely survived pogroms. Everyone went into therapy—even my grandpa Seymour, who did his time with the Mick Jagger of the psychological world, Alfred Adler.

My mother not only went into therapy, she lived it. Her second husband was a psychiatrist and her first husband was actually crazy (she chronicled this craziness in her book, the aforementioned *Fear of Flying*, which was a cornerstone of the sexual revolution). My dad was husband number three (she's currently on number four). When I was growing up my mom went to a meshugenah shrink who was both very fat and very famous. She wore paisley muumuus. She treated lots of famous people. Sometimes she would tell us stories about these famous people. Sometimes she'd share their phobias and their foibles. Never a model of discretion, this shrink would always meet a patient's story with a story of her own. "It's very interesting you wanted to sleep with your mother's cocker spaniel," she would reply, "because [insert name of famous actor here] actually did!"

This shrink was married to an ex-cop and together they ran the therapy group that was the inspiration for the therapy group in the book *Heart-*

burn. The two shrinks lived in a huge penthouse apartment surrounded by foliage-covered terraces. Sometimes the ex-cop would fall asleep during the group sessions. On the days when I came with my mother to individual therapy, the fat shrink would give me candy or hideous rhinestone-encrusted pins shaped like flags. I loved that candy. I still love candy. I never liked those pins.

Dad also put in his time with the fickle mistress. In fact, Dad went back to school and became a professor of social work. My father's sister also became an analyst, and then married an analyst. In my family, if you are not in the helping profession, you are in the opposite profession—writing.

For my whole life I knew (as did the ten million readers of *Fear of Flying*, which seemed to include every therapist I was sent to) that my family was crazy. So it shouldn't come as any surprise that at the ripe old age of four I went to see my first shrink. I balanced out the backbreaking work of kindergarten with hours on the shrink's high chair.

When I got into first grade (at the glitzy Dalton School on East Ninety-First Street) I had a huge realization: I wasn't crazy because I'd been in therapy for three years at the age of seven. I was just like everyone else. Everyone at Dalton had a shrink. Of course they were all high-class *yekkes*, German Jews, the opposite of my family's low-class *ostjuden*, Polish Jews (or, as we were called on the Upper East Side, herring merchants).

Did I mention that I was a fat kid? Well, that was another reason, according to Upper East Side logic, that I clearly needed treatment for a psychological disorder. I was a very fat kid by Manhattan standards, while I would probably just have been considered a healthy eater in the Midwest. According to the shrinks, my fatness wasn't the result of me sitting around watching hundreds of hours of TV and eating junk food, but an intense psychological and moral failing. In Manhattan, there is no sin, no crime, that inspires more guilt than being fat.

While I am no shrink myself, I have to wonder whether there was also some connection between the many extra pounds I carried and the many shrinks I saw. You see, I began to rank the shrinks by whether or not they would give me candy. Those who did were my favorites and I would happily go see them again. Those who didn't were out. I was a brutal negotiator: Give me candy or I'm going home to watch *Diff'rent Strokes.*

Perhaps my parents hoped that therapy would do more than cure me of fatness. Perhaps it was an optimistic preemptive strike against the fact that they divorced when I was four. Therapy did help me, but perhaps not in the way it was expected to: The more time I spent lying to the funky adults who billed by the hundreds, the more I realized I wasn't crazy at all.

As they assaulted my eight-year-old mind with theories of sexual repression, I felt no guilt over humoring them, over telling them what they wanted to hear. After all, what did they expect when they asked me that fateful question? Was I sexually repressed? I don't think I even knew what the word repressed meant. But I didn't want to hurt their feelings, so I would nod and say, "Yes! Yes I am! May I please have some candy now?"

Not all my shrinks were bad (or good), but some did have more impact than others. Earnest Doctor A made me play stupid therapy games and did not give me candy. I was seven. She had stringy brown hair and gesticulated like a Chihuahua on crack. I hated her. Lying to Doctor A was the only way I could deal with her. As I got older I got better at lying to shrinks. I learned and used words with them like "transference," "countertransference," "repression," and "vagina dentate," even if I didn't always know what they meant.

Sometimes Doctor A would do art therapy. Sometime she'd make me talk. Doctor A and I would argue. Doctor A's office was dark and filled with dusty brown furniture. She'd sit in a huge armchair, which even at age seven I knew was a Bloomingdale's knockoff of a fancy mid-century modern armchair. Sometimes she'd arrange her hair and ask me if I felt "repressed" because my mother "wrote dirty books." I would say yes, because I sensed that was what she wanted to hear.

By far the worst thing about therapy with Doctor A was that she truly believed she was helping people. Here's a tip, Dr. A: Treating rich kids on the Upper East Side for three hundred bucks an hour isn't altruism— it's a lot of things, but a selfless good deed it is not. Sometimes when she wasn't looking I'd try to change the time on Doctor A's enormous eighties-style digital clock so that I could leave. The only advantage I can see in hindsight is that with her, the forty-minute hour really felt like an hour.

Doctor R was next. She gave me candy. Doctor R was a social worker with a long Greek name and an apartment on Central Park West. She'd come via a recommendation from a truly sadistic middle school teacher who also had a long Greek name. I thought Doctor R was truly stupid. Sometimes she would listen to her answering machine and open her mail during our sessions; those were the times I liked her best. Sometimes Doctor R would give me orange juice and spice drops. Doctor R had short blonde hair and very little body fat. Like Doctor A, she sat in a Bloomingdale's knockoff of an expensive mid-century modern armchair.

Sometimes she would stare at me and ask things like, "Do you feel repressed because your mother writes dirty books?" I was eleven. By now I was a pro. I would say, "Yes, yes, yes! I do feel repressed! No one's ever asked me that. It shows what a good therapist you are, that you're able to put together two complex ideas like that. How did you figure that out?"

Doctor L did not give me candy but did seem to have some clue as to what he was doing, which made him totally stand apart from Doctor R and Doctor A. Doctor L had a fancy office between Madison and Fifth Avenues. Doctor L looked like an owl, and this was wildly amusing to me because his initials spelled O.W.L., too. Once he gave me a piece of white chocolate cake (sadly, he didn't have any forks, so I had to use my hands). I also liked him because his professional-looking office, with its old leather couches and expensive dried flower arrangements, was an actual office and not just his living room.

Doctor L (or Owl, as I began to call him when I talked to myself, which was more often than not) convinced me to stop already with the doughnuts, or at least to stop eating quite so many doughnuts. Doctor L cured me of fatness, or at least he got me to do something about it, although fat cells would continue to plague me like locusts.

Doctor L wouldn't let me play with the dollhouse in his office, but then again, when I started coming to him for therapy I was fourteen. I was now a seasoned professional. Sometimes when I would get really bored I'd ask good old Owl if we could draw pictures instead of talking.

Sometimes he'd say yes to this. Then I'd draw pictures of monsters and say that I wanted to kill myself because my psyche was so tortured by the fact that my mother wrote erotic novels. The truth was far more tragic than that; the truth was my psyche was just very, very bored.

Doctor F was cute and had gone to very fancy schools. She wore flesh-colored panty hose and perhaps that traumatized me in some way because I have a serious aversion to them now. Doctor F was pretty and seemed to always be pregnant. She had two children during my tenure with her. By now, in my teens, I had moved from sugar candy to drug candy. I was the only patient whom she ever had who got substantially worse under her care. Doctor F ultimately sent me to rehab. Of course, that was after months of my falling asleep on her sofa. She believed my falling asleep on her sofa was due to what psychoanalysts call "resistance." The truth was that falling asleep on her sofa had more to do with hours of cocaine-propelled partying before our sessions. Pretty Doctor F felt really bad about sending me to Minnesota in November for thirty long days, but it was one of the best things that anyone in the psychological profession ever did for me. I would have liked her more had she not stumbled into asking me that fatal question: "Do you think your mother's erotic novel writing has been a negative influence in your life?"

Doctor B was the doctor I went to after I graduated Hazelden, clean at nineteen. Doctor B is my grown-up shrink, the one I still see whenever I feel I need a mental tune-up (or every week, whichever comes first). Doctor B loves marshmallow Peeps and has two children. He wears skinny tan suits in the summer and skinny gray wool suits in the winter. Doctor B has a tendency toward bow ties. He does not give me candy of any kind, and has never asked me about my mother's writing unless I brought it up.

Doctor B reminds me of my beloved childhood shrink, Owl, who convinced me to stop gorging on doughnuts. I love Doctor B and will probably continue to seek treatment from him until I am either cured, or one of us kicks it. Not that I want either one of us to die—at least I don't want that consciously.

I am a Jew, though my idea of being Jewish has less to do with going to temple and more to do with praying on a shrink's sofa. Maybe seeing a shrink isn't just a Jewish thing. I have plenty of goy friends who get tons of couch action. But therapy is different for them—it's not expected. Some of these friends are the first in their family to yammer on about themselves one, two, even three times a week. I am just continuing a family legacy. The Jews I know have never been shy in the relentless quest for a place to kvetch, which I imagine makes them much better therapy patients than the goyim who come in from Connecticut and find themselves in New York and newly neurotic.

While being analyzed may not be restricted to Jews, we did invent it. It is considered by some the "Jewish Science." We talk about it obsessively and write about it all the time. The members of the Maidstone Country Club aren't complaining openly about their shrinks being gone for the month of August. We are. This is one area in which Jews can declare themselves definitively superior: We're better at therapy! Or maybe it's just that after losing six million of us so recently, we tend to not mind being known as a little zany.

Did all the therapy work? I don't know. I don't smoke crack or hate my family, but I don't feel perfectly mentally healthy every day either. Maybe it was my fault the therapy didn't take completely. Perhaps it was the way I humored the shrinks, my inability to be honest with them, or maybe it was my innate resentment and belief that these people were out to make a buck on my neurosis. Despite all my therapy I still feel guilty, even about committing my family's and my own insanity to print in this essay (but at least I'm not the first in the family to do it).

Which brings me back to my mother. I like her books, and don't feel repressed by them. I like the fact that she has the chutzpah to write about her sex life. I think it's funny. I think she's cool. And if it does bother me I close the book and talk to her—the real live person who raised me, whom I love and admire, and who still takes me to Bergdorf's to go shopping when we have an afternoon off together. And then, sometimes over coffee, like any normal Jewish child whose parents have paid for thousands of dollars of therapy, I tell her exactly how she screwed me up.

Among the Holy Schleppers

*

JENNIFER BLEYER

My journey to find a place where I belong as a Jew has been a long adventure with rather unlikely origins: I was sixteen and tripping on acid at a Grateful Dead show in Ohio. This was when I first heard of Rabbi Shlomo Carlebach.

Breaking through thick clouds of patchouli and pot smoke at the Richfield Coliseum, my brain was thoroughly blown into another dimension when a bearded face swirled in front of me—a man who wore tzitzit under his tie-dye and a colorful knitted yarmulke. His smile was gentle and his eyes intent. "Hey, sister," he said, "are you Jewish?"

Given the psychedelic circumstances, the question took a minute or two for me to process fully, and even then I wasn't sure what to say. Well sure, I was Jewish. But I didn't feel all that connected to it. I wasn't a stereotypical Jewish American Princess, like many of the girls at my high school. I wasn't religious or a Zionist, as my parents had raised me to be. I didn't feel any particular attraction to klezmer or Yiddish, and as a vegetarian, the very thought of pastrami made me want to puke. But still, I did have the feeling that there might be something there, something worth tinkering with and exploring in a quiet, personal way.

The bearded man continued, "Sister, if you ever go to New York City, you have to go see Shlomo Carlebach. You won't regret it." He pressed a business card into my hand that said "Shlomo Carlebach, Rabbi" with an address on West Seventy-Ninth Street in Manhattan. Delirious and hallucinating, I stuffed it in my pocket along with other concert detritus and wandered off.

It so happened that two years later, I moved to New York to go to college. My first semester at Columbia was mostly spent drinking 40s at punk shows on the Lower East Side and making zines, but eventually I decided to seek out this mysteriously recommended rabbi. I was in that frame of mind that you've probably also been in at some point, before you had things figured out. That kind of splayed-open-at-the-seams curiosity, when every conversation with a homeless man or a store clerk or a bartender or the person next to you on the subway seems to be exactly what you're supposed to hear at that moment, rife with hidden instruction on how to navigate reality. I had held onto that business card for two years, suspecting that it might lead me to some such interesting conversation.

So on Shabbat during Hanukkah, I went to the address on West Seventy-Ninth Street. The synagogue was a two-story sliver of a building in the shadow of the Upper West Side's prewar corridor. Inside, it was the essence of plain: Pink walls, rows of metal folding chairs, a simple ark for the Torah, a disorganized bookcase teeming with prayer books, and a lace-curtained room divider separating men and women. Some people davened. Hanukkah candles were lit on the windowsill. At the back near the door, a cherubic older man rocked and prayed. Turning, he saw me and asked my Hebrew name. "It's Chaya Sarah," I said, feeling funny to say a name that had been out of commission since grade school. Reb Shlomo smiled, kissed my forehead, and said, "Chaya Sarah! I am *so* happy to see you."

Reb Shlomo descended from a lineage of prominent Hasidic rabbis. In the '60s, he broke away from his prescribed path and established the House of Love and Prayer to serve the tuned-in, turned-on, dropped-out hippie Jews of Haight-Ashbury. He then spent years traveling the globe, singing, playing guitar, and establishing his own style of New Age neo-Hasidism. He had a moshav in Israel, the little shul in New York, and followers everywhere. To be sure, he was controversial and deeply flawed: I learned much later that he had allegedly sexually abused numerous young women. But I was less wooed by Shlomo in particular than the notions he suggested: That Jewishness was not the exclusive province of its official adherents up in the castle, but something that belonged equally to those of us who live way out beyond the moat. Next to the usual Jewish pegs of fear and guilt, he offered a radically different narrative, one born of love and joy. Standard-issue American Judaism seemed to me to suffocate under the hulking weight of its own dour authority. But Reb Shlomo's Judaism was buoyant with contradiction, madness, and transcendence.

I saw him as more of a signpost on a road than a destination, a sign directing me simply to think about Jewishness and look the contradictions and madness straight in the face. Curious, I went back to the shul periodically as Reb Shlomo overturned my stock image of rabbis. Those I had known growing up were politicking figures who sat at the helms of overstuffed Midwestern suburban congregations. They wore funny choir garb, solicited hefty donations, and delivered snoozy sermons about the fawning allegiance we owed to Israel, and the evil bogeyman threatening our survival in the guise of intermarriage. They were perfectly nice, but seemed more like social club impresarios than spiritual guides.

And yet here was Reb Shlomo, rumpled and austere, hobbling everywhere with a volume of Talmud under his arm, greeting everyone who crossed his path with the most effusive declarations of love. On Purim, he sang and played guitar for hours, keeping us dancing in drunken manic circles. On Passover, he gave each person at the table a long personal blessing for the year to come, and the all-night seder ended well after dawn. On Saturday mornings, I would stop by for a little while and listen to him tell stories—stories told in such a way that his eyes rolled back in uncontrollable waves of bliss during the telling. He would wave his hand through the air and invoke the legends of the great Belzer and Kotzker rebbes, the Ishbitzer and Lubliner rebbes, and of course Rebbe Nachman of Breslav. I could almost see their spirits lassoed, for a moment, back to earth.

The polyglot congregation on West Seventy-Ninth Street also overturned my stock image of who synagogue-goers were. I had grown up in congregations where the aisles were used as catwalks during the High Holidays. Here, worshippers were freaks, geniuses, outcasts, and eccentrics— definitely more like members of the tribe to which I imagined myself belonging, if not in substance at least in essence. One was a former yeshiva student who now favored various Hindu gurus, but still kept Shabbat. One was a Kahanist alcoholic from Transylvania. One got arrested for aiding a runaway teenager, and other congregants rallied to help bail him out of jail. Reb Shlomo referred to all of them fondly as "holy schleppers." They were the sort who hadn't necessarily done that well with money or love. They weren't the best looking or the most socially adept. But they flocked to this little shul to sing and dance until the roof shook.

A year after I met him, Reb Shlomo died. But his presence stayed with me, especially in having been encouraged to seek a place of my own within Judaism. Years passed and I continued to fiddle around in the liminal spaces between Jewishness and everything else. I met others who seemed to do so as well, consciously or not, and became sort of fascinated by how many other Jews there were like me.

"LIKE me" meant someone who had hitchhiked across the country a half dozen times, traveling up the Pacific Coast highway with surfers, along Route 66 with Cherokee women, and across Interstate 80 with a shoe salesman. It meant someone who had worked as a waitress, housecleaner, temp, bike messenger, city investigator, typist, zoo guide, researcher, barrister, and fajita vendor at traveling festivals. It meant someone who had been in and out of relationships with a punk boy from Memphis, an Ecstasy dealer from Toronto, a chain-smoking sculptor, an activist saxophone player, and a self-fashioned motorcycle adventurer. It meant someone who had fallen in love so deep as to know, beyond any shadow of a doubt, that she was the happiest girl in the whole city, and someone who had experienced heartbreak so deep that the tears flowed without shame at outdoor cafes and on subway cars. It meant someone who had glimpsed the divine with other seekers at Sufi zikrs, Hindu kirtans, Buddhist meditations, pagan equinoxes, and Native American peyote ceremonies. It meant someone whose urban tribe was black, white, Indian, Mexican, Dominican, Asian, Arab, and West Indian—a sprawling group of friends who showed me that, yes, life is complicated, but it is also glorious.

Like me also meant someone who had been reared on Solomon Schech-
ter Day Schools, Shabbat dinners, and bat mitzvah lessons. Someone
who was second-generation American, named after a great-grandmother
who had been killed in Auschwitz, and who had grown up in an atmosphere thick with European accents, foods, and melancholy. It meant someone who had studied in an Orthodox women's yeshiva in Israel, and who
felt that maybe, just maybe, there is a Divine Source who expects something more from us than intellectual appeasement and Western liberalism.

I had never been to a shrink, had never had a Jewish boyfriend, and
had no special feelings of identification with the characters on *Seinfeld*,
but nonetheless I felt Jewish in some inexplicable way, and was forever
wondering how that jived with everything else.

For some people, I began to think, being Jewish was the big honking
main-course brisket on their identity dinner tables. Everything they do is
Jewish, everyone they know is Jewish, everything they see is through a
Jewish lens. Maybe they have a couple of side-dish identities, like being
a woman, a litigation attorney, or someone from St. Louis. But by and
large, they are big Jewey Jews.

But then, there were people for whom identity itself is more of a dim
sum experience, their Jewish part of it like one small, tasty (mock) ham
dumpling amid a variety of other yummy treats. I was a dim sum Jew,
and so were most of my Jewish friends. I had the idea one autumn day to
make a magazine for us. This magazine, I decided, would be called *Heeb*.

It took about a year and a half for me to get my magazine going—to
procure some seed funding, cobble together a volunteer staff, set up a little office in my Brooklyn apartment, solicit and edit content, and find a
designer who would work for nothing. I got a rudimentary Web site up,
figured out how to accept online subscriptions, made a subscriber data-
base, screenprinted T-shirts in my living room, and organized a launch
party. I had been working eighty hours a week and was just short of losing my mind. Finally, the first issue came out.

That first issue had some funny pictures of Jewfros, hip-hop reviews
by the grandmother of one of our editors, and a Neil Diamond center-
fold. It had a dry hysterical analysis of the connection between Nazis and
Pizza Hut, a memoir of one young male writer's teenage affair with Allen

Ginsberg, and a bunch of staged photos of a sexed-up Jewish wedding. Nothing too declarative or even definable. It was an attempt to capture what was Jewish by side-glance rather than head-on.

There was an odd publicity blitz—the sort of thing that happens all the time when the media's slobbery maw opens around a cultural curiosity of momentary interest, chews it up, and spits it out. In a flash, I was interviewed by the *New York Times*, the *Los Angeles Times*, the *Chicago Tribune*, the *Hartford Courant*, CNN, ABC, *New York Magazine*, the *Village Voice*, and more. It was weird and disembodying, and the press was generally either adoring, mocking, or fascinated. But through it all, the magazine clearly became a symbol that young Jews had arrived—and we weren't afraid to make fun of our ourselves. I found myself to be the movement's unwitting spokesperson, and thought I was done with it until a call came one afternoon from Howard Stern's show inviting me to come on the air the next day.

As an NPR-and-Pacifica kind of gal, I had actually never heard Howard Stern before and didn't know what to expect. It was basically like being stuck in a room with a bunch of fourth-grade boys making fart noises and sex jokes for forty minutes—more bizarre than insulting, really. Howard railed against my magazine, commenting on the unforgivable offensiveness of its name (what it must take to offend Howard Stern!) and making various tangential remarks about gas chambers and the ovens at Auschwitz. I tried to steer the conversation toward things that I thought might be mutually agreeable to discuss, like circumcision and marijuana legalization. He also got me to show him my ass. The show finally went to a commercial break. Howard leaned over, shook my hand, and said, "Sounds like a great magazine. Good luck."

Back home in Ohio, my proud and defensive parents had to fend off the inquiries of people at their synagogue on Shabbat, asking if that had really been their daughter on Howard Stern. I received shocked e-mails from friends I'd known in junior high, people who'd dutifully taken the law school-and-chuppah route after college. They knew nothing of what I had done with my life except that I'd lifted my skirt (under truly irresistible pressure) on Howard Stern. I mean, who needs an alumni bulletin when you have something like that?

The media spotlight passed, and I continued to publish *Heeb* from my Brooklyn apartment. In many ways, it was exactly as I'd intended it to be: secular, irreverent, political, and funny. It was my own subconscious writ large and distributed at Barnes & Noble. Therapy probably could have afforded me a less-revealing sphere in which to work out my questions about what the hell this Jewish thing meant, but the train had already left the station, its direction set and its whistle blaring.

As it turned out, it was a train that other people wanted to get on as well. Clearly the response indicated that my subconscious was shared by many other people. *Heeb* found a fan base of a size and fervor that I would never have predicted. Hundreds of e-mails and letters came in from everywhere—Montana to Missouri, Long Island to Las Vegas—essentially saying variations on the same thing: *"Finally."*

The cumulative effect of it, along with the whole *Heeb* vibe, spoke to some deep longing that people seemed to have—a longing to be cool in their otherness, a longing to belong to a subculture that was theirs alone.

They wrote in about their dating angst, their neurotic families, and their seder stories. They wrote lurid tales of what really happened to them at bar mitzvah parties, summer camp, and Hebrew School. Some wrote about having been raised in Israel or Russia or (gasp!) Texas, or having been the rabbi's daughter, or having *shtupped* the rabbi's daughter (on the bimah, no less). Some letters came from parents who grabbed at the magazine like a life raft, subscribing to it for their cheeseburger-eating, shiksa-dating children. Some came from the unapologetically cheeseburger-eating, shiksa-dating children who essentially said, keep it coming with extra bacon. Some letters came from kvelling grandparents who said we evoked memories of Catskill-era cheekiness. Others came from fifteen-year-old kids who reported that a single copy had made the rounds of their classroom, flipped through until dog-eared and memorized word for word. People sent in stacks of submissions, writing about everything from the connections between Scrabble and Kabbalah, to the stylistic evolution of the JAP, to whether good bagels can be found in California (to that question, a resounding no).

Heeb became more and more entrenched in its own little corner of the subcultural universe. But as more people heard of it or got into it, the more disconnected I felt. After a while, it was like I was putting out a magazine for people with brown hair. Sure, I have brown hair, I like having brown hair. But I can talk about it only so much until it feels utterly irrelevant, not to mention self-indulgent. Being the poster girl for hipster secular Judaism wasn't really me. And although I was glad for *Heeb*'s success and worked very hard for it, the popular conception of its message was, roughly speaking, that being Jewish is cool. "Being Jewish is cool?" I mean, seriously. Being Jewish, cool? Um, dork factor: ten. Being Jewish isn't cool. It's not cool now, it never has been, and it never will be. But still, this was the message taken from *Heeb* by many people, and I was its rather mortified messenger.

I far preferred the definition of Jews as the very definition of outsiders—as nerdy, different, uncool. That I bore this ridiculous message of Jewish coolness into the world made me want to crawl under a rock. I finally felt true Jewish guilt. I felt like Dr. Frankenstein, having created and unleashed a monster against my core beliefs. I didn't want to be a "cool Jew." If anything, I wanted to be a holy schlepper.

So after four issues and almost three years creating *Heeb* magazine, despite the very New Yorkish assumption that acclaim and success trump all else, with an easy exhale, I left.

Not long after leaving *Heeb*, I was having coffee with my friend Moishe. Moishe, who grew up Hasidic in Brooklyn, had been a *Talmud chohem*, a true Torah scholar. He had been sent to the most prestigious yeshivas, where he learned day and night. His brilliance was renowned, such that from a very young age, the rabbis predicted he would be among the greatest minds of his generation. He loved learning Torah and was very good at it. Except for one thing—he couldn't find proof that God existed. He attacked the idea from every possible angle, but nothing could help him overcome his persistent doubt. So at age twenty-seven, Moishe shaved his beard and got rid of his black hat. He went to live in the secular world, which he found terrifically cold and alienating compared to the richness of his Hasidic community, but at least there, he felt he was no longer living a lie.

Moishe and I were talking at a diner until four in the morning. One would be hard-pressed to find two people with more divergent Jewish journeys than the two of us, but still, our conversation rambled easily over vast terrain. At some point in the night, he told me this story:

Once, there was a young rabbi. People came from near and far to hear this young rabbi speak, because the way he spoke about Torah made them feel like they were flying through the air. And when the rabbi spoke, he himself felt like he was flying, such was the enjoyment he received from teaching Torah. But once he met with his own rabbi, a great rabbi, in the privacy of his study. There, he confessed that he didn't believe a word that he said. He didn't believe that the Torah was true.

"Oy," said the young rabbi, "how can I go on like this? They hang on my words, and I enjoy teaching them, but this is hypocrisy of the worst sort!" The great rabbi looked at him and replied, "So you enjoy it, and they enjoy it. You get joy from it, and they get joy from it. The only one it's bad for is hypocrisy!"

I thought of how far I had drifted from the eighteen-year-old kid who hung out at Shlomo Carlebach's synagogue between acid trips and punk shows. Back then, I had my own weird little search going on for a place within Judaism. It was something I tinkered with in a quiet, personal way. But when the tinkering turned loud and public, it ceased to be mine anymore. It belonged to everyone else, becoming part of their own searches, I suppose.

The waitress came over and filled our coffee cups. Moishe and I looked at each other, he who had left his prodigious Torah study, and I who had left *Heeb*'s Jewish hipster posturing. They were things we were good at, things that gave others joy. But they were lies of a sort, and the guilt of that hypocrisy was too great to brush aside. It felt more truthful—more Jewish, even—to be outsiders.

But at some level, even though Moishe wears jeans and a T-shirt now, he is still a Hasid. And at some level, I'm still someone who would think that there should be a big noisy magazine for Jews like me. Those who don't quite fit into the tradition they were raised in, but can't turn their backs on it altogether. Those whose irreverence is a sort of twisted prayer. Those whose Jewishness grows through the cracks.

Guilt Judo

RACHEL KADISH

THANKSGIVING dinner. My friend—like me, the grandchild of Holocaust survivors—settles into the seat next to his grandfather. The two
exchange pleasantries. Then my friend mentions that he's recently taken
his toddler on her first choo-choo ride.

"*Trains*," says the grandfather. He splays his hands on the tablecloth,
and sighs. "I remember when they put us on a train. This was during the
transport from the ghetto to the first work camp."

The story of the grandfather's wartime suffering—tragic, inexorable,
hypnotic in its familiarity—spins out as the Thanksgiving meal is brought
to the table, served, and consumed.

"But that's history," the grandfather intones at last, as the plates are
gathered. "Life is for the young."

A college buddy of mine—Jewish, though not a descendant of
survivors—once observed that his family dynamics follow the rules of a
sport: Guilt Judo. The sport requires a range of moves: arm-twists, throws,
the art of the pin. Grace and style matter, and it is of course imperative
to master that most fundamental skill: learning to fall without injury.

Oh. You're home.

No, it's just that I thought you'd be home an hour ago.

*It's okay, it's just that the dinner got dry and ruined in the oven. And your
uncle went home. He was upset not to see you, though he didn't want to let
on. So tell me, how was your drive?*

To play successfully, my friend maintained, you need to understand the rules. Family obligations pin the needs of single people. The needs of the elders pin the needs of the young (except when said young are infants). Safety pins punctuality. (*Q: Why were you late? A: I wanted to come earlier, but the roads were wet . . . I just didn't want to take the chance.*) You get the idea.

The Holocaust pins everything.

Many Holocaust-survivor families—at least the ones I've encountered—have powerful vocabulary for everyday troubles. The missed phone call is terrible, as is the stained blouse. The over-seasoned soup? Disaster. Disaster, in fact, lurks around the most innocent-looking corners. Mountains hang by a thread. I've known survivors who are impossibly controlling in day-to-day life—worried about the weather and the canned goods in the pantry; consumed with planning for traffic patterns; beside themselves because you haven't made reservations, dressed for the cold, put a dust ruffle on your child's bed ("It's hygienic!"). They seem nearly undone by humdrum disorder. Yet in an emergency, they shine. They turn into the heroes you always knew them to be. To varying degrees the same goes, I believe, for us children and grandchildren of survivors. Calm waters may disorient us, yes; small matters may evoke overblown responses. But when you're raised to anticipate disaster, it's no big deal when it comes. (The one time when, living in a group house in college, I actually had to say, "Mom, I have to get off the phone, the house is on fire," my mother barely batted an eye.)

Here is what my mother says about her own mother: She would threaten to jump out the window when she was upset. She would open the door of a moving car and threaten to jump.

Though I didn't have many years with my grandmother—she died when I was five—I adored her. She was a brilliant, artistic, beautiful, rebellious woman who'd lost her community and most of her family in the war. Her hard-won law degree (no small achievement for a woman in 1930s Poland) was useless in postwar New York.

"She would say she was going to kill herself," my mother says, "then lock herself in the bathroom for an hour."

It was only in my twenties that I read Helen Epstein's *Children of the Holocaust*—a book first published in 1979, with page after page detailing nearly identical behavior. Children standing anxiously outside bathroom doors. Parents enclosed in darkness.

My grandfather told me to have six children. ("They killed one-third of us. We need numbers.") He said I wasn't safe in the U.S. ("We thought we were safe in Poland.") He counseled me endlessly to remember the stories of the Holocaust. If we grandchildren did not remember, no one would. This truism was solemnly echoed in my Jewish school and summer camps. To remember, to remember actively, was to ensure that these things could not happen again. To forget was to let the survivors' experiences wither away. To forget was to let Hitler's victims die all over again.

There was never any danger, for children and grandchildren of survivors, of forgetting.

Look on the bright side.

A friend who once worked for a famous newspaper confessed, years after growing disillusioned and quitting, that she'd probably never lose her sensitivity to her former employer's judgments . . . would never lose track of who was up and who was down in the paper's hierarchy of prestige.

I could not fathom this. Institution-worship is for people who grow up believing there is one university; one newspaper of record; one country to live in. My grandfather thought the Jagellonian University in Kraków was the center of the universe; then, abruptly, it wasn't. Cataclysm gives you perspective. The edifices of modern culture? They think they're all that. They're not the center of the world. Hollywood isn't. Neither is Harvard. Neither are the celebs, the think tanks, the exclusive clubs, the political elite. Neither is the publishing world.

Neither are you—you outsider reading this essay. Want to reject me? See if I care. My people have survived worse than you.

See? There's a bright side.

T HAT, in case you didn't recognize it, was a pin.

I N my childhood, Holocaust guilt seemed a private matter. By the time
I was a young adult, though, the Holocaust had become a prominent
part of American cultural education. The survivors and their children
were telling their stories, and the importance of Holocaust memory had
come not just to Jewish but to national attention. Today the most popular
attraction on the Washington Mall—by far outranking the Smithsonian—
is the Holocaust Memorial Museum. Universities routinely offer Holocaust
Studies courses; archives brim with videotaped survivor testimonies. For
better and for worse, now everyone has something to say about the
Holocaust. A creative-writing teacher I know relates that a Midwestern
college student of hers, non-Jewish but determined to write outside his
own life experience, began a short story with this line: "Morning call
came early at Auschwitz, but that was okay because David was a morning person."

What was private has become public, and now everybody—Jewish
and non-Jewish Americans alike—owns a share of the stories, the moral
urgency, the guilt. We've arrived at a point of Holocaust saturation, where
never forget is not only a moral imperative, but a thriving industry.

As Abba Eban said, "There's no business like 'Shoah business.' "

A T every Holocaust-related lecture I have attended, there is one. She
stands on line for the Q&A microphone—it's usually a she. You can
see her coming. Waiting behind distinguished professors, PhD candi-
dates, and a few elderly Holocaust survivors who wearily, politely, offer
small corrections of fact to a scattering of interested hums.

She waits on line. Pent up, straining forward, her hair white or perhaps heavily dyed. Something about her dress is often strange—the colors too bright or the blouse askew, the buttons of her sweater misaligned.
When at last she reaches the microphone, she seizes upon something one

of the speakers has said: the American graduate student's stray assertion that most refugees traveled a certain route, or perhaps the French professor's assessment that in the wake of Chirac's historic speech and the creation of a commission to enact individual restitution, the French government's rapprochement is, at long last, finished.

No. This woman's hand chops the air. *My uncle traveled this route. My aunt was imprisoned. My cousin traveled a different route so this is not true what you say, that Jews traveled only the Vladivostok route. There was another.* Often she holds documents, which she reads from in a quavering accented voice: the aunt's prison papers. Her voice strains with fury at the betrayal she has just heard. *Here is the documentation. I brought the documentation. My family was in France. It is not finished.* The sheaf of pages rattles. Her voice is thick with rage.

This is an academic setting. It is not a place for fury. Of course her specific case may be true, but this is irrelevant to larger historic questions. Speakers are lined up behind her, eyes averted, faces impassive; the session is running late; every extra minute is coming out of the lunch break. Someone rises—everyone has been waiting for someone to rise—and takes the microphone from her. Thank you. Others are waiting. Your contribution is appreciated.

I come to think of this woman—this survivor who refuses to be polite—as a Jewish prophet, a wrathful Job or omnipresent, ever-witnessing Elijah. Long after the last of the survivors has died, she will continue to appear at lectures: throwing a wrench into academic discussion, rattling her sheaf of papers, raging with the choking grievances of Lamentations.

I am wrong about this. She will not visit these gatherings eternally. In a few years she'll be dead.

I N college and after, I was periodically asked to speak at Holocaust-commemoration events. At first I accepted every invitation. Later I became more selective. I didn't like the way it made me instantly exotic. People's faces changed as soon as I identified myself as a descendant of survivors: They turned reverent. I didn't deserve reverence; my grandparents did. I didn't want to use the Holocaust to make myself heroic.

Nor did I wish to make myself one-dimensional, declaring myself a "Holocaust Girl" (see S.L. Wisenberg's sobering 1994 piece by this name) at the expense of my American identity. My father's family came to the United States decades before the Holocaust. I grew up hearing stories of the Great Depression from my grandmother; my father served in the U.S. military during the Vietnam War. These are my family stories, too.

Still, I could make the Holocaust personal for an audience of strangers. I've been entrusted with stories. I've researched and written fiction and nonfiction about the Holocaust and its aftermath. I've felt, all my life, fiercely protective of survivors; and now, as I watch them enter old age, many with a prodigious, stunned contentment at having made it there at all, I understand it's my job to keep the flame lit.

But does that mean suiting up for a lifetime match of Guilt Judo?

Perpetuating memory, passing on the stories of the survivors I love: I've been committed to these things as long as I can remember. The horrors that were done, and the pure human evil displayed by the doers, need to be known and pondered and used to catalyze action today and always. But I don't think that gives me carte blanche to use the Holocaust in any way that happens to feel satisfying. And I don't believe the point of *never again* is to render everyone reverent unto silence; to pin everyone else's suffering to the mat until the end of time.

I refuse to be so intimidated by guilt that I don't speak up against what I see as misuses of the victims' memory. I've seen Holocaust-education programs that seemed so invested in emphasizing Jewish annihilation that they can't tolerate acknowledging that some Eastern European Jews are still alive (the March of the Living, an international program that brings teens to visit the Polish concentration camps, initially prohibited Polish Jewish teens from participating). I've met students who can tell you all about Auschwitz but nothing about the pre-genocide lives of the Jews who were murdered there. I've been rebuked for my participation in German-Jewish dialogues ("I can't believe you *talk* to them") by a second-generation writer who told me he thinks a five-year-old German today is culpable; I've heard the same writer tell audiences, to applause, that Jews have no business living in Europe today. (Isn't that what Hitler said?) And if each of us has one incident that sums up what's worst about certain types of Holocaust-remembrance, then here's mine: A prominent American congregation member, on a mission to Poland to donate a Torah in honor of a murdered community, was overheard to say, with the Torah scroll in his arms, "You know what I want to do with this Torah? I want to take it and shove it up the asshole of the first Pole I see."

Does the Holocaust mean never having to say you're sorry?

By birthright, I'm a natural-born black belt. I know the moves. But here is what I now wish I had asked my college friend: What happens to the people who win at Guilt Judo? If we pin all comers, what then? What is the game's endpoint?

I've been to Poland twice now, to research a book about Holocaust reparation and restitution claims—a subject both personal (some of my relatives are involved in a claim) and riveting, because it makes Guilt Judo concrete. In the legal battles over property and compensation, each match is played out visibly—the winner receiving a check, the ownership of a long-lost painting, the deed to a building.

In Kraków's old Jewish square, a neighborhood my grandparents knew well, loss runs under everything like a low hum: under chipped brick and broken panes and blackened window frames; under bright new facades standing flush with burnt-out shells. Half the buildings are still abandoned ("abandonment" being, of course, exactly the wrong term for what took place there), but in the last few years an odd thing has happened. This neighborhood—which stood forsaken and drug-infested for decades—is being renovated. Hammers and drills start at daybreak. Half the buildings lining the square have been converted into "Jewish establishments," their freshly painted signs advertising food, books, mementos. Since the early nineties, when this renovation was seeded by a handful of committed locals—men and women who are one-eighth Jewish; one-sixteenth; possessors of a tallis found in an avowedly Catholic grandmother's attic or just a complex affinity for things Jewish—business has grown steadily, benefiting from the tourist boom that followed the filming of *Schindler's List* on this spot.

Almost no Jews live here. The Jewish Book Store is run by Catholics. The klezmer musicians who perform nightly at the restaurants are—unbeknownst to the Jewish tourists who flock to hear them—non-Jewish Ukrainians. Lining the walls of the tourist shops, on shelf after shelf, sit rows of carved wooden Jews. Most of these figurines are Orthodox men with beards, though some are women in traditional dress. Some of the wooden Jews play instruments. All look mournful. The figures, I am told, are bought by tourists eager for a bit of "authentic" Jewish Poland . . . and also by Poles, some of whom may buy them out of nostalgia, some because they believe the figurines are good luck for business. The wooden Jews do not represent the actual pre-war Jewish population of Kraków, a large portion of which was cosmopolitan and non-Orthodox. I can't imagine what my grandmother, who loved Chopin, philosophy, modern dance, and skiing, would have said of these miniature people who are supposed to represent her lost world. But the figurines sell as quickly as the local carvers can produce them.

Every day I walk—partly to see the city, partly to combat the loneliness: a leaden mass in my throat that I couldn't dislodge if I tried. A few blocks from the Kraków square I encounter samples of a popular graffito, featuring a Jewish star on a hangman's noose. A Polish acquaintance explains quite earnestly that this has nothing to do with anti-Semitism. *See there? The word Cracovia is spray-painted beneath. This is graffiti about the Cracovia soccer team. It's nothing to do with Jews. Calling Cracovia "Jews" is just a way of insulting the team.*

Anti-Semitism is thick here, and largely unexamined. While it's true that there's been a recent surge of philo-Semitism, exemplified by the huge non-Jewish crowds at Kraków's vibrant Jewish Cultural Festival and a palpable interest in Judaism from Polish intellectual circles, in Poland it can still be physically hazardous to declare oneself Jewish. Among much of the population here, any sympathy for Jews is outweighed by outrage that the plights of non-Jewish Poles have not been redressed. Person after person here will prove, in a litany of conquest, oppression, and murder going back centuries, that they have suffered worse than the Jews. Worse than anybody. Poles are the Christ of Europe. It is Poles who are owed. As for the Jews' former homes? During the war, Poles found these buildings and moved in. The buildings were empty. The Poles have lived in these buildings for decades. Now, Rich Jews From New York want to take these homes away. *We're poor people who can't afford new homes. We're a struggling nation. Are you trying to bankrupt us? We, who suffered under both Hitler and Stalin?*

The day before I'm to leave, I meet with the director of Kraków's Jewish Cultural Center. At the conclusion of our interview, he invites me to a reception in the Center's art gallery. I follow him down the stairs, mulling the fact that neither he nor a single member of the Center's devoted staff is Jewish.

In the gallery, I flip through the guest book, scanning those entries written in languages I understand. "Bless you! Bless you for all you have suffered!" read inscriptions signed by tourists with obviously non-Jewish names. It's not clear whom these writers are addressing, as there are no Jews here. The guest book, crammed with a sweaty philo-Semitism, seems shorthand for whatever Poland's Jews represent to these conscientious visitors: Spirituality? Endurance? An opportunity for serious moral reflection? A confessional where one may at last declare guilt, sorrow, a desire for personal amnesty?

These people are playing on our side. Is it ungrateful to find their efforts creepy?

Here at the Kraków Jewish Cultural Center, at a crowded reception at which I feel like possibly the only live Jew on the planet, I'm greeted. A Polish woman approaches, her eyes shining as though we're long-lost friends. Her husband translating, she gives her name, tells me she's a sculptor, then stands there beaming while her husband begins a peculiar interrogation. Do I know Rafael Stern; Helena Frankel; Avram Rosemann? The list goes on. None of the names means a thing to me until I realize he's enumerating the Jews he once knew in pre-war Kraków— a relentless litany clearly intended to prove something.

Soon the woman interrupts. She wants to know when I'm leaving Kraków. Tomorrow, I answer. She is disappointed. Her husband translates so softly I barely catch the words—something about not enough time to sketch me. She stands back and looks at me hard. Her gaze is neither friendly nor unfriendly; she has simply stopped interacting with me as a person. After a few seconds she smiles. "I won't forget." She taps her temple. "Now I have your face in here."

I am still smiling at this nice Catholic couple in this crowded gallery, though I know something is wrong. I'm smiling because it's what people do. Because it will take a few more heartbeats, a few uncertain steps out the door of the building, to understand the role I've been conscripted into in these strangers' absolution; to imagine it, high on a tourist-shop shelf: my own face, notched into wood by a blade.

This is what a Guilt Judo victory looks like.

As I stand there, the woman moves alongside me and folds my arm under hers. She touches my cheek, then lifts my glasses.

"Beautiful eyes," she says. "Beautiful dark eyes."

L IKE it or not, we're in this sport together—descendants of victims, of bystanders, of perpetrators, locked in our holds, straining. Guilt Judo isn't going away any time soon, because the sport has a purpose. It's a wearying but sometimes necessary way of making sure unredressable wrongs are at least acknowledged—making sure you get *heard.* We all know how to play it, whether recreationally or in self-defense, in our families or in politics.

Of course, this endless contest is not limited to those affected by the Holocaust. Look around and you'll notice that most of the globe—at least wherever the philosophy of *might makes right* has evolved into *blessed is the lamb*—is engrossed in its own inter-group matches. Black vs. Jews (*how dare they compare slavery to the Holocaust . . .*). Native Americans vs. African Americans (*. . . slaughter to slavery . . .*). Palestinians vs. Jews (*. . . their suffering to ours?*). Catholic vs. Protestant vs. Jew vs. Muslim vs. Hindu. The Hatfields have suffered—but the McCoys have suffered more. You say your population was decimated? Decimated is one-tenth of your population wiped out. Decimated would have been an improvement, compared to what happened to *us.*

But exactly what—in our homes, in our political conferences—is the point of the game? What is the point of determining who hurts more; whether my tears were more important than yours; whether the Holocaust was worse than slavery? Does it render the opponent's suffering lesser, unmentionable? Does it guarantee sympathy? Love? Compensation? A better future? Does it work?

We all conduct ourselves as if we believe it does. And sometimes we're right—sometimes Guilt Judo is an effective tool for important practical ends. But it's also, if we're not careful, poisonous.

You were only in Auschwitz for two weeks. I was there two years. What did you survive? You have no right to call yourself a survivor.

The person who makes such a declaration is not malevolent; he or she has simply been destroyed in spirit.

MAY I say something, now, about guilt? I think it has a bad name. American culture presumes guilt is something manipulative, something to be washed away with a good jet of therapy. Guilt, though, is nothing more than a cue that we have a choice to make: Do something to repair the situation, or accept it and move on.

Guilt is a powerful, important road sign. The trick is to remember that it's only a road sign and not the destination. In truth, it's a fundamental error to believe that the word for the burden we all carry, we children and grandchildren and neighbors and acquaintances of survivors, is guilt. I don't feel guilty about the Holocaust. (I didn't do it.) Nor do I feel guilty because my family survived. And now that I'm an adult, I no longer feel any guilt about the contrast between my own privileged life and the traumas my family endured. My grandparents wanted me to have a good, safe life; if tragedy should befall me, I know how fervently I'd wish my own children a joyous life. My family's legacy neither devalues my own experiences nor makes me somehow holy. It just means I inherited a history, transmitted by people doing the best they could. So now I need to do the best I can.

What I feel is not guilt—it's responsibility.

I am absolutely serious now. I am not playing. This is not a pin, it's just the truth: I don't care who suffered the most. All I care is what we do about the Holocaust's legacy now, for the generations behind and ahead of us. Getting mired in guilt (mine, yours, theirs) is a waste of all our time. There may be infinite ways to feel guilty about the Holocaust, but the "Your life is good and they died" varieties and the "How dare you compare other people's suffering to ours?" varieties are moral dead ends. The only one worth sweating over is the one that asks, "What are you going to do about it?" I have a responsibility to carry on my relatives' stories; to speak out about anti-Semitism and racism when I encounter them; to do my small part to keep cross-cultural dialogue going; to make sure victims' individuality isn't lost in thickets of tragedy; to respond actively when I see harm being done. And to avoid posturing and self-importance in the process. I have a responsibility, too, to make sure I enjoy life's wonders to the fullest. I would be remiss if I neglected to laugh; to make the most of this country's freedoms; to teach my toddler how to imitate a pterodactyl, talk to the moon, and delight in a train ride.

Memory fades. Tomorrow's children will never know survivors. The responsibilities I bear have no statute of limitations; I'll always do my best to protect the survivors and their legacy. But that doesn't change the fact that the history of the Holocaust will grow distant, even abstract. No amount of Guilt Judo can prevent this. And while strenuously broadcasting that the Holocaust was worse than any other human suffering may be justified, it can't keep the survivors alive any more than it can undo what happened . . . and it is going to damage us.

If the memory of the Holocaust recedes, let it not be because I failed to do my part to keep it alive—I'm committed to that labor. But if the Holocaust comes, in some unknown number of generations, to occupy a smaller place on our cultural landscape, I don't see this as cause for guilt. The point isn't to pin everyone else ad infinitum, but to carry forward the important pieces of memory so that people see, and understand, and act differently in the world because this happened.

If we can accomplish that, then whenever it comes, the inevitable decrescendo of memory—which some will call abomination and others will call healing—will be, in truth, neither. It will simply be life. It won't signal that we've failed—that we've let down the Holocaust's survivors or, worse, its victims—but rather that we've simply, regretfully, tragically, hopefully, moved forward. And that has nothing to do with wrestling each other to the mat, and everything to do with standing up.

What Will They Think?

*

TOVA MIRVIS

THOU Shall Care What Other People Think: For my family, this has always been the eleventh commandment. It looms large; it produces the guiltiest of all guilt. More than God, it is the community that watches over and induces guilt, not a voice within or above. If Sartre had it right and hell is other people, well, here, so is guilt.

I can trace this guilt back to my great-grandmother, who once picked a fight with my mother about her clothing. I imagine the scene, my mother at sixteen or seventeen, trying to find herself, to pull herself out from an abundance of expectation, and my great-grandmother, beautiful, proper, impeccably dressed. Was it about needing to dress up more, to style her hair, to wear more makeup, to wear more ladylike shoes? It could have been about any of those things, my mother says. She doesn't remember anymore. But underneath the details of clothing, this fight, and so many others, was about how terribly much my great-grandmother cared about what other people thought.

What my mother does remember clearly is how she tried to silence her grandmother. "It's going to end with me," my mother proclaimed.

It's this parting line that she now looks back to as a pivotal moment. It's also the part of the story that I like, with its foreboding air of finality. But for all its drama, this wasn't a truthful statement. It didn't end with my mom, this caring about what other people think. This quality was passed down one more generation, as if it were part of our genetic makeup.

But it's not all genes. It's where we've lived, too, in the particular nexus of communities my family has been part of, in Orthodox Jewish Memphis. This seeming disjuncture existed only on the surface. Really, Orthodox Judaism meets Southern life in near-perfect harmony. Both are communities well ordered, tightly constructed. Everyone has a place, and everyone knows where that place is. In both, the desire to belong reigns supreme. The fear of finding yourself on the outside keeps actions and thoughts in check. With eyes and ears lurking everywhere, nothing goes unseen or unheard.

My great-grandmother came to Memphis from Poland as a teenager and was determined to fit in. She had, as the story goes, beautiful long auburn hair that she carefully styled every morning. She was proud and harsh with her children; she always wanted more for them, more for herself. She cared, deeply, desperately, about what she wore. She shopped at sales and held up the price tags, with their numerous markdowns, as trophies. My grandmother, who grew up under this scrutinizing eye, became Orthodox on her own, when she was a teenager. She too wanted to feel like she belonged, but she didn't have the clothing to fit in at the wealthier Reform temple where her family went. So, as this story goes, she took the streetcar to the then-poorer, smaller Orthodox synagogue and didn't look back. In this community, where she eventually settled, married, raised three children, and helped to found an Orthodox day school, she could feel comfortable in her own clothing. But for me, it's a world where it's sometimes hard to feel comfortable in my own skin.

To be Orthodox is to live in a web of rules. It is a system built of minute laws, where every aspect of life is delineated, legislated, parsed, and commanded upon. There are rules of food, rules of dress, rules of time, rules of place. Obligations, requirements, and forbiddens abound. The rules spawn out one from another; they multiply with each subsequent text.

At the Yeshiva of the South, a cross between a high school and a finishing school for Orthodox young women in Memphis, we were well versed in the rules of social propriety and religious observance. We kept, as if by second nature, the complex laws of kashrut. Observing the laws of the Sabbath was a given as well. We studied the prohibitions of food preparation on Shabbos and knew the most minute application of the law: how to pour boiling water from cup to cup before making tea, how to warm up food, how to stir soup, how to peel vegetables, all without trespassing a single law. We studied the Bible and the Prophets and the meanings of the prayers. We were taught to believe in reward and punishment, the world to come and the possibility of *kares*, being cut off from your people. We were taught that what we wore determined who we were. Skirts had to cover the knees. Collarbones and elbows were to be hidden away. Pants were forbidden. Boys were forbidden, too. Talking to one of the three boys who populated, in entirety, the separate and equally unhappy high school was a risky endeavor. We were also taught that contact with these same boys or their equivalents would become permissible when it was time to get married, which we would all of course do, preferably in the few years following our high school graduations. We were taught, in more subtle ways, that girls needed to be good and pleasing and kind. We were taught to agree, uphold, affirm. We were taught that there was one right way to be, and many wrong ways.

Guilt was crucial, an integral part of the mechanism. It was never a quantity that could be separated out and gazed upon. It was simply the flip side of observance. If we didn't follow the letter of the law, we were guilty. And it wasn't only large transgressions that produced sizable guilt. The smallest details mattered as much as the large commands; in the strict eye of the law, they were often one and the same. I believed that every action, however tiny, was being recorded. Every word, every thought was visible and evaluated; they could all be divided into categories of allowed or forbidden. There was little room for ambiguity. The world and all its inhabitants could be plotted out on a grid, good versus bad. God did not exist on high, removed from the daily dealings. God lived in the here and now, inside the most private and seemingly insignificant moments. Living in this world was like looking at a stalk of a plant, a tiny organism under a magnifying glass. The most minute particles of life were enlarged, swelling in importance, to a size worthy of God's attention.

Despite all these rules, God could be lenient. If God were a police officer handing out speeding tickets, at least He was one who could be argued with. Deals could be struck, compromises reached. But there was no appeasing a judgmental neighbor. Though the laws claimed their power from a divine source, that alone wasn't enough to ensure their enforcement. They required another deity, one far more powerful, this fear of "What Will They Think?"

But who is this ubiquitous "They" after all? Not that it matters. Those who use the phrase "What Will They Think?" and those who are made to hear it, know the answer to this almost instinctively. It differs from house to house, mind to mind, but that doesn't change the power of this superhuman, supernatural "They." "They" is the embodiment of your shortcomings, fears, and secrets. "They" hovers in the bushes, can see through walls, into houses and private, locked rooms. But can "They" see into your head? Is that finally the only private space?

For me, it was. Growing up, I was one thing on the outside, someone else on the inside. I projected an outward image of the good girl, but inwardly I plotted my escapes. In high school, I mastered the art of the adjustable skirt. My skirts were rolled up and down, their length determined depending on who was looking at me. My classmates and I, those who shared in this endeavor, reveled in who could get away with the shorter skirt. We discovered that short, flared skirts were more malleable than stiff, knee-length denim. We took pleasure in walking the line. The transgressions themselves didn't need to be large to feel powerful and transformative. In a world so delineated, when life is lived under this magnifying glass, small transgressions take on the power of larger ones. When I went home from school and changed into pants, I felt as if I were traversing the lines of the forbidden. I knew what the rabbis were so worried about. I did feel different in my jeans, oddly powerful, alluring, and strong.

This abundance of rules created an unintended side benefit, a world replete with the thrill of getting away with something. Of kissing boys when I wasn't even supposed to be tapping them on the shoulder. Of skirts just above the knee, the naked feeling of legs set free in a pair of shorts. How sweet the trespasses were, this tantalizing underbelly of guilt. The journey into forbidden territory, the crossing of boundaries, these were an inextricable part of the pleasure. Nowhere else could guilt be so pervasive and so delectable.

This is true, I suppose, only for those who chafe against rules, those who do not easily fit into the "They" of community. Maybe for some, what others think and what they themselves think is identical; the community only reinforces the individual belief. But I think more about those who are chafing, those who, like myself, come up with this gap between the voice of a community, and the internal voice. I think, for example, about a friend of mine who had once been strictly, devoutly Orthodox. She always had her arms and legs covered; she always wore stockings, or socks, even with sandals, even in the summer. Then, she stopped being so religious and she could never bring herself to wear socks again, not even in the winter. She said her feet needed to be free. She preferred cold toes to covered ones.

I think about my friend's toes a lot. But like her, I wasn't always chafing. After my four years of high school, with its attempts at rebellions and pseudo-short skirts, I left Memphis. I was going to college, to Columbia, but first, I was spending a year in Israel, something most of my six classmates, all five of them, were doing. In Israel, I studied at a women's yeshiva. The classes might have been similar to what I had studied in high school, but the approach was vastly different. Here we were encouraged to question. We were supposed to wrestle with the texts, not simply swallow them whole. It didn't matter that this women's yeshiva was at the left-wing edge of Orthodoxy, deemed radical by many for its willingness to teach women these texts, for giving them the skills to lay their own claim. I fell in love with these texts, the oversized folio pages of the Talmud, the cryptic unpunctuated lines of Aramaic, the tiny scripted Hebrew letters of the rabbinic commentaries. For the first time, the rules were not something imposed; I saw how they progressed from a biblical line to a Talmudic explication to a rabbinic dictate. I felt part of their evolution.

I look back to that year as the time I felt most comfortable in this world, most engaged, most fully within. This respite continued for several years, through college, until I got married. So much so that when I first got married, I covered my hair, as is required of Orthodox married women. I did it out of a belief in Halacha, Jewish law. I also did it in the most lenient way possible. I wore baseball hats and berets, and tried to make them look like a fashion statement, not a religious statement. I thought about the more modern explanation for it, that it is a sign of marriage, that it is a woman's equivalent to a man's yarmulke. But at the same time, what also moved me to go out and buy all those hats was my desire to be like everyone else in my community, to look the part of the cute young married woman I had been raised to emulate. It was my attempt to cast my lot with this group. After the novelty wore off, two or three months in, I complained that the hats were too tight. They made red lines where they rubbed against my forehead. I hated the brim that impeded my sight. But this I could have overlooked. What I realized after a few years was that the hats were too tight in other ways as well. I felt constricted, covered over. I felt quieter, shyer. I felt as if the purpose was not to cover my hair, but to cover my self. When I ripped my hat off my head, the second I walked into my apartment, I felt like I could be myself again. Once I was walking down Broadway and caught a glimpse of myself in a mirror. A voice whispered out from underneath the hat: This is not who you are.

I stopped covering my hair and thought of it as my coming out. I worried for a few days what people would think, and then it became a relief. I had learned to hide away what I was thinking, as if questions and doubts could be covered over as easily as knees and elbows. But I was finally ready to have my hair, and myself, exposed. This time, I didn't care what anyone thought. Covering my hair sparked in me a discomfort, one that didn't subside, even when I gave my hats away to a friend, when I got an expensive haircut, or when I decided to let my hair grow long. Through my observance, I had grown more at odds with my religion than ever before. It was the beginning of a change, or maybe the first explicit manifestation of one that had been a long time lying in wait. It unleashed other disagreements I had with Orthodoxy, about women, about creativity, about authority and more, and it became my self-acknowledgment that I wasn't going to fit in here as seamlessly or as easily as I had once tried to.

I remember a rabbi who once said that during his own crisis of faith, he had decided that he couldn't live his life on the fence. This was when I was in high school, at an Orthodox youth group convention that served the function of trying to bring people closer to Orthodoxy, as well as give us one of our few chances with guys from out of town. He hadn't been sure of his belief, and knew he didn't want to live this way, with not knowing. Though of course I knew which way he had decided—one look at his beard and black hat dispelled any possible doubt—I badly wanted to hear him lay out his doubts and his resolution. I think I wanted to hear someone else name this feeling, admit to it, wrestle openly with it. With us sitting pin-quiet and still in a circle around him, he offered us various "proofs" of God's existence. I remember so well feeling moved by them, in awe, and elated at the certainty being offered.

But the certainty didn't last the week. I often wonder about him, how or if he really climbed off the fence and stayed there. I'm still, and maybe always will be, on the fence. This change is not primarily in action, or maybe it's not right now. It's in my mind where I feel this distance, this growing fissure most. When asked to define myself, I hedge the definition of Orthodoxy, or load it with adjectives to qualify it, or explain it so it is more true to who I really am. I don't feel guilt, not exactly. I have a fascination and envy for those who have left it unequivocally behind, fascination and envy for those who exist wholeheartedly within. Mostly I feel uncomfortable: I wish that I felt more resolved. I wish that when my five-year-old son asks me a question about why do we do this or don't do this, I knew better, more easily, what to say.

I've also found, more and more, that any attempt to pin it down is not about determining what I think; it is about someone else trying to decide whether I am in or not. What I really don't believe in anymore is this notion that belief can be plotted, that religiosity can be kept in an account ledger, that these large questions of belief can be settled with finite answers, that communal eyes and ears need to be heeded. I no longer believe in the voice of a "They" that is censorious, that wants to control what is said and thought, that tries to stifle dissent and questions. And I no longer think that I am the only one feeling this way, even if all around me, there is such a deep-seated reluctance to talk about it. I don't know yet what I do think, what I will think. For now, that means living in a tenuous middle ground, sometimes moving closer, sometimes moving farther away from my Orthodox world.

I'M writing this in late summer, when the last days of the season are racing by and I wish I could hold onto them, to keep the pleasure of sandals and exposed arms and legs. For me, summer officially ends not with Labor Day but with the approach of the high holidays. Starting roughly a week before Rosh Hashanah, the *slichot* "forgiveness" prayers are recited, leading up to the detailed confessional of Yom Kippur. With fists clapping chests in unison, we sing out in confession that *Ashamnu, Bagadnu, Gazalnu,* we have sinned, we have transgressed, we have stolen, we have rebelled, we have scoffed.

Though the tune is plaintive, there is something oddly celebratory about the moment. There is nothing quiet or private about this confession, nothing hidden away. It turns out that not only is guilt communal, but so is penance. With the plural of words like *Ashamnu, Bagadnu,* and *Gazalnu,* there is room to hide. There is, finally, comfort offered from other people's presence. The plural lets us stand as a group, that we can hide, at least a little bit. What feels most like a relief to me, though, is the acknowledgment that we, all of us standing here, are human after all. God doesn't require perfection, orthodoxies of practice or belief, even if such acknowledgment has to come in the formulized, safer words of prayer. It's not a call to guilt, but an acknowledgment of humanness. The confession is a moment not to cast away our humanness but to embrace it.

But at the same time, I long for the quiet, singular voices underneath these communal ones. My favorite image of the high holiday season is that of a blank page reserved for each of us. Between all the lists of sins, I seek out the quiet space where anything can be written, be said, be thought, be explored. This year, as it has been for many years past and will be, I'm sure, for many more years, I find myself with a belief that has fractured, opened, widened, loosened, lessened. The proverbial neighbors, I can easily conjure up what they would think of this, of all this. But God, I always imagine, is so much more benevolent.

The Last Jewish American Nerd

*

DARA HORN

I remember the first time I was humbled into learning. When I was
seven years old and had already become one of those annoying smart-
aleck children that people want to smack in elevators, I told my mother I
had some questions that I wanted to ask a rabbi. My mother, always encouraging me, took me to meet with one. I suspect that she thought I
was on an earnest quest for wisdom, as I now assume of my own students. What she didn't know was that my real motives were far less innocent. I was convinced, at seven years old, that I had personally uncovered
gaping holes in the fabric of Jewish thought, and that I was the first person in the history of the world to discover that the whole religion was a
sham. I was on an obnoxious mission to catch the rabbi in a trap.

In the rabbi's office, I could see right away that the man behind the
desk—who seemed strangely normal and unauthoritative without a tallis
on his shoulders or the bimah beneath his feet—was putty in my hands.
He smiled at me like I was four years old. (I was seven, thank you.)
Clearly he had no idea that I was about to shatter his self-esteem and destroy his faith in his Torah and his God. It would have been sad, if it
weren't so much fun. My mother introduced me, and the rabbi kept smiling the smile for four-year-olds as he waited for me to begin. I leaned
forward, thrilled, and asked my first devastating question.

"Did Adam and Eve have belly buttons?"

The rabbi answered, "No."

This was annoying. I had seen a fig-leafed picture of Adam and Eve in
a children's bible, with belly buttons, so I knew this should have been

good. Instead, the rabbi had simply given his answer as if it were obvious, the way the worst teachers did at school. My mother almost laughed.

In the wake of this humiliation, I skipped over some of the other
questions I had prepared (if Adam and Eve didn't have any daughters,
where did all the people in the world come from? if God wanted to kill
the whole world in the flood, then why didn't he want to kill fish?) and
decided to go straight for my best weapon, the question where I had science to back me up.

"In the Torah it says that animals were made on the fifth day, and
then people were made on the sixth day. But in school we learned that
the dinosaurs were on earth for 65 million years, without any people at
all. So how could God have made the world in six days?"

The rabbi looked startled. Now it was my turn to grin. He was trapped.
But then he grinned back at me, and before I knew it, he was asking me
a question.

"How do you know when a day is over?" he asked.

Again I was annoyed. I was supposed to be the one asking questions
here, not him. But my mother was watching me. "When it gets dark," I
muttered.

"When the sun goes down?" the rabbi asked.

I nodded, not sure where this was going, but feeling extremely
uncomfortable.

"And when was the sun created?" he asked.

I knew that one. "The fourth day," I said, proud to be right.

"So how long were the first three days?"

I was dumbstruck. Beneath my astounded silence, I heard him say, "A
day could be millions and millions of years."

The girl I was when I entered that office would have given him a
smart retort. She would have smirked that the dinosaurs were made on
the fifth day, after the sun was created, so his answer didn't explain anything. But the girl I had just become was too busy thinking to speak. In
that moment, in the same way some children are awakened to science,
or music, or sports, I was awakened to metaphor. The universe opened
before me like an enormous unwound scroll, and I saw things I had never

seen before: That in words, an ocean could fit into a single salty tear-drop, or a thousand ancestors could fit into a single belly button, or 65 million years could fit into a single day—and that in a single moment, I could realize that I wasn't as smart as I thought I was.

IT has been said that Jews are the people of the book, but really we are the people of the school. The word "Torah" derives from the root *yarah*, to aim or shoot—figuratively meaning instruction, or pointing someone in the right direction. The Shema, our central statement of faith in God, doesn't remind us even once to read our books, but reminds us twice to teach and repeat their contents to our children. After the biblical era, prophets were replaced by sages, and the study of Torah—not the reading of Torah, but the *study* of Torah—became the defining element of Jewish life. Intellectual life was not merely praised, but cultivated through compulsory education and then even bred into the genes as scholarship, or even a family history of scholarship, became the most sought-after quality in a potential spouse. It shouldn't be surprising that this appetite for learning has followed many Jews into the secular world. What is surprising, I think, is that even when the texts we are studying are not the Torah, so many of us still believe that scholarship is not merely desirable, but necessary and even sacred. And our guilt from failing in it—from disappointing our teachers or our students—can be exceedingly great.

But there is a larger reason, too, why our academic failures weigh so heavily upon us. Part of growing up American is knowing that your life is yours and yours alone, to live as you desire. But part of growing up Jewish is knowing that the supremacy of the individual is really a lie. The truth, Jewish tradition suggests, is that your life is not merely yours. It also belongs to all the people who made you who you are, and to all the people who you made who they are—your parents, your grandparents, your siblings, your spouse, your children, your grandchildren, your teachers, and your students. Your life, no matter what it may mean to you, is also an act of service to them. Being American means that you are responsible for creating yourself out of the void, but being Jewish means that three thousand years before your birth you were already standing at Sinai, already at school, already being taught who and how to be, whether you wanted to be there or not.

And such is the guilt of both the Jewish student and the Jewish teacher: The secret knowledge that no matter how much we learn, or how much we teach, it will never, ever be enough—that our parents, our teachers, our children, and our students are watching us, and so is everyone else, that eternity is breathing over our shoulders, waiting to see if we will notice.

A student facing these expectations needs to be constantly humbled, to be reminded again and again that everything she already knows is nothing more than a tiny spark in a night full of infinite stars. Fortunately, American education has a built-in set of checks and balances to insure the humility of anyone likely to receive an A: the shaming of the American nerd.

Much to the chagrin of people like me, the real tests of school don't take place in the classrooms, but in the hallways, the gym, and the parking lot. And those were the tests that I repeatedly failed. As the years passed since my embarrassing moment in the rabbi's office, it became increasingly clear that the things that mattered most to me were precisely the things that mattered least to my peers. Studies have shown, for example, that no one in the entire world (except possibly your mother) will ever care how you did on the AP physics exam. But you can be damn sure that every single person in the entire school will know who failed the driver's test. As my fellow high school alumni could probably still tell you today, that was me. And no matter what my teachers and parents said, it was painfully clear to me which of these two tests actually mattered. Similar humiliations abounded. My classmates were always powerfully attracted to me when it was time to pick a lab partner; strangely, no one among these admiring hordes was interested in taking me to the prom. By the time I made my first (and only) television appearance— as co-captain of the quiz bowl team, on a show for a local public access channel that might as well have been called "Nerds Versus Nerds"—I knew that this was not the sort of thing one brags about. The shame was mine alone.

But it was in Hebrew school that I really saw how irrelevant my interests had become. To everyone else, the various afternoon and weekend Hebrew schools we attended were a joke. My classmates ridiculed the teachers' Israeli accents, made up new English parody words to liturgical Hebrew songs, and threw things in class. Oddly, in the social atmosphere of the strange parallel universe called Hebrew school, the guilt that is traditionally associated with Jewish learning had been reversed. As my peers dropped out of these various Hebrew schools one by one without guilt, they and their parents agreeing that sports or music or other pursuits were more worthy of their time, I realized that if I were going to continue caring, there were no rewards on the horizon. It was going to be *Torah lishma*, learning for its own sake, and it was starting to look like I would have to go it alone. Was I the last Jewish American nerd? If I was, I knew I needed help. And I knew that there was only one way to find it: through my teachers.

I am now completing my doctorate and teaching Jewish studies courses as a visiting college instructor, perched on the edge that divides teacher from student—and I feel at all times, and from all sides, the presence of all the teachers I might have learned from and all the students I might have touched. Every teacher and every student feels it. As individuals, we might believe that each person is responsible for his or her own mistakes and missed opportunities. But as teachers, we know that influencing and even dramatically altering someone else's approach to life isn't an impossible dream. It is our professional responsibility, plain and simple. Changing our students—making them more informed, more aware, more insightful, more perceptive, more appreciative of and involved in the world we share—is our job. When students fail, it means that we have failed, too.

Like every student, I often found myself over the years in classes that I took not out of passion, but because they were hurdles I needed to jump over—classes where I didn't care much for the professor or the subject matter, but where I nonetheless knew I needed to succeed. Rather than concentrating on the subject in these classes, I paid close attention to the phrases the teacher liked to repeat, to the students' comments that the teacher appreciated most, to the points of view the teacher preferred. Then I chose research projects on topics that I knew the teacher would love, and mastered the art of churning out work that gave the teacher "what she wants."

But when I loved a class, and loved the teacher, I never cared what the teacher wanted. Instead I cared about what *I* wanted—to follow the teacher out of the room to continue the conversation, to race to the library to find the book that the teacher had mentioned only casually, to push aside the assigned reading so as to be able to read more, to write my paper on whatever idea was squeezing its way between the words said in class, even if it meant ignoring the suggested topics, or researching until there was no time left to write. I sometimes got better grades in the classes I hated than in the classes I loved, but in the end it was irrelevant. I knew what I had learned. And I knew what I had wasted.

It would be easy to brush off the guilt of these wasted moments simply by saying that a person can't love everything—not every subject can be compelling, and we can't expect every teacher's personality to click with ours. But every student knows it's not that simple. We've all been surprised by classes that we expected to hate and then came to love because of a teacher who made the subject shine. And we all know that, more often than not, teachers who don't click with one student don't click with the next student either. There is almost always a consensus about whether a teacher is good or bad. If we truly value learning, then there is no excuse for the waste of all the opportunities that might have enlarged our world—no excuse for bad teachers, and no excuse for students who indulge and encourage them. Now that I am on the other side of the seminar room, I often look at the students in front of me and wonder: Are they trying to find out "what she wants," or are they trying to find out what they themselves want? And if they are only trying to find out what I want, then why have I failed?

These are not casual questions. The great secret of education is that one doesn't learn by being smart, but by being aware of the limits of one's own knowledge—by finding those limits and then plunging over them, as if jumping off the edge of the world. The student has to know that the edge is there, and the teacher who coaxes the student over the precipice has to catch the student when she falls. It is a sacred trust.

There is only one way to alleviate the eager student's guilt in trying to discover "what the teacher wants": what I will call teacher love. I don't mean illicit liaisons between students and teachers, but rather an entire category of loving that belongs in its own distinct place in our collective toolbox of emotions, alongside romantic love and parental love and sibling love and all the other varieties of love. Teacher love happens when you fall in love not with a person, but with what that person knows. You fall in love not because that person flatters you into thinking that you know everything, but because that person makes you realize that you know nothing—and you aren't embarrassed, but intrigued. You fall in love with what you don't have, with what that person drives you to find, with the powerful underground spring that you have walked over all this time without knowing it was there. And you beat a path to where that person tapped the spring, and then you sit in the dust at the feet of scholars and drink in their words.

My mother fell in teacher love when she was eight years old. Her parents had sent her to Hebrew school, where they told her she would learn "Jewish." She was delighted that she would soon understand her parents' secret Yiddish conversations, and only several months later did she realize with great disappointment that she was learning the wrong language. But in the meantime, she fell in love. Her Hebrew school teacher had such a passion for Jewish history, life, language, and texts that she followed him home one day and found herself in a vast private library of books full of ideas she had never known to exist. She returned nearly every week for the next fifty years. She followed him to the university where he became a professor and received her doctorate from him, and later she brought me and my brother and sisters to his home as we grew up, so that we too could drink in his words. As a child, I knew that visiting him wasn't the same as visiting a relative or my parents' friends, because he wasn't a relative or even really a friend. He was a teacher, and it was obvious from the moment one walked into his house, when he would begin pulling books off the shelves and ritual objects off the tables, a constant show-and-tell of things he had discovered. He taught me to read Torah, taught me to play chess, loaned me books from his jeal-ously guarded library, guided me through college research projects on Hebrew poetry, fact-checked my first novel. When he died suddenly sev-eral months ago, I realized that even with all of the words we drank in at his feet, he had still left us with the thirst.

Teacher love is like other kinds of love: It might sneak up on you the first time, but once you have experienced it, you will never be able to live without it, and you will always search for it again. When I went to col-lege, I knew I needed to find a teacher the way other students knew they had to find boyfriends or girlfriends. And one day I took a course in modern Jewish literature and fell in love.

It happened by surprise, the way it had for my mother. Because of my mother's teacher, I had already fallen in love with Hebrew literature, and I took the class because there were a few Hebrew works on the syllabus. The rest of the books were mostly translations from Yiddish, about which I knew nothing and cared even less, but I was confident that I could figure out what the professor wanted.

I quickly saw, however, that this professor didn't want much. She wanted us to read the books—not necessarily to like them, but to read them, and to take them seriously. These were books by authors whom I had never even heard of, and they were masterpieces. One was a novel by Yankev Glatshteyn, an American Yiddish poet whose works had almost never been translated. The novel had been translated, but it was long out-of-print; in class, we read it from wilted photocopies. I read and was amazed by how good it was—and by how similar it was to one of my favorite books, a Hebrew novel of the same era. It was then that I mus-tered the courage to venture into the hallway after class, to ask the pro-fessor if I could write my paper comparing the two. It was like asking someone out.

I was nervous, but nothing can describe my excitement when she said yes. And when she confessed that she was currently writing a chapter of her own book on exactly that topic, I was smitten. But it was when I en-tered her office for the first time that I knew I was in love. Her office, like my mother's teacher's home, was overflowing with books about things I had never heard of, in a language I couldn't read. And just the way my mother once had, I looked around at those books—nearly all of them old, crumbling, out-of-print, and in Yiddish—and saw the frightening edge of my own knowledge, the vast world that lay just beyond the precipice. I learned Yiddish the following year.

In the Jewish tradition, teacher love is almost a requirement. "Make for yourself a teacher," the Mishnah advises us, "and acquire for yourself a friend, and when you judge all people, give them the benefit of the doubt." The three parts of this verse have bothered me in turn as I have grown up. But only now do I see that they are all pieces of the same relationship: The creation of the teacher by the student, the bond that grows between them, and the readiness to love—the courage to know that love can only emerge when we are open to the possibility of changing someone else's life. And when you have seen the power of that possibility, you feel the enormous guilt of accepting anything less.

In any subject, the teacher's guilt for not inspiring every one of her students is acute. But in the field of Jewish studies, it is colossal. If I were teaching English literature and failed to ignite my students' passion, I would know in the back of my mind that those students might still brush up on their Shakespeare with the professor down the hall. But because I am teaching Hebrew literature, which few people in America have ever studied, and Yiddish literature, which fewer people in the world have even heard of, there usually isn't anyone down the hall. When I walk into my first day of class each term, I know that this course is very likely the last time my students will ever stand at the door to a room full of thousands of years of buried treasure—and I am the only one holding the key. If I fail to engage their imaginations, the loss is not merely mine or theirs. Thousands of forgotten words lie buried beneath each mediocre paper, thousands of vanished thoughts are hidden behind every get-out-of-class excuse. For the key I am holding is not an ordinary key. It is attached to a golden chain of teachers, linked from one student-turned-teacher to another, stretching across generations and leading all the way back to Sinai. I am only twenty-seven years old, but already I am looking around at my students, wondering whether I will succeed in passing it along—or whether I will become the last of the last, the most diminished of scholars, without students to follow me, fading away while still holding the key in my hands.

Too often, love hurts, and I felt that heartbreak in the very first class I ever taught. I was only a year or two into my doctoral program, and I was a teaching assistant in a course in modern Jewish literature, responsible for enlightening and evaluating seventeen students barely younger than I was. I invited them to sign up for individual appointments with me during my office hours; I told myself that I was helping shy students come out of their shells, but really I did it for me. I was looking for love.

I was thrilled when the first student—*my* first student, the very first student I ever had in my life—arrived at my door. I faced him, nervous. He waited expectantly for me to speak, until I finally found the courage to ask him about himself. He leaned forward, and my heart rose with hope. Then he pounded the table with his fist and said, "I'm a biology major, I'm a junior, I'm applying to medical school, and I need an A in this class."

I braced myself against my desk, remembering what I had been like years ago—all those smart-aleck questions when I didn't yet know just how much I didn't know—and didn't laugh. Instead, I gave him the benefit of the doubt. For the next two months, he sat right at my side at our seminar table, took notes furiously, and raised his hand at every opportunity. He then proceeded to plagiarize his first paper. Needless to say, he did not receive an A in the class. But I was the one who went home heartbroken—because when you are a teacher, every student's failure is partly your own.

I'm still only an apprentice teacher, about to jump out of the world of being a student and into the great beyond. And I am always aware of the guilt one must bear when love fails. But last semester, a student took me by surprise.

He was a freshman, and he came into my office with a confused look on his face and a familiar complaint. "I just don't know what to write my paper about," he moaned.

It's a lament that I have long learned to translate in my head as a request for "what she wants." Before I even answered him, I felt the key falling from my hands. I offered a few suggestions, each with less enthu-siasm than the last. But at one of them, for reasons mysterious to me, his face lit up. He returned the following week carrying an enormous stack of books, explaining that one thing had led to another, and then another and another, and would it be okay if his paper was a little longer than what he had been assigned? I sat stunned behind my desk, looked at the stacks of Hebrew literature photocopies littering my office, and won-dered if it was love.

When the class ended—after he had turned in his excellent paper—he made a strange confession: He had taken my course by accident, after being bumped out of his first-choice class. But here he was, still revising the paper he had already turned in, wondering if I could give him more reading recommendations, and asking what class I planned to teach next.

It's summertime now, and I'm looking forward to fall, hoping he'll be there—and relieved to know, finally, that I am no longer the last.

Holy Guilt Trip

*

Rabbi Sharon Brous

As a rabbi, I am a living, breathing trigger for other people's guilt.

Over the past 12 years, nearly every social encounter has been punctuated by some variation on the classic: "Oh my God, you're a rabbi? I'm *such* a bad Jew. I haven't been to services since my Bat Mitzvah." People feel compelled to expose either their greatest vulnerabilities—"I've just never been attracted to Jewish women. Am I a traitor?"—or their family's—"My brother intermarried. Is that really bad?"—before I can even get their names.

Apparently, something about me elicits reflexive, often involuntary confessions. It's as if my very presence reminds people of all of the ways that they fall short—they're not good enough, not religious enough, not doing enough to fight poverty. Each time it happens, I am shocked and flattered that people trust me enough to offer up their deepest insecurities as small talk. Sometimes though, penitents get so caught up in their confessions that they don't notice that I'm holding an hors d'oeuvre plate in one hand and a crying baby in the other, and am just trying to make my way over to an empty seat in the corner. I'm starting to understand why so many rabbis appear to the untrained eye to be socially challenged—avoiding eye contact, abruptly cutting conversations short, and slipping out the back door whenever possible. It's about survival.

I am also the ultimate buzz kill at a party. "Oh, I'm so sorry, rabbi," after a crude joke. "Excuse the language, rabbi," after an accidental curse over a spill, "I'm so embarrassed that you had to hear that, rabbi." And, commingling with the apologists are the rebels—those who feel the need to flaunt their freedom from the bonds of institutional religion by deflating the grandeur of the holy rabbinate. Once, on the way out the door, a congregant leaned over to me and whispered, "My girlfriend and I have to go home now—*to have crazy sex!*" I have a decent sense of humor, but this comment, accompanied by a pretty gruesome hand gesture, was almost enough to send me running to the *mikvah*. Whether it manifests itself as apology or defiance, I'm certain that it's all rooted in the same fervent desire to reclaim power from The Religious Authorities, whom I apparently represent.

The great irony, of course, is that I, as a woman rabbi, am an even greater disappointment to those authorities than are any of the heretics who confess their sins to me. Forget the guilt about not attending second-day Rosh Hashanah services; I bear the guilt of knowing that most of the religious world holds me accountable for chipping away at the last vestiges of our sacred tradition in the modern world. My years of therapy in a clip: I am an eternal teenager, trying desperately to secure an invite to the cool party, until finally, resisting rejection, I sneak in through the back window only to realize that most of the people inside don't even want me there. And that it isn't that cool anyway. Nevertheless, I refuse to walk away.

My falling in love with Judaism was born out of a feeling of isolation and alienation from everything that was supposed to be my own. I grew up in a family of devoted adherents to a bizarre and confusing blend of ritual observances. We were, I later came to understand, *haredi* Reform: We ate bacon regularly, but never ham, God forbid (we weren't *goyim!*). We worked on Shabbat (my parents were in retail), but wouldn't think of sewing a button on a shirt until the sun went down Saturday night. We sat through Yom Kippur services in desperate boredom, just waiting for the rabbi's sermon so we could pass judgment as two-thirds of the congregation inevitably exited for their snack break, leaving only my family and the elderly and infirmed—the folks who literally couldn't leave—to hear his remarks.

While I chose my college partially for the great Jewish life it promised,

I was decidedly uninterested in studying anything Jewish. Luxuriating in the stacks of my secular liberal arts university, I was well trained in political discourse, high on history, sociology, and psychology, and far more knowledgeable about the dangers of theocracy than the nuances of theodicy. I found myself doing what I thought all good Jews were supposed to do: immersing myself in study, volunteering pretty regularly, reading the *New York Times* over coffee and bagels, and generally trying to be a decent human being.

Then one night, I was invited to Shabbat dinner by a religious classmate who asked me to bring salad dressing. I'll never forget her frantic scream after I placed the unopened bottle of Italian dressing on her kitchen counter, insisting that I had, "totally *treyfed* up the kitchen by bringing in *unhekhshered* food." *Treyf? Hekhsher?* I was mortified and guilt-ridden—as much by my stupid mistake as by the fact that I didn't understand half the words she was shouting at me.

I went on to have one humiliating experience after another that year and the next—trying to find a place for myself in the Jewish community, but ultimately realizing that I was more an alien invader than a fellow traveler. I was ashamed of my ignorance and resentful of the judgment I encountered among the religious. I suppose that most people would respond to that shame and resentment by bidding farewell to the strange world of head coverings, scruffy beards, and long denim skirts, but I'm such a sucker for guilt that I chose to do the opposite.

I decided that it wouldn't be enough to peruse the Jewish section at Barnes & Noble or take an Introduction to Judaism class. Instead, I booked my first trip to Israel. My hope was that a semester in Israel would help me understand what my parents and grandparents had so artfully rejected, and at the same time I'd acquire some tools to slap back the next time I felt persecuted by the religious.

Despite my desire to learn and engage, I remained quite cynical. I suppose that's why I was surprised to find myself, a few days after arriving in Jerusalem, weaving through the crowded plaza of the Western Wall, driven by an acute need to confess my failures as a Jew and a human being to God.

"I'm sorry," I sputtered awkwardly. "I'm sorry that the highlight of

Rosh Hashanah every year was sneaking out of services with my sister to stick *'Fur Is Dead'* cards in the pockets of the minks in the coatroom. I'm sorry for kissing Josh Schwartz *in the sanctuary* on a Shabbaton in '89, for watching *The A-Team* and *The Dukes of Hazzard* instead of doing something meaningful with my early adolescence, for taking perverse pleasure in stumping my pathetic religious school teachers, for not trying hard enough to make sense of the jumbled mess of my Jewish identity."

"*I'm sorry!*" I said again, this time slightly irked by the dramatic silence. "I'm not a bad person. You've probably forgiven people for worse."

"True enough," God finally replied, in a dismissive calm apropos only to the Creator of Heaven and Earth. "I just don't know why it took you so long to call."

So I had finally garnered the courage to leave the comfort zone of secular, rational, academic thought to try to have a conversation with God, and I got scolded for it. Not only that, but the encounter took place at the Western Wall in Jerusalem of all places—how trite! How uninspired! And yet, this was my story, unfolding before my teary eyes. My heart raced and I stood there, bundled up in the long wraparound skirt generously provided by the Orthodox establishment to protect heretical women from revealing themselves in T-shirts and jeans before the ancient bricks of the Temple retaining wall.

My big mistake was in believing that the guilt trip would end once the conversation with God began. Little did I know this was only the beginning. My unexpected conversation with God inspired a year of intensive Torah study and deep spiritual seeking. I quickly realized that I was far more stimulated by the study of Talmud and the quest for meaning than I ever had been by my secular studies. It dawned on me that attached to my Western brain there was a Jewish heart that also needed cultivation.

I spent my evenings in Jerusalem's bars, in purposeful conversation with a number of people interested in saving the lost souls of wandering Jews from suburban America. These soul savers, whose lifestyle intrigued and aggravated me, tried to convince me of the virtues of *halakhic* living, of Orthodoxy, and I challenged, debated, and struggled to understand their beliefs and practices.

It was a lovely, dynamic engagement until the moment I realized that

I had fallen deeply in love with Torah, and God and I had sort of made up. I wanted, I *needed* everything that these religious people had—just in a way that would preserve my dignity as a woman and a human being. I had to find a way to build a Jewish life that would affirm who I was as a woman, an activist, and a thinker; one that would engage, not undermine, all aspects of my identity.

It dawned on me with a certainty I had never known in my life: I would become a rabbi. Convinced that my path had chosen me even more than I had chosen it, I dared to utter the words out loud to one of my shepherds.

"A *rabbi?*" my soul saver asked, in horror. "What's wrong with becoming a *rebbetzin?*"

"I don't want to *marry* a person in love with Torah and God," I responded. "I want to *be* that person."

It is still unusual for a young woman to choose the rabbinate. Ordination of women rabbis began in the mid-seventies, but the male–female ratio at rabbinical gatherings makes the Senate look generous to women. It was a particularly unnatural and illogical step for me because I grew up on the tough streets of Short Hills, New Jersey—a world in which the choices a youngster could make were three: law school, medical school, or business school. A few iconoclasts chose a career in the arts, but we only spoke of such people in hushed voices. The rabbinate was practically unthinkable—a path appropriate only for those who could not get into law school. Even with a legacy.

What I didn't know at the time was that deciding to become a rabbi for a woman means deciding to become a *woman rabbi*, itself a distasteful oxymoron in much of the religious world, and an inescapable source of angst even in the liberal Jewish world. I quickly learned that there actually *was* something worse than being an ignorant, illiterate, High Holy Day Jew who didn't know that salad dressing had to be kosher. My very being—as a strong, serious, spirited woman in love with Judaism—posed an existential threat to the Jewish people, and my passion for Torah and tradition only added insult to injury.

I have come to understand that guilt is axiomatic to a career in the rabbinate. It seems to be something of an institutional necessity for all clergy members—maybe the price we pay in return for parsonage. The great miscalculation I made was in assuming that my guilt tab would be limited to the two biggies: family and congregants. Explaining to your kids why you can be present for the intimate moments of everyone else's family but never seem to have time for your own is a classic. And explaining to the random couple you bump into in the supermarket why you don't remember every detail of their marital woes, despite the fact that you counseled them for an hour seven years ago, is not easy either. The fact that it's not humanly possible to do everything, or to remember everyone, doesn't make people any more forgiving—or clergy any less guilt-ridden.

But guilt for women rabbis is far more complicated. Over the years, I have become masterful at inadvertently inviting, then sidestepping, the ugly interdenominational rage that manages to transcend the norms of social conduct. At my brother's wedding in Jerusalem, I was stopped by an Ultra Orthodox woman in the hotel lobby.

"Excuse me, what do you think you're doing?" she asked me snidely.

"Um, trying to celebrate my brother's wedding," I replied.

"No, I mean what's that on your head?" she asked.

"Oh, this?" I offered, taking it off to show her up close, as if she were legitimately asking. "This is called a *kippah*—Jews wear it as a sign of humility and reverence before God."

"Jewish *men* wear *kippot*," she reprimanded me. "You ought to be ashamed of yourself!"

"Thank you," I said sweetly, purposely oblivious to her insult. "I'll take that as a mazel tov!"

I think I could handle my perpetual alienation from the religious world were it not that my religiosity simultaneously renders me virtually crazy in the secular world. As a rabbi, I embody for many people all that is wrong with Judaism, God, Torah, and the cosmos.

To those critics, I say, "Look, I'm sorry that Judaism's not an easy entrance religion. I'm sorry that Religious School was so lame. I'm sorry that Hebrew makes your head spin. I'm sorry that Rosh Hashanah services are so damn long. I'm sorry I don't have a big white beard. Most of all, I'm sorry for *musaf*—but it's really *not* my fault! Everything worthwhile takes hard work and discipline." I wonder if one day I'll ever just be *me*. People have projected so much anger and judgment on my shoulders that my back is literally starting to hurt.

In seventh grade, in an act of evil genius, the administration of my suburban junior high school decided to deal with the cataclysmically awkward social development of adolescents by forcing us to confront our worst fears head-on. On the first day of school, we had to choose three friends with whom we'd be bound to share a table in the school cafeteria for the next three years.

I went through utter turmoil trying to decide on my seating assignment. I knew I didn't really have a shot at the popular table, I wouldn't go near the nerdy Jewish table (where I probably belonged), I couldn't even pretend to fit in at the bad girl table, and even though I played clarinet, there was no way I wanted to sit with the band geeks. I found this challenge utterly stupefying. I am a little bit of all of these things. Why are they making me decide?

As a grown-up, I think of that agonizing seventh-grade decision all the time. I am religious, which makes me a traitor to the women's movement. I am a feminist, which makes me a categorical pain in the ass to traditional Judaism. I am a human rights activist, but I am in love with the state of Israel. I am a spiritual leader of a community, but sometimes feel that I don't have a right to pray. My husband is a sweet Jewish guy, but he has a penchant for writing teen sex comedies. Sometimes there are so many complexities to struggle with, so many things to feel guilty about, and so many people to let down that I resent Shabbat for making me take a break from it all.

But ultimately, it is precisely Shabbat that gives me the strength to persevere. As the sun falls on Friday night, I am able to move beyond the guilt, the judgment, and the disappointment and be present to the holiness around me. On Shabbat, I remember why I am doing all of this in the first place. I find myself in a place where it's safe to breathe, to sing, to sit in silence, and to dream with God about what is possible, rather than be mired in what is. And for a Jewishly illiterate, borderline popular, somewhat nerdy kid from Short Hills, that's not half bad.

Our *Bubbes*, Ourselves:

Trying to Please the Family

American Express

*

Cynthia Kaplan

About four or five years ago I got my grandmother an American Express card that was attached to my account. This was, in my opinion, the coup de maître, the masterstroke, of what had become, over time, a veritable catalog of lifestyle "improvements" I'd attempted to impose upon her in her late eighties. At that time, she was beginning to show the first symptoms of what I at first presumed to be a garden-variety, age-appropriate forgetfulness, but turned out to be the onset of Alzheimer's. While I'd had limited success with some earlier catalog entries—hearing aids, sneakers, and, my personal favorite, nonstick pans—I felt confident that an American Express card was the perfect antidote to her growing confusion during shopping expeditions. Now she wouldn't have to worry about counting cash or writing out checks. She could buy anything she wanted, anywhere she wanted, with The Card, and she could just pay me back later. It seemed like such a reasonable idea, especially since I knew she wasn't the type to stay up till all hours ordering a year's supply of Victoria Principal beauty aids from the Home Shopping Network, or suddenly decide one morning while cooking Cream of Wheat that what she could really use is a ten-thousand-dollar Garland stove.

Up until then the only credit card she ever had was a B. Altman's card. When it came time to pay a bill, she went to the store and hand-delivered her payment, in full. I'm not sure my grandmother even waited for the B. Altman's bill to arrive in the mail before she took the bus back across town to the store to pay it. In fact, this was how she paid all of her bills. Once a month we walked her rent check to the rental office of her building complex. The telephone bill was brought to an AT&T storefront on Eighth Avenue.

Maybe she just didn't trust the United States Postal Service, which was odd because there was a view from my grandparents' window of the old post office at Twenty-Ninth Street. A very long time ago, when we were young and short, my brother and I used to stand on the two-foot-high radiator cover beneath the window in the den and watch the postal trucks navigate the rooftop parking lot on the federal building next door to it. It all seemed on the up-and-up. But these were the Reagan years, and perhaps my grandmother, a socialist, felt particularly disenfranchised.

When she paid in cash, my grandmother withdrew any one of several combinations of bills and coins from her billfold, her change purse, an inside pocket of her pocketbook, and a second, smaller billfold. Occasionally, she pressed into service the extra twenty she kept in the pocket of her skirt.

The American Express card never quite caught on. Primarily, it turned out that its Enormous Buying Power, such as I was able to describe it to her, was antithetical to my grandmother's sense of privacy. Who needed someone to know so much about you? Where you shop, what you buy, how much credit you have? My grandmother didn't like anyone to know *anything* about her. A person could ask the most innocuous question— where she grew up or if she'd ever traveled to Norway—and she would say later, "What does she need to know that for?" and, indignantly, "She asked me if I'd ever been to Norway! Can you imagine?" My grandmother read judgment into personal questions, as if they were questions on a quiz and there were a right and wrong answer. A wrong answer might mean she was provincial. A right answer might reveal she was too bourgeois. So my grandmother would say, "Oh, I've been here and there." Her tone would have been coy, but her intent clear. She may well have danced the tarantella with Henrik Ibsen on a moonlit night in Oslo, but if she did, it was no one's business but her own.

I can see now, too, that the American Express card was too open-ended for my grandmother, its functionality so wide-ranging as to render it irredeemably vague. Who exactly was American Express, anyway? Wasn't it a travel agency? At one point, she asked me if we were going on a trip. I should have dropped the whole enterprise then and there. My grandmother had always been literal-minded, even before the Alzheimer's. Moreover, in her prime, with all her faculties intact, it would never have occurred to her to buy things she could not pay for with the money she had in the bank. Buying on credit was too precarious, too fraught with the possibility of blowing it all, all the gains, all the sweat and struggle. It was even, perhaps, a little unsavory. Where were they going to get this money, anyway, when it came time to pay the piper? Nobody wanted to be chased down Ninth Avenue by a thug named Pinky. My grandparents lived in the same two-bedroom apartment for over forty years. It was neat and clean and very comfortable, but not too fancy, nothing bought on an installment plan. Besides, fancy was dangerous. Fancy meant that it was always possible that the socialists would come one day, revoke my grandparents membership, and occupy the apartment in their name of The People, as they did Ralph Richardson's mansion in *Dr. Zhivago.*

My grandmother's B. Altman card was more a symbol of customer loyalty than an expression of financial free will. It was a permanent record of her proud affiliation with the store, which may be why she carried it long after B. Altman's closed. It remained in her wallet like an I.D. card. In a way, it was. B. Altman's sold quality clothes, well made, not flashy, and of good value. That's what my grandmother wore. That is who she was: well made, not flashy, good value.

My grandmother grew up in Russia in poverty. She rarely spoke of her childhood, but I have gathered, from the little she has told me, that her father was the great love of her life. (That is, aside from *my* father. I'm sure she loved my grandfather, too; they were married for sixty-seven years, but, well, *twin beds.*) My grandmother's father was a feckless fellow, not much of a breadwinner, but, by her account, merry and charming. My grandmother was the eldest of four girls and he treated her as though she was his son, which, in the old days, was a great compliment. He took her everywhere, often on his shoulders. Maybe that last part isn't true. But it's a visual image I have of them now, jaunty and quixotic, extrapolated from what my grandmother told me, or maybe just from a look on her face. Her father became ill and died when she was nine or ten. After that the family burned the furniture for firewood. Or something like that. Then the Revolution came and they got out. They sailed from Constantinople to Marseille to Ellis Island when my grandmother was sixteen. At least she said she was, so she could work. When she got to Ellis Island she went into the ladies' washroom, took all of her clothes off, washed herself and the clothes in the sink, and then put the clothes back on. That's what they mean when they say they had only the clothes on their backs.

I go to the nursing home today as I have done innumerable times. As I exit the elevator, I see through the giant fish tank that makes up most of the wall between the hallway and the rec room that it is TV time. Rows and rows of wavy figures seated in wavy wheelchairs face a large TV screen. Through the oxygenated, undulating water it looks like an Impressionist painting, blurry and vivid at the same time. *The Old and Infirm in the Evening at Westchester.* I'm not sure what they are watching; it is probably a rerun of *Matlock* or *Murder, She Wrote.* I don't know why but I wish it were something incongruous, like World Cup Soccer. It sure isn't PBS, which is too bad; my grandmother was a lifelong supporter of Channel Thirteen. She drank her lukewarm coffee from its mugs and carried her book-club books and rubber rain shoes in its canvas tote bags. During her last year in the apartment she had become an ardent fan of *Riverdance.*

From the doorway it is not hard for me to spot the back of my grandmother's little white head and bent neck. Even if she were dressed in a Santa Claus outfit and sitting in a sea of Santa Clauses, I would still recognize her from behind. Isn't it funny how that is? Once I would have been happy to find her so situated, in the company of others, but now I am saddened. The old Grandma would never have willingly joined in any such gathering. She would have wandered around on her sturdy, ankleless legs, doing her own thing, chatting up the desk nurses with her nonsense, snidely refusing to partake in group functions. Sometimes I am sorry my grandmother never swore. She would have been well served by the expression "Fuck that shit."

Tonight she is wearing an outfit I do not recognize. It consists of a white blouse and a faded-to-white floral print thing that is wrapped around her waist, and I can't tell if it is supposed to be a skirt or what. These items are not hers. Sometimes it still amazes me that I know every single piece of her clothing. Underneath all this is a thin white layer that appears to be a full slip. My grandmother dabs her nostril with a corner of the skirt. It is not totally unreasonable to believe that she might have mistaken this for a hanky. I am sure she first searched for a pocket in which she hoped to find a Kleenex, because that is where she always kept one or two, neatly folded, along with her key, which was safety-pinned to the pocket lining. I come up to her and touch her shoulders. Hi, Grandma, I say. It's Cindy. Who, who? she asks. I put my face right up to hers. It's Cindy. Who? Oh, my Cindy. I wheel her away to the winter garden to look out at the falling leaves.

Once, not so long ago, my grandmother, a dressmaker by trade who expertly sewed many of her own clothes, would have as soon wiped her nose on her skirt as she would have sent a holiday card to Richard Nixon. She took enormous pride in her appearance—her smooth, ironed blouses and soft cardigan sweaters, her fully-lined wool skirts with their neat on-seam pockets. My grandfather once told me that one very warm evening, not long after he first met my grandmother, he ran into her at a concert in Philadelphia's Fairmont Park, and my grandmother pretended not to know him. So, partway through the concert, when he found her sitting on a bench with an open book in her lap, he suggested to her that she had brought the book along so people would think she was an intellectual. He told her he doubted that she had even read it. Insulted, my grandmother stomped away, but it was so hot out that her white skirt stuck to her thighs and she had to peel it away in full view of my grandfather. I like to imagine that perhaps this was why, for as long as I knew her, even through dementia, she never wore a skirt without a lining or a slip.

My grandmother also took pride in her hard-earned accomplishments, her spotless apartment with its all-over, moss-colored carpeting and clean white walls, painted every two years. Over time the light switches had become harder and harder to locate, obscured beneath fifteen layers of

Benjamin Moore China White. When my grandmother first saw the tiny, charming brownstone apartment I lived in when I was single, with its hardwood floors and wall of exposed brick, she was appalled. She knew from experience that that is how the poor lived. Certainly it's where the pogroms, should they return, would find you huddled, perhaps in the pitiable glare of a bare lightbulb because someone this poor probably wouldn't have lampshades. Nice people, people whose grandmothers had B. Altman cards, for example, had rugs and paint.

We are told that sometimes now my grandmother is found sleeping in other patients' beds, and they in hers. Her bras disappear on a weekly basis; occasionally it is clear that she is not wearing one. Among the pictures on her bureau is one of a little girl none of us know. I call her Missy. I like to imagine her to be the sister my grandmother referred to when the Alzheimer's got her to thinking I had one. The photo album of our *actual* family, the one I made for her a few weeks after she moved to the nursing home, has long since disappeared, and I fear some other resident, one with a milder case of dementia, will look through the photographs and gasp in horror because, for the first time, *she does not recognize her own family.*

At first we railed against the system. My mother sewed name tags into my grandmother's clothes, as she had into mine and my brother's when we left for sleepaway camp. (She probably just snipped a bunch of Kaplans from what was left of the thirty-year-old roll of Cindy Kaplans.) So, where are my grandmother's things? Sometimes I worry that people are dying in clothes labeled Kaplan. We demand an accounting of the garment situation from the social worker. She has none. Or rather the answer is obvious. My grandmother's fashion sense is a thing of the past. Perhaps the more unrecognizable she is to me, the easier it will be.

She has also become too frail to take out of the nursing home. Nothing pleased my grandmother more than getting into our car for the five-minute ride to the local diner. The food there was very mediocre, which was exactly how she liked it. She was ecstatic just to see the car pull in at lunchtime to pick her up and was equally thrilled after the meal, as if she hadn't seen the very same car in years, much less an hour and a half. She praised it lavishly. "That's a beautiful car you have." Or "Oh, my goodness, that's your car? Since when?" It was there at the diner that, with a supernatural power often attributed in the movies to the aged or to four-year-old Victorian-era children previously thought to have been drowned, she intuited that I was pregnant. One winter day, as we waited for my husband David to pay the bill, and apropos of nothing, my grandmother smiled and patted my stomach. "Ahh," she said, and "Well, well, well."

There was a long time during which I felt that I could not have a child while I was helping to take care of my grandmother because, in a sense, she was my child. Then she went into the home and I had a son. It is the natural order of things. The King is dead, long live the King. But so have I been usurped. She loves the baby, *loves* him, but she hasn't said my name unprompted in a long time. I have begun to miss her, the old Grandma, as she once was. I have thought all along that the baby filled the space but I see now that it is a different space. She and I used to hold hands all the time, even while we were sitting around. "I just need *you*," she would say, clutching my hand, holding it to her cheek. I have stopped holding her hands, because, well, now I am holding the baby. But is there anything in the world that feels or looks like an old person's skin? The baby's? No, not the baby's. The baby's skin is opaque, it is made up of layers and layers of constantly multiplying cells, it is all promise. My grandmother's skin is transparent, blue-tinged and smooth like something worn down to its essence, like sea glass. It may not withstand the tides another year. Soon it will disappear.

Sometimes days go by now and I don't think of her.

S UDDENLY, American Express promotional offers are coming to my apartment addressed to Dorothy Kaplan. Does she want to join my gym and get a half-price facial? Is she interested in European travel excursions? Does she want to shop at Michael C. Fina or stay in a Hilton Hotel for a special price if she uses The Card? I'd like to know where they were when she *had* the card. I'd also like to know why they are not offering any of these discounts to me when I have been a Loyal Card Member Since 1985. Perhaps some small cog in the American Express marketing wheel has been digging up obsolete records in order to fill a quota. The first time it happened I was startled. No, shocked. Seeing her name like that—it was as if I had received a piece of mail addressed to Rip Van Winkle. But at the same time, I secretly thought: Hmm, Dorothy Kaplan, why these are not concerns of mine anymore. Oh, the relief, now that she was in the home. Which is a terrible thing to feel, I know. I used to sit in her apartment sorting her mail into its various categories—junk mail, bills I would pay with her checkbook, things my father should look at when he comes, letters addressed to my deceased grandfather—while thinking of the million other things I had to do, *wanted* to do. And it was, well, really wonderful not to worry that she would become lost in a blizzard, fall in the bath, or leave the stove on. But all this relief was fleeting because with it came an admonishment, as though each letter, each postcard posed the burning question: *What have you done with Dorothy Kaplan?*

I wrote about the terrible day we put my grandmother in the nursing home for a newspaper. After the piece ran, letters came to the newspaper, some addressed to the editors, some to me, an almost unanimous outpouring of sympathy. Many people just wrote because they wanted someone with whom they could share their own agonized stories. I was sent e-mails and letters from around the country, books on Alzheimer's by their authors, and even a tape of Alzheimer's-inspired music. What that kind of music sounds like I still do not know. My dread of it outweighs my curiosity.

But there were a couple of other letters. Rebukes. One in particular from a Japanese man who indicted our society, American society, as a whole, asking why we do not care for our loved ones as they did for us, why we let someone else pick up the tab. We have broken the natural cycle of family life, he wrote. People all over the world attend to their elderly in their own homes, he said, and it should be an honor to do so.

Oy. Well, why *was* she in a nursing home? Why wasn't she at home or with her family, where she could still get mail? Where she could avail herself of promotional discounts like any American has the right to do? For one thing, it had gotten to the point where she needed twenty-four-hour supervision, something none of us could have provided. As it was, my parents, my brother, and I had been locked in a fairly tight, near daily rotation of visits to my grandmother's apartment for the past couple of years. In fact, we probably waited longer than we should have to get her professional help—she still liked to stand on a chair to change a lightbulb. This doesn't sound like a big deal until you factor in that the chair was on top of the kitchen table. And another thing—had my grandmother moved in with my parents, we would have had to send my *mother* to a home.

O N a cold, grim day in March, with my father at her side, my grandmother dies. We bury her next to my grandfather. There is no formal funeral, only a graveside service presided over by a local rabbi whom none of us know. I do not cry, which is uncharacteristic, because I am an accomplished crier, but I hadn't seen my grandmother in the weeks before her death and I am not one hundred percent sure that she is gone. All that mixing and matching in the nursing home. Perhaps Mrs. Perlmutter, from down the hall, was laying in my grandmother's bed dressed in her herringbone blazer with the ORT pin on the lapel when she stopped breathing. In my mind it is likely that I will drive up to the home a few days from now (or a week, or however long I put it off for) and my grandmother will still be there. In fact, during the funeral, I take almost no notice of my grandmother's casket until we are preparing to leave the cemetery. But as I walk away I cast a last, cursory glance back, and I am so startled by what I see there that I do a noisy, neck-wrenching double take, like Lou Costello in *Abbott and Costello Meet the Mummy.*

Someone has placed a little ivory figure of a harp seal on top of the coffin. *Her* little ivory figure of a harp seal. It had lived, along with a Wedgwood ashtray, a University of Pennsylvania shot glass I had given her, and a jade something or other, on the top tier of a three-tiered occasional table in her apartment for as long as I can remember. Its sudden apparitional appearance is deeply and utterly spooky. I grab my mother's arm and point to it. She, too, gasps. Then she remembers that my grandmother had given it to her grandnephew, Michael, who was eleven or twelve. He must have decided to return it from whence it came. Clever boy.

They say that the older memories are the ones that endure. That when you can no longer work the telephone or the washing machine, other stuff, stuff that's been in deep storage, is extruded through those gaps and floods the consciousness with ancient goop. A family trip to the seashore in 1908, say. Or the time a horse kicked you in the forehead. I say *you*, to be inclusive, but I mean my grandfather, specifically, who liked to reference his scar on a regular basis. I had not seen that ivory seal in years, but now I will remember it to my dying day. I will picture the variegated whites of its ivory body, the perfectly rounded curve of its head, and the graceful tilt of its tail. I will remember how, as a child, I loved the hard, smooth feel of it in my hands. I would stroke it tenderly and then I would hold it to my lips and cheek, where it felt cool. It will come back to me at odd moments of my life. It will appear in my dreams and find its way into my stories, like a kick in the head from a horse. And it helps, somehow, to think of my grandmother reunited with it. I hope she will know it when she sees it.

So, why did I want my grandmother to have an American Express card? Why? Why did I want her to have hearing aids and sneakers? Why, for God's sake, did I want her to have Teflon? Was I trying to make her last longer, to keep her sharp, to stave off what was more and more obviously the inevitable? Yes, I was trying to save her, but I was also trying to save myself. When my grandmother died I would no longer be a grandchild. The last little part of my childhood that belonged to me still, because I had a grandparent who was alive, would end, and the prospect of that ending seemed to be something that must be prevented, even at the risk, however unlikely, of a Garland stove. No matter that I was already a grown-up, or that I worked and had a husband. No matter how badly I'd wanted my *own* child, I still wanted to *be* one. That sounds incredibly selfish but there it is. I am notoriously nostalgic for my childhood and I had counted on my grandmother to be a conduit. The relationship between grandchildren and grandparents is established early and is constructed of some fairly basic elements—playing Scrabble, building houses with playing cards, flipping drink coasters, divvying up small treasures. And who else but a grandmother ever fried bologna?

What is remarkable is that these elements do not change with time. They do not age with you, they do not become obsolete. At least they did not for us, perhaps because my grandparents never bought any new games. But that is not why as adults my brother and I often sat on my grandparents' living-room carpet and built card houses. We did it because we still could. And now we can't.

I suppose I wanted my grandmother to have The Card for exactly the reason she did not want it. For its endless possibilities. I felt that if she could learn to use an American Express card she could learn anything, do anything, except go to the Olympics, of course, where Visa still purports to have a stranglehold. It was a test really, which she failed not only because it was her nature, but because she had already begun to suffer from Alzheimer's. She had begun, despite my many protestations, her transformation from the grandmother of a child to the grandmother of an adult. And I had begun a transformation of my own.

Land of My Father

*

AYELET WALDMAN

THE spring after I graduated from Wesleyan University I reported, as instructed, to the draft office near the Megiddo intersection, outside of Afula in the north of Israel. I had hitchhiked there from the kibbutz where I had been living for the past few months. These were the days when everyone in Israel still hitchhiked, even twenty-one-year-old American women on their way to be given their induction dates for service in the Israeli Defense Forces.

I made some concessions to safety, hauling back my thumb when I saw the telltale blue or green license plate that indicated an Arab from the Occupied Territories, sticking it out more aggressively when the plate was acceptable Israeli yellow. By the time I arrived at my destination, I was thirsty, dusty from standing at the side of the road by the fields of feed corn and alfalfa, and chewing my nails from anxiety.

I was also excited, enamored of the romance of wearing a uniform and strapping on an Uzi (or—since I am female—more likely a steno pad) on behalf of the Israeli government, her people, and the ideal of a Jewish nation.

My family is Labor-Zionist the way other Jewish families are Reform or Conservative. We did not go to synagogue when I was growing up, even on the High Holy Days, and none of my father's six children had Bar or Bat Mitzvahs. We observed only two holidays: Hanukkah and Passover. Our seder was an abbreviated one that deleted all references to God, substituting a theology cobbled together from parts of the Haggadah, a little watered-down Marx, a dollop of Herzl, a smidgen of Martin

Luther King, Jr., and a dash of Yosef Trompeldor. On my parents' walls hang engraved vistas of the temple mount in Jerusalem—and not because they believe that the high priests will be sacrificing pure red heifers there as soon as the Messiah comes.

My father brought me up to believe that Jews are strangers in all lands but *Eretz Yisrael,* and that a Jew cannot feel patriotism toward any other country. Despite the fact that he was born in Montreal, he never felt any real allegiance to Canada. My father moved to Israel in 1948 to fight in the War of Independence. I was born there, as were my older brothers and sister before me.

My family left Israel in 1967 when I was two years old, just weeks after the end of the Six Day War. It was my mother, an American, who insisted on returning to Montreal. She hated living in Israel and refused to stay any longer. All through my childhood, my father made it clear that he was on his way back to Israel any day, or next year, or as soon as the kids finished college, or when he retired. Any day now he would go home.

We moved from Montreal to the United States when I was seven, and in all my years of public school I never said the "Pledge of Allegiance." Not from second grade in Teaneck, New Jersey, through my graduation from Ridgewood High School. I stood respectfully silent, my hands by my side, because I had learned from my father that that flag was not mine and I should not, I *could* not, promise fidelity to it. I stood separate from the country in which I lived, not quite American, despite my American passport, despite being the daughter of a mother born in Brooklyn. I stood silent, because I owed my allegiance to the blue and the white.

As I sat on the long bench at the draft office in Afula, sipping a Kinley orange soda, I wondered idly whether an old friend of my father's, the retired director of military intelligence, might be prevailed upon to pull a few strings for me. I imagined I would make a pretty good spy, intelligent and sophisticated, quick-witted and sly. I would be a character in a spy thriller, luring terrorists with my irresistible sexual magnetism and then garroting them with my own two hands. The fact that I have never been capable of keeping my mouth shut for longer than three minutes at a stretch did not trouble my fantasy. Perhaps I had just not had time to think through the ramifications of a secret agent plagued by an insatiable confessional impulse.

Finally, I heard my name called over the crackling public address system. My moment of glory was at hand. I reported to a uniformed clerk sitting at a desk and she pointed me into an office. Her boss, the commander in charge of the Afula draft office, sat behind a drab metal desk, ancient and scuffed. It was piled with folders of a kind I've only ever seen in Israel: long and pale blue, fastened with a little metal clip, stuffed with lined paper, flimsy, thinner than the paper we use in the States. The officer waved a folder at me, motioning me to a chair in front of his desk.

His glasses sat on his forehead, not on the crown of his head, to hold back his hair, but centered directly over his eyebrows. He squinted at the file and then looked up at me.

"You're American," he said. It was a statement rather than a question.

"Sort of," I said. We were speaking Hebrew, of course. My Hebrew was excellent, almost perfect. I spoke like a native, but a rather simple-minded one, with an impeccable accent, and the occasional grammatical mistakes of a toddler.

"My parents live in the States," I explained. "But I was born here and my father lived here for nineteen years. We left in 1967."

The officer sighed, as if this information made him very sad, as if it pained him to hear of a pair of Jews who had chosen exile among the shopping malls of New Jersey over a pioneering kibbutz in the middle of a reclaimed desert. I sighed along with him. It made me sad, too.

"You'll be a very expensive soldier," he said. I knew that. I had a college degree, which made me immediately eligible for officer's training, an expensive course of study that results in higher pay. More to the point, with my parents out of the country, the army would shoulder the burden of my living expenses. This is something the Israeli army does for all soldiers whose parents live in the Diaspora. The army pays not just for military barracks and board, as they do for every other soldier, but gives the soldier of foreign parents an additional stipend sufficient to provide all the comforts a family would—an apartment, a telephone, whatever a young soldier on leave might need. They even fly the soldier to visit his or her parents abroad. Each soldier from out of the country costs the Israeli army tens of thousands of dollars every year.

The officer flipped through my file for a few moments, his eyebrows knotted under his glasses, his expression ever more dismayed. Then he looked up at me and said, "Do you want to be relieved?"

"Relieved?"

"Relieved of duty. We're relieving an entire class of girls this year. Budget cuts. I can relieve you, too, if you want."

I stared at him. Relieved of duty? Did he understand how long I had been planning for this? I had spent my sophomore year of high school in Israel, on a kibbutz in the Galilee, where we had converted our bomb shelter into a disco and slow-danced to Elton John's "Daniel" while the Ketusha rockets fell. Did he understand that during the course of that year I had determined that I would join the army?

Did he understand that I had spent my junior year of college at Hebrew University barely attending classes, because most of my time was spent waiting for my soldier boyfriend to make it out of Lebanon on his weekend leave? Didn't this commander realize that I knew then that I'd be joining my boyfriend in uniform?

How could he imagine I would want to be relieved of the duty my father had shouldered so willingly? If he only knew, he would understand that I would never want to be relieved of the duty that inspired the most wonderful of my father's stories, the stories that made up the most, the only, magical moments of my relationship with him.

My father is a reserved man, even taciturn. Or at least that's how it felt to an overly dramatic girl trying to communicate with the back of the *New York Review of Books* or the spine of a worn and well-thumbed history of Stalin's second Five-Year Plan. Only in the car could I reliably count on my father's attention, and then only if I triggered one of his expansive moods by asking a certain kind of question, eliciting a story about one specific part of his past—the decade encompassing and immediately following the Israeli War of Independence. Then my father would talk: animated and excited, his eyes bright, his hands in motion.

I loved these stories of my father's. I loved the image of him as a young man, sleeves rolled up, dusty feet in leather sandals, bent over the stalled engine of an ancient John Deere. I could see an alternate version of myself as a child, riding on the wing of his tractor through the alfalfa fields instead of in a red Dodge Aspen station wagon along Route 17 in Bergen County, New Jersey. I loved to hear about the nightly battles in the dining hall of the kibbutz about politics and ideology, the bitter squabbles over Trotsky and Engels.

This was a more intellectual life, I imagined. Idealistic and true, meaningful and profound. It was the life people like my father and I were meant to have. There was danger in my father's stories, too. There was a friend from Montreal who rode a white horse nine miles through the countryside to visit my father, managing in the process somehow to foil an attack launched by a neighboring Arab village. My father told me about how he recruited soldiers for the War of Independence, units formed of boys who'd known each other growing up in Montreal. I loved this image of my father as a secret agent.

We'd ride in the car, my father would tell these stories, and my imagination would take off even further. I could picture him in the Displaced Persons camps in Europe, recruiting soldiers, buying up arms from crooked military men or from sympathetic officers, officers who, perhaps, had seen Bergen-Belsen, had liberated Dachau, and were willing to help even the score with the shipment of a spare half-rusted tank or a few cases of machine guns. In my mind my father wasn't just a grunt soldier, he was an operative, like one of George Smiley's men (I liked that John le Carré). After all, my father did have friends with connections, didn't he? There was that man in military intelligence.

My father's stories were romantic, but they were not love stories. He never talked about love—not about the woman he married before my mother, nor about my mother. But he told tales of the romance of pioneering, of the romance of danger. I longed to be a part of the world that he described. I longed for my own chance to risk my life for something greater than myself, for something that meant more. For my *people*.

My father, in those drives throughout northern New Jersey, swept me up in his saga, his love affair with a strong Jewish people. The people of his stories did not crawl miserably into the ovens of Auschwitz; they rode tanks through the Sinai desert and stormed their way through an invading army. My father was one of those liberators, and when he told me about himself and the rest of them, I fell in love with it all—with Israel, with the kibbutz, with the army, with him.

All unhappy families have stories they tell about how misery overtook them, why their luck was spoiled, where it all went wrong. Everything went bad for us, our story goes, when we left Israel. The lifelong brooding that affected my father can be traced to his longing for his land, and to his remorse over having left it. My brothers' and sister's various miseries are due to their having been torn from their one true home. Sometimes in our house things get more specific, and we blame it all on leaving the kibbutz. Had we not left the kibbutz, we say, everything would have turned out differently. Had we never left Israel, had we never left the kibbutz, my father would have been happy.

The mythology of my family is that the gloom and despondency that has characterized my father's mood for most of my life is a direct result of living here, in America, instead of where he belongs, where we all belong, in Israel. My father spent his career as close to Israel as he could while not living there. My father was a fund-raiser for the United Jewish Appeal, the Jewish Federation, Hebrew University, Tel Aviv University, Asaf HaRofeh Hospital, and on and on. He was one of an army of men and women who eased their conscience about having left Israel by milking American Jewry for money and showering the proceeds on Israel.

Instead of strengthening Israel by living there, as he meant to do, he was part of an American movement resented by Israelis that created a false economy of charity, and made Israel a supplicant nation, unable to survive without the gift, but resenting the giver. My father hated this work, and he was stunningly ill suited to it. He was and is a misanthrope, whose gloom comes close to lifting only when he is alone, closeted with a dusty tome on the history of collective agriculture in the southern Baltic region or on the geopolitical ramifications of the War of 1812. But my father the warrior could inspire a crowd to unanticipated generosity when he entranced them with the tale of the battle to liberate the Western Wall.

I believed in my father. I believed in him when I rode alongside him in the car, listening to his stories, and I believed in him when I heard him regale a crowd of thick-walleted and misty-eyed suburban Jews. It is simplistic and insufficient to say that I wanted to make my father happy. I wanted to be happy *for* my father. I wanted to live in Israel for him, and fulfill the contented and gloried life my mother had denied him. She wouldn't live in Israel. She wouldn't struggle on behalf of the Jewish people on a spit of rugged land surrounded by ferocious enemies. But I would.

As soon as I was old enough, in tenth grade, I went to Israel. I spent all my subsequent summer vacations on kibbutz, and then my junior year of college in Jerusalem. I loved it there. I loved the landscape, the food, the heat—but most of all, I loved "passing." I loved being taken for an Israeli. I dressed like an Israeli, I spoke like an Israeli, I affected that Israeli sarcastic click of the tongue and shrug of the shoulders, and I condescended to all things American. I acquired a kibbutznik boyfriend whom I kept, much to my mother's near-desperate panic, for six years. After graduation, I "went up." I made aliyah, moving to Israel once and for all. I knew this meant I would serve in the army. I was ready to go.

THE commanding officer of the draft office in Afula shuffled his papers and turned back a page of my file, waiting for my answer. He reached into his desk drawer and took out a stamp, an inkpad, and a multipaged form interspersed with carbon paper.

"*Nu?*" he said. "Do you want to be relieved of duty?"

"Yes," I said.

UNTIL I accepted the draft officer's offer, I had not realized how much I wanted to leave. In the six months since I had moved to Israel, my dream had gone sour without my even noticing. The life I had imagined for myself, my father's life, had begun to seem so small, so unsatisfying. The kibbutz where I lived was not a place where dogma was debated and intellect was prized. It was a place where only the elderly still bothered attending the weekly meetings and few could even state with any confidence the ideological principles on which the community was based. It was a place where women accepted their jobs as nursemaids and kitchen workers without complaint, without any questioning that this was their logical employment.

Worse, I discovered that the kibbutz was a place where most people worked only so hard, never harder, where mediocrity was rewarded and excellence punished and reproved, or at best greeted with confusion and distrust. Moving to the kibbutz revealed to me the pernicious and unpleasant truths underlying the glorious mythological tales of socialism my father had been telling me my whole life.

But had my disillusion been only with the kibbutz, I might have been disappointed, I might have been sad, but I would not have greeted the draft officer's offer with such profound relief. After all, there is an entire country in Israel outside of the kibbutz. I could have moved to Ramat Aviv, to Jerusalem, to a moshav in the Negev. I did not even consider any of those options.

When presented with an unexpected choice, I realized an unexpected truth: I wanted to go home. After a lifetime of being a stranger in America, a patriot to a sliver of land across the globe, once I was finally in the place I'd been taught was my homeland, I felt like nothing so much as a displaced American.

The sensation of being utterly disconnected to the country that is supposed to be our homeland is common to most Americans who come to Israel. It is not merely a foreign country, but a Middle Eastern country, despite its thick veneer of Western commercialism and cultural identity. My family was supposed to be different, however. I was supposed to be different. Because of my ease with Hebrew, because the people in my family were war heroes, because I was born in Israel, I was not like those other American Jews. At least not until I faced the prospect of living out my father's dream.

Suddenly I felt like a displaced person. I gobbled up the English contents of the kibbutz library and spent what little money I had at English bookstores in Haifa and Tel Aviv. When I listened to my Israeli friends deride America I felt a surge of defensive patriotic fervor that was utterly foreign to me. When I met an American with whom I could converse in English I felt my personality shift, like an automobile into a smoother gear. I was myself only in English, not in Hebrew. I felt so disconnected, but I wouldn't admit it to myself. The thought horrified me. The sensation was so shocking to me that I refused to identify or even acknowledge it until the commanding officer of the Afula draft office offered me a way out. Then I grabbed it with both hands.

I was *homesick,* and my home was in America. Three months later, I left Israel.

T HAT was almost twenty years ago. Ask me now and I will tell you that the Zionist dream, the very notion of *Eretz Yisrael,* the idea and the ideal for which I expected and was prepared to fight, has turned bitter in my mouth. When a friend recently told me that her Israeli husband longs to go home, and that she was considering a move, I was ashamed to hear myself discouraging her, recounting every story of every American woman I know who has fled from Israel after years of miseries, tiny and large, when she realized that if she did not leave soon, her son would be riding in an armored vehicle, dodging rocks and shoulder-launched missiles while guarding some fanatical Jew's hothouse tomatoes in the Gaza Strip.

I sent my elder daughter to a Jewish Day School, but pulled her out after a year, in spite of her contentment, and in spite of my own feelings of deep pleasure at hearing her recite the *Modeh Ani* prayer at the beginning of every school day. I could not stand to see her waving her handmade, construction-paper, blue-and-white flag while Ariel Sharon was prime minister. Instead, I try to raise my four children with strong Jewish identities that have nothing at all to do with Israel.

When I first married my husband, I brought with me into the marriage all the biases with which my father had inculcated me. Hebrew words were to be said with perfect Israeli, Sephardic pronunciation. On our first Hanukkah together, my husband and I had an ugly squabble, complete with shouting and slammed doors, about the proper pronunciation of the name of the candle that lights the others. He called it a *shames.* I derided his Ashkenazi pronunciation and refused to allow it, insisting he use the proper word, *shamash,* accent on the second syllable.

Now we are Yiddishists in our house. We light the candles on Shabbos, and on Yom Kippur I help wrap my husband in his *tallis*. Although the Zionist ideology on which I was raised dismissed Yiddish as the language of the ghetto, we embrace the Diaspora's intellectual and cultural history, as well as Yiddish's inexhaustible well of profanity. How better, after all, to curse a person, than to wish that a healthy cholera seize his belly or that she grow like an onion with her head in the ground? Neither English nor Hebrew can compete with that.

I am, in a very real sense, the daughter my father made. It is not that I love all things American, God knows. What I love is exile. As a people, we Jews are meant for exile. We flourish when we exist as separate within other nations, cast out from the dust and sandstone of Zion.

Only as separate within others can we retain our distinct character, our unique perspective. As artists, writers, scientists, philosophers, exile becomes us. It is the loss of the temple that inspired the rabbis to create the Talmud; they substituted the word, the symbol, for the red heifer. Those rabbis invented a religion of learning that wound chaotically, yet somehow inexorably, from Maimonides to Wittgenstein to Spinoza to Derrida. What I love best about Judaism are laws like the ones that strictly proscribe destroying fruit trees in time of war. And the absolute preeminence of the prohibition against taking a life.

America is a fine nation in which to be exiled, to be displaced. I like our Constitution, our Bill of Rights, and if the forces of evil do not succeed in chipping away at them entirely with their Patriot Acts and their Constitutional Amendments against gay marriage, I think they will continue to provide decent enough protection for the Jews; the best we can hope for at any rate.

I like, too, the new and raw history of this country, despite its brutal aspects. It has its anti-Semitism, of course, ugly and pernicious, and yet I think it's less likely to bubble over and overwhelm than that of Europe. The roots of anti-Semitism in Europe are gnarled and deep, and cannot be dislodged, not even by images of stacked corpses, starved children, cattle cars, crematoria, and millions murdered. They are eerily familiar in the rhetoric of the most righteous condemnation of Israel in Europe today. There is no room there for our continued exile. America has its own history of hatred, but it is also a country formed on the notion of freedom of religion.

I have a friend whose grandmother used to warn with classic pessimism, "Never forget, you're just around the corner from an oven." I don't forget, and unlike most Jews of my generation, I share her foreboding. I believe the fact that any of us at all survived the pogroms and the Holocaust was entirely fortuitous. We will always be a target. Like Tom Lehrer so famously sang in "National Brotherhood Week," *everybody hates the Jews.* To the classic argument that Israel is our only haven, that Israel can be our only sanctuary if they reopen the oven doors, I ask: When a nation can be wiped out by a single bomb, what difference does a nation make?

And yet, with my father I never talk about any of this. We do not talk about Israel, or the politics of the Middle East. I am sure he knows of my beliefs, of my shift away from Zionism, and I'm sure he is dismayed. But we are not a family that speaks of our emotions, and certainly not of our failings. I will never tell him that I am wracked by guilt for having betrayed him, for failing to believe in the ideal, and, even more, for having failed to be happy in Israel in his stead.

My ideological battles, the struggles that engage my intellect and heart, do not involve socialism and Zionism, but rather racism, poverty, prisoners' rights, feminism. The literature I enjoy is all in English; even Israeli writers I read only in translation. I don't toil with my hands, working in the dairy barn or the cotton fields or even the plastics factory. I am a writer, and though I know my father is proud of me, I can't help but wonder if sometimes when he looks at my children, he thinks about what they would have been like if we had never left Israel, if we had never left the kibbutz.

But the thing about these stories that families tell themselves, the legends of unhappiness, is that they are not very often true. My father's story is precisely the one we Jews have told ourselves for two thousand years. Exile is the cause of our misery and despair, and only when we return to Zion will we be happy. My father lives in New Jersey and thus my family's myth can continue, but we Jews have returned to the land of Israel and must confront the truth.

Has the end of exile made the Jews happy, has it solved our pain? Has asserting dominion over this land given us comfort and belonging, a sense of home? This question is a complicated one, and I know there are those for whom the bitter misery of suicide bombings and razor-wire walls do not serve to dispel the existential security of living as a Jew among Jews, governed by Jews and guarded by Jews. For many, though, I am certain that aliyah to a nation forced to occupy lands populated by millions of poverty-stricken and enraged enemies has brought insufficient comfort and joy.

Like the melancholy of the Jews, my father's sadness is not geographical. His despondency is not a function of Diaspora, or even of circumstance. I have come to understand that my father's unhappiness is as much a part of his personality as is his love of obscure Soviet history. The entire enterprise of my childhood and adolescent dream was doomed to failure. I could no more bring my father joy by ending my exile than I could bring myself joy by living in a country where I felt so wrong.

I am as my father made me, displaced and uncomfortable, a Jew in America. But my happiness is here with a husband who feels, unlike me, absolutely American. I am raising four American children who do not even know that I do not entirely belong.

I once saw a photograph of my father taken sometime in 1948 or thereabouts. He is wearing a haphazard uniform, wrinkled, the shirt not matching the slacks, the combat boots scuffed and worn. He is holding a rifle and his eyes are squinted against the sun. He is handsome, his face narrow and lean, a trace of a beard on his cheeks. He looks very dashing, a weary soldier caught in a moment of repose.

I cannot tell from his expression if he is happy.

My Private Caller

*

LORI GOTTLIEB

I'M in the checkout line at Best Buy paying for an eighteen-feature Panasonic phone when I realize I might finally be free of my mother. It says so right on the box: The phone that will change your life!

It's just an ad slogan, but to me it's a sign, maybe even a message from God. At the very least, it's validation from the universe that getting Caller ID for the sole purpose of screening my mother's calls won't give me cancer, as my guilty conscience fears, but might actually "change my life."

"Whoa. . . ." I say to the cashier while pointing at the bright orange letters so she can share my life-changing moment. But she just looks at me like I'm retarded or stoned.

At home, I gleefully unpack the phone, programming in my numbers, learning how to work the Caller ID. It's an ordinary white cordless model, but I treat it with reverence, like it has magical powers. It will take magic to keep my mother at bay.

Don't get me wrong: My mother's not abusive or even mean-spirited. She's just, well, Jewish. Which means she loves me more than life itself, but nothing I do is good enough, even though I'm perfect, because, after all, I take after her. A dubious honor, but still.

It's not that I want to avoid my mother entirely; I just need a good three rings to prepare for voice-to-voice contact. Forget WMD, those elusive Weapons of Mass Destruction. My mother is a PMD, a Person of Mass Destruction. She can—with a phrase, a sigh, a glance (which whooshes through the fiber-optic cable along with each "tuh, tuh")— utterly destroy the fortress of selfhood I've carefully constructed in my adult life. There's something about my mother, the PMD extraordinaire, that turns me into a PSD—a Person of Self-Destruction. So I've purchased the first line of defense.

I scan the Panasonic box for more empowering messages when my phone starts ringing. *Private Caller.* Huh. I wonder who would block their name or caller ID. It can't be my mother, the woman who announces her entrance into a room with bugles and a receiving line, who broadcasts her name from across the supermarket parking lot so that the entire neighborhood hears her call out, "Sylvia! Over here, doll! It's ROZ!" She's not exactly known for subtlety.

"Hello?" I say confidently into The Phone That Will Change My Life.

"Where have you *been?*" my mother bellows through the phone line. "I've been calling you for five hours! What if there had been an emergency? Next time, think about other people for a change, will you?"

THE phone rings and I glance down at the Caller ID: *Private Caller.*

Oh shit, I think. In just two days, I've noticed that lots of people have Private Caller—most of whom get on my nerves. It seems like all the annoying people have figured out that this is the only way anyone will take their calls. I stare at the phone. It could be a telemarketer, an ex-boyfriend, an editor asking for a rewrite. On the upside, it could be Rachel, who got Private Caller in order to stalk her ex-fiancé. Then again, it could be my mother. And who wants to risk *that?*

I let it go to voice mail. No message. Must have been my mother. It's her passive-aggressive way of guilting me into calling her. Even the telemarketers leave messages: "Hi, this is John from Prudent Health Plans. I've called you twice this week and I'm surprised I haven't heard back." Telemarketers leave the same message my mother would—if she ever actually left one.

I won't call her. If she wants to talk to me, she can leave a message. I decide to call Rachel instead. I pick up the phone and dial.

"Hi, Mom," I say. *D'oh!* I hate myself. I have no willpower.

"Lori? Is that you?" I'm her only daughter, and she can't figure this out from "Hi, Mom"?

"Did you just call me?" I ask.

"Why would I call you?" she replies. Our phone conversations are like high-level chess games that would put Garry Kasparov to shame.

"I don't know, because I'm your *daughter*." Suddenly I'm worried that she didn't call and hang up after all. Doesn't she think about me? Doesn't she care?

"Anyhow," she says, changing the subject. "What's new?"

"Not much." I've got an entire catalog of neutral phrases developed over the years, my linguistic Switzerlands. "You know, the usual."

"Then how come you're never home when I call?" she says. I *knew* it! I love that she called, but I hate talking to her. Maybe I'm schizophrenic.

"Mom, I'm busy," I say.

"Okay, go do 'the usual'—whatever that means," she sighs, sending intravenous guilt through the line. "I'll go call your brother. At least *he'll* talk to me."

"Mom . . ."

"Love you," she says and hangs up.

"Hi," I say. "It's me." Silence. "Lori, your *daughter*."

"Oh, hi, honey," Mom says. "You sound different—do you have a cold?"

"No, maybe it's the speakerphone." I pick up the receiver on The Phone That Will Change My Life. "Is that better?"

"A little," she replies. "But you still sound different. It must be that I haven't heard your voice in so long." We just spoke two days ago.

"How are you?" I ask.

"Oy!" Mom begins, her signal that "big news" is about to follow. "Did you hear about Kim? She just had twins. It was a C-section! Remember that shower I gave her . . . of course you don't, you didn't come. Anyhow, she's a doll. And John! Oh, Lori! If only you could find someone like John! His brother just got engaged but he would have been too *young* for you anyway. And Herb is in the hospital again. Cancer. Of the whatchamacallit. It's terrible, just terrible. You remember Herb, right?"

Whenever I ask "How are you?" Mom thinks it means, "Who's about to croak?" "Who's off the dating market?" and/or "Who just had her uterus sliced open?"

"Yeah," I say. "That's terrible." I have no idea who Herb is. But if I ask, Mom will accuse me of lacking interest in other people's lives. It's a trap.

"You should send Herb a card," she says. "He's at St. John's."

I imagine sending a card to St. John's, addressed simply to *"Herb— patient with cancer of the whatchamacallit."*

I walk over to my fax machine and dial my cell phone so it starts ringing.

"Mom, I've got to take this call."

"Okay, but honey, are you all right? Are you happy?"

"I'm happy, Mom, but I have to go."

"If you were so happy, you'd have time to talk to your mother." Mom's the queen of non sequiturs.

"I'll call you later," I say, pretending to answer my cell phone. Then I paste a Post-it over my desk: Do NOT Call Mom.

Later, I see the Post-it on my bulletin board and imagine getting hit by a car, after which my grieving parents enter my empty apartment and find the note. I wonder if it will seem cryptic to them, my own personal Rosebud. Then I realize that most of my Jewish friends probably have similar messages peppering their work areas, their nightstands, their journals. *Do NOT call Mom. Be nicer to Mom. Respect Mom. Respect yourself.* I picture these Post-its sewn together into a quilt, a blanket testament to our ambivalent relationships with loving but lethal mothers.

"L ISTEN," I tell my friend Rachel.

"I've heard it three times now," she sighs.

"Just listen to the way her voice drops when she says, 'Talk to you soon' and tell me what you think it *means*." Most women sit around analyzing their boyfriends' voice-mail messages; I'm analyzing my mother's.

I stare at the blinking light, still shocked that my mother left a message at all. It's unprecedented. I hit the star key again. BEEP!

"Lori, it's your mother. Remember me? Since you haven't called me back, I have some information for you and I suppose I should tell your, uh, whatchamacallit . . . Hello? Is this thing working? Anyhow, tomorrow's party starts at seven, and that means exactly what it sounds like: *seven*. I know you and those friends of yours think seven means seven thirty, but in our world—the normal world—it means just plain seven. Oh, and if you have to wear black slacks, wear black slacks. But please try to wear a nice blouse with some color. It's a party, not a funeral. And also, would you please put on a little lipstick, honey? You know how I feel about lipstick. Why do you have to be so stubborn? Would it really kill you to try a nice gloss? Last time I asked, you said you'd wear some and you didn't. Merv and Arlene thought you looked pale and sickly. Why do you want to hurt me? Okay, sweetie, talk to you soon."

I look up at Rachel. "Does 'talk to you soon' mean I should call back now or talk to her at the party tomorrow?"

"I think it means I should lend you my lip gloss," she says.

THE phone rings and I glance at the Caller ID. *Private Caller.* I decide that if it's Mom, I can always get off by pretending that the line's breaking up. I've used this excuse so often that once she wrote a series of complaint letters to Pac Bell and they sent out a technician. When he asked what the problem was, I shrugged and said, "My mother."

"Guess who I ran into today?" Mom says.

"Who?"

"Just guess!" she says

"Um, I don't know . . . Barbara?"

I'm not sure that my mother knows a Barbara, but I don't have much to work with. Her friends are very competitive with each other in a "keeping up with the Jewesses" sort of way, so I try to stay out of her social life.

"Not Barbara," Mom says with annoyance. "Barbara just had a mastectomy. She's in the hospital. I *told* you about that. Don't you remember?"

"Oh, yeah," I lie. "How's she doing?"

"She's having *reconstruction*," Mom whispers, like someone's bugging the line. Then she perks up. "Guess again!"

"Um . . . Estelle?" I'm pretty sure she knows an Estelle.

"You know very well that Estelle's in *Europe* for Katie's *wedding*." She sighs so loudly that the line starts to crackle.

"Oh. So who'd you run into?" I ask.

"Try one more time!" she practically squeals. "You'll never guess. Not in a million years!" I love that: I'll never guess, but I should try to guess.

"Ophelia," I say.

"*Who?*"

"Ophelia," I repeat.

"I don't know any Ophelia," Mom says, puzzled.

"Yes, you do," I insist. "She's Alison's mom." Ha! There is no Alison, there is no Ophelia, and Mom's too proud to admit that she doesn't know these people! Checkmate! I win! I do a little Victory Dance in my office.

"Oh, *Ophelia*," Mom covers. "I didn't hear you the first time. Is that a new phone?"

"This is silly," I say, clicking on e-mails. "Just tell me." I keep myself alert by doing the Victory Dance again, first in slow motion, then at warp speed, then in slow motion.

"Well, if you must know," Mom says, pausing for effect. "I ran into Danny."

I stop mid-Victory Dance. Several years ago I lived with Danny.

"Did you talk to him?" I ask. I imagine them chatting about his wonderful life. I bet he's won the lottery or something. I feel light-headed and have to sit down.

"No," she says. "I was across the street." *Saved!* "But I heard he has kids now. Two girls." *Ouch.*

"Really? Who told you that?" If she says, "Guess!" I'll kill her. I'll put arsenic in her Folgers.

"Hmm, I don't remember," she says. *She doesn't remember?* It's an emotional felony for me not to remember that Estelle-I've-met-maybe-once is in Europe at Katie-I've-never-met's wedding, but it's okay for her not to remember where she heard that the man I lived with for three years is married with two kids?

"Besides," she continues, "what difference does it make? Are you really surprised that Danny got his life together after you left him? Will you break up with Doug, too?"

"I don't know," I say. "Maybe." Doug and I have been dating for a year and a half. Everybody loves Doug, but he's too earnest for me. He's vegan and does yoga. I would have split six months ago if I hadn't been so worried that my mother would think I was making another Big Mistake.

"So," I try again. "Who told you?"

"Who cares who told me! Why can't you be normal?" Mom asks, like this is a reasonable question with a logical answer.

"Why are you being such a bitch?" I say. I don't care how inappropriate this is. How can she taunt me with this information? I want to call her a "manipulative bitch"—so the way I see it, "bitch" is really a euphemism.

"I'm going to hang up now," Mom says. Mom went to a single therapy session after her mother died six years ago, but her only two takeaways seem to have been "I'm going to hang up now" and "I'm sorry you feel that way."

Then I remember what my own shrink advised when it comes to my mother: detachment. "It's like letting go of a gangrened limb," he'd said. Sitting on his sofa, I closed my eyes and imagined my left arm being chopped off with a meat cleaver. "It's still better than no arm," I told him.

Another time he put it this way: "She's toxic." It seemed elegant, like a haiku. Loosening my grip on the phone, I picture myself in a Hazmat suit, tossing my mother into a toxic waste dump. I can actually feel myself "detaching."

"I'm sorry," I lie.

"I know you are," she lies.

"Mom?" I say.

"What?"

"I'm going to start wearing more lipstick." I don't know where that came from. I have no intention of wearing more lipstick.

"That's fabulous!" she says. "Go see Sheila at Saks. Tell her I sent you—she'll give you a discount."

THE phone rings and I glance at the Caller ID: my brother. I pick up.

"Your brother says you screen my calls," Mom says. She actually called from Brad's phone to see if I'd answer. "How many people screen out their own mothers?" Mom asks indignantly.

I want to say: *Most of my peer group. And they have normal mothers!*

"You know what?" Mom says. Uh-oh. I never want to "know what" when righteous indignation is involved.

"What?" I say.

"One day I'll be dead, and then you'll be sorry that you *can't* take my calls."

Oh, boy. Here we go. Lecture #23. Mom has approximately thirty well-crafted speeches on deck at any one time, and all she has to do is fire a neuron that signals "play" in her brain. Boom! Insta-lecture.

This one is about how I didn't help her through breast cancer. It's a moving speech, one that often makes me cry. But not because of her Meryl Streep–level performance or the rousing you-only-took-me-to-chemo-once climax. No. It's that the one time I did sit with her in the "chemo lounge," watching the fuchsia poison drip into her veins, I felt something for my mother that I've never felt in my entire adult life: pure, unadulterated love. And I hated loving her. It was so . . . awkward. Afterward, as I drove her home, she asked me to lunch. She couldn't possibly want food—who wants lunch after chemo? I didn't realize that she probably just wanted an excuse to spend more time with me.

"You shouldn't eat right after chemo," I'd said in the car. I felt more nauseated than she did. At home, I tucked her into bed and fled. I couldn't stand another second of loving her so much.

Or maybe I didn't want the feeling to go away.

I place Mom on the speakerphone so I can grab some Kleenex from across the room. I need to wipe my eyes. She's nearing the end of Lecture #23, and she's about to launch into the part about how I'm a terrible daughter, a bad seed, while my brother's a saint.

"Your brother's a saint," she says, as if on cue. "An absolute saint!"

"He's a Mama's Boy," I retort. (My shrink says I have to stop responding, but I can't help it. "You're a writer," he told me. "Rewrite the dialogue. Rewrite the script." "I can't," I replied. "My mother gives me writer's block.")

". . . and your brother cares!" Mom continues. "He calls!"

"You think it's healthy that a thirty-six-year-old man talks to Mommy every single day?" I wonder how often other people call their mothers. Once a week? Once a month? Or how about once a new boyfriend? Once a new outfit? Once a new haircut? At least we'd have something new to talk about.

"I'm getting my hair cut tomorrow," I say, changing the subject to something safe.

"Make sure they cover the gray," Mom says.

"I don't have any gray," I explain for the umpteenth time. Mom got her first gray hair in her twenties and she's convinced that I'm lying about my natural hair color. Who lies to their mother about their natural hair color? How low could *those* stakes be?

"Well, you will," she says with an air of foreboding. "You have to be very, very careful."

"Okay," I say. "I'll prophylactically cover my future gray hairs."

"ARE you losing weight?" Mom asks when I call back after another of her stealth hang ups. "You sound like you're losing weight." What does *that* sound like, I wonder.

"My weight's fine," I say.

"Is it really? Millie and Sam were driving in your neighborhood and saw you walking down the street. They said you looked too skinny."

I have no idea who Millie and Sam are, but all my parents' friends function as a de facto secret police force that vigilantly reports on my whereabouts.

"I'm perfectly healthy," I say, logging on to my e-mail. Mom is worried that men think I'm too scrawny, that I'm not "filled out" enough.

"I don't believe you," she says.

"Why not?"

"Because you're acting very shady. Next time, look at me when I'm talking to you."

I stop clicking on e-mail. "Over the phone?" I ask.

"What?" she says. "You think I can't tell when you're not paying attention?"

"Mom, I've got work to do," I interrupt as she runs down this week's births, engagements, and carcinomas.

"You work too hard," Mom says. "You seem stressed."

"I've got five things due," I say. "Of course I'm stressed."

My mother doesn't understand the concept of work stress. The most stressful thing about her life is that she has two unmarried children in their thirties. She once told me that she feels like a pariah, and ever since, I imagine my mom, Hester Pryne–like, walking down Beverly Drive with a big "P" and a wedding cake couple circled with a line through them emblazoned on her Gucci jacket.

"Get a facial, it'll cheer you up," she says. Sadly, she's being sincere.

"I don't have time for a facial," I say.

"What do you mean you don't have time? It takes an hour."

"I'll call you later, Mom."

"Wait," she says. "Are you happy . . . with your work?"

Wow—a real question, something of substance. It's shocking coming from her. I crave this from my mother.

"I am when I'm not on a deadline," I quip. She's silent, listening. All I can hear is her breath. I decide to take off the mask.

"When I'm writing something I care about, it's like . . . being high," I say. This is the first honest exchange we've had in a long time. I get a tingle in my spine. "It's like an addiction to this amazing drug."

"What are you saying . . . you take drugs now?" Mom asks, concerned.

"It's an analogy," I sigh. "Jesus."

"Don't swear," Mom says. "I just want to know if you're happy."

"I thought we were talking about my work," I say.

"You know what your problem is?" she says. "You think too much. Do you think you can try thinking a bit less?"

My heart does a nosedive into my belly. "I'll think about it," I say.

"**I** BROKE up with Doug," I say when Mom answers. I need chicken soup and hugs and words of encouragement. I need a shower.

"Oy, vey! What made you do this?" she gasps, like I just robbed a bank or injected heroin.

"I don't know. He expanded my mind but not my vagina," I say to piss her off.

"I'm going to hang up now," Mom says.

"I'm sorry," I say. Why do I always apologize when she's wrong?

"No, *I'm* sorry," she says. "I'm sorry that you always throw your happiness out the window." I look out the window for my happiness splattered on the pavement below, but all I see are two kids with purple hair walking by.

"I wasn't happy, Mom. I was bored."

"Let me tell you something about marriage," Mom says. *Uh-oh.* We're entering dangerous territory. It should be cordoned off with rope and guarded by militia carrying Uzis. I don't want to hear about my parents' marriage. Theirs is a match made in denial, and I'll do anything not to have that kind of life.

"Marriage is boring," Mom continues. "If you keep having these . . . these *crazy* ideas about love, you'll be alone for the rest of your life."

"Loneliness is better than boredom," I say.

"No, it's not!" she insists, but I wonder if she's right. Loneliness is pure longing, whereas boredom is, "Hmm, should I see a movie or read a book? Should I get a manicure or slit my wrists?" Boredom is exciting—there are lots of options. Loneliness isn't about options. I fall into a manhole of self-doubt, but then I think about listening to Doug's lectures on bottle recycling each night and I realize I'm right. HBO reruns and a vibrator are much better company.

"Look," I explain. "I want to get on a better path."

"And you're on the path to loneliness!" Mom yells. "I don't know what you and that shrink of yours think you're doing!" Mom thinks my therapist is out to get her. She thinks going to therapy is like becoming a Moonie.

"Mom . . ."

"Either he's brainwashed you or you've really lost your mind!"

"Why don't you trust my choices?" I ask. "Why do you always criticize me?"

"I don't criticize you, honey," she says soothingly. "I'm trying to improve you."

"You haven't called in a while," I say when Mom picks up the phone. "I was worried about you." I've never uttered these two phrases before in my life. I wonder if I'm suffering from Stockholm syndrome, the way Patty Hearst overidentified with her captors.

"We've been busy," she says.

"Busy with what?"

"Social engagements," she replies, like she just popped out of a Jane Austen novel.

"With whom?"

"Oh, friends," she says. My heart starts pounding—something must be wrong. She's not tossing strangers' first names at me and shaming me for not knowing them.

"Mom, what's going on?"

"Nothing's going on," she insists, but I know something's up. She's being as evasive as me.

"The cancer's back, isn't it?" I say. My voice starts to crack. I feel like I might faint. "You don't want to tell me because of how I acted last time, but it's back, and you've been in treatment, and . . ." I open my calendar to try to figure out which days I can take her to chemo. I vow to take her to lunch whenever she wants.

"I'm fine," Mom interrupts. "If you must know, your father and I bought plots at the cemetery, and it's taken up a lot of time."

"You *what?* Where?"

"It's called 'Serenity,' " she says proudly. I give her the hairy eyeball through the phone. "Serenity" sounds more like a fragrance than a cemetery to me.

"*Why?*"

"Well, it's a new cemetery, and we went to visit and thought it was just lovely. We read a review—it was a rave—and then last week, Jackie and Phil said they got theirs and so did Dave and Ann and everybody's talking about it, so we thought . . ."

Ah, now it makes sense. This isn't about death—it's the morbid equivalent of a restaurant opening.

"So nobody's sick?" I ask.

"No, honey. We even got one for your brother—and he's healthy as a horse."

"You got one for Brad?"

"He wanted one. He was worried we might get separated . . . later on." What a freaking Mama's Boy.

"Why'd you get one for Brad and not for me?"

"We didn't think you'd want one. You're always avoiding family occasions."

"This isn't a family occasion!" I say incredulously. "I don't want to be a homeless dead person! What if I'm all alone?"

"You won't be alone," Mom says. "Just don't be so picky with men."

Suddenly it hits me: Mom left me plot-less so I'll go out and marry the next guy that asks, just so I'll have a burial partner. She's devious.

"So I should get hitched as insurance for the afterlife?" I ask.

"Well, I wouldn't put it like that," Mom hedges. "But you know what they say: happily ever after."

Even Mom knows how ridiculous this sounds. We both begin to laugh, deep belly laughs—each building on the other's until we're so loud I can't tell her laugh from mine. We try to calm down, but we're like two schoolgirls who can't stop giggling in class.

"Anyhow," Mom continues, chuckling, "no matter where your father and I are buried, I'll always be a phone call away."

"You think they have Caller ID in the afterlife?" I ask. I start to breathe normally again, but Mom's still making hiccupy noises through the phone.

"Mom," I say. "It's not *that* funny."

It takes me a moment to realize she's crying.

THE phone wakes me up. I get out of bed to look at the Caller ID: *Gottlieb, S & R.*

When did Mom get rid of Private Caller?

"Oh my God! It says it's my *mother*," I tell Adam, who's still half asleep. I don't want Mom to know about Adam yet. Or maybe I do. I want her to know that he understands more about me in the month we've been together than she has in my lifetime. My mom may possess my soul, but Adam can see it.

"Don't make any noise," I tell Adam. "She can't know you're here."

"Mum's the word," he says. I don't even mind his puns.

I pick up the phone, but the call has already gone to voice mail. I punch in my code: no message. Typical. I get back into bed.

"Do you want to call her?" Adam asks.

"No," I say.

"You do," he says, tickling me.

"I do," I laugh. "But I won't."

"Yes, you will," he laughs.

"Of course I will," I say, reaching for the phone. It starts ringing before I pick up. I glance at the Caller ID: *Gottlieb, S & R.*

"It's her again!" I scream, astounded by the digital letters. I let it go to voice mail.

"Hey, look at that," Adam says a minute later. The message light is flashing. I punch in my code and put it on speaker. BEEP!

"Lori, it's your mother. I know you're there . . . can you hear me? Are you ignoring me? Do you think this is funny? You must be there. Where else would you be? You don't wake up this early. And you're not seeing anybody. So I hope you aren't out sleeping with some stranger. It's unattractive at your age, it really is. You'll get diseases and nobody will want to be with you. So please, honey, pick up. Hello? Are you in the shower? Maybe you're in the shower. Call me back, sweetie. Bye."

I press delete and get back into bed when the phone starts ringing. I cover Adam's ears with my pillow. "Answer it," he says, "or she'll never stop calling."

I grab the receiver: *Private Caller.*

"It's not her," I say, picking up the phone. "Finally, we're free!"

"What, you think I don't know about Private whatchamacallit?" my mother yells before I can say hello. "Is this what I have to do to get my own daughter to pick up the phone? And who were you talking to anyway? Are you sleeping with a stranger?"

"Mom, I can't talk right now," I say. "I'll call you later."

I put down The Phone That Will Change My Life and realize that it hasn't changed my life one bit. I feel like a victim of false advertising, but I have only myself to blame.

I curl up in bed with Adam. A minute later the phone rings again. I get up and turn off the ringer. I don't even look at the digital display. I hand Adam the phone, grab the manual, and together, we begin to disable the Caller ID.

Philosophers with Wombs

*

REBECCA GOLDSTEIN

ALTHOUGH I was married shockingly young, right after my freshman year of college, I postponed having children for some years. I was moved by large and inexplicable ambitions. No woman I knew had the ambitions I did. The women's movement was in its toddler phase. In the Orthodox Jewish world in which I'd been raised, we hadn't heard a peep out of it. So where did I get off thinking that I had important things to learn before I could even contemplate duplicating my genes? I have no idea.

I'd always had the thought of motherhood tucked away on my list of to-dos. I loved kids, I more than looked forward to having one or two of my own someday. Yet the pressure to have children right after marriage—so universal in my family's community as to go without saying—was as unwelcome to me as the thought of never having kids at all. I wanted to be a mother, sure, but I didn't want to be a mother who wore housedresses.

The housedress is a garment halfway between a bathrobe and a proper dress. It allows you to change out of your nightclothes without allowing you to leave the house. A woman can respectably answer the door in it, but she can't step out of the door. Sometimes they are called "housecoats," cruelly pouring on the irony: coats that keep you inside.

They are cut like coats, boxy and waistless. In fact, they are the most singularly unsexy garments imaginable, designed perhaps to banish any innuendo of peekaboo sensuality hovering around nightgowns, negligees, or lingerie. The woman who wears a housedress might not be fully clothed, but she isn't in a bedroom sort of way either.

My mother got up and put on a housedress almost every single day, except of course on the Sabbath, when she got dressed up and went to synagogue. (Dressing up always involved another esoteric garment of those days, the girdle—but that's another essay entirely.) Housedresses were my mother's working uniform and they always made me feel uneasily sorry for her. They represented a life of terminal drabness, the foreclosure of adventure. To get up and put on something that didn't allow you to tread over your threshold and stride out into the great wide world seemed a renunciation so capacious that it left almost no room for stepping around in.

When I tried as a child to picture myself all grown, I'd see some vaguely female form hidden in a housedress, and I'd feel my spirits sag. So when grown-ups called me a little girl and then ostentatiously corrected themselves—"Oh, of course, you're a *big* girl"—their silly subterfuge never went over well with me. I was trained, as Orthodox girls invariably are, never to answer back or evince any sign of inner dissent. But what I would have wanted to respond—and vehemently, too—was, "Of course, I'm a little girl. Why do you think that I'd want you to say that I'm not?" The insult was that they thought I'd be insulted by their stating an obvious truth. It was no shame, to my mind, to be little; rather what seemed to me a crying shame was to have to get unlittle, to grow up only so that you grew into a housedress.

There was a queasiness that the housedress provoked in me, though I didn't have the words to express it. My mother was fastidious to a fault—she ironed everything, including the bedsheets, our little footed pajamas, and, of course, those housedresses of hers. Still, there seemed to me something slovenly about life spent in a state of dishabille. A life in a housedress was a life of too much intimacy with the body, and I confess it made me squeamish.

Simone de Beauvoir's *The Second Sex*, which I read in college, finally gave me a means to explain the queasiness that mothers in housedresses—that *my* mother in *her* housedress—stirred up in me. I read de Beauvoir's classic in the English translation, which has been criticized as not only mutilating her existentialism but as exaggerating her misogyny, making her appear too dismissively contemptuous of the life of the majority of women—of those who hadn't gotten doctorates in philosophy from the Sorbonne and become the consorts of Jean-Paul Sartre.

I confess, however—and judge me as you will—that I didn't find the descriptions I read in *The Second Sex* as biased against women. Rather I read them with the startled satisfaction of hearing one's most private inchoate thoughts given polished public expression. The suggestion of an unseemly intimacy with the body that I'd felt, even as a little girl, in the life my mother led in her housedress is laid bare in de Beauvoir's unsentimental pages. "The species takes residence in the female and absorbs most of her individual life; the male on the contrary integrates the specific vital forces into his individual life." Those specific vital forces turn the individual male outward, merging his identity with "projects" by means of which the ultimate project of transcendence can be pursued.

But woman, though she too has her intimations of transcendence, softens and liquefies in the rising tides of reproductive destiny, "the life of the species," even when that destiny is unfulfilled: "[E]ach month all things are made ready for a child and then aborted in the crimson flow." De Beauvoir's description of female life, stuck fast in immanence, is rife with references to viscous fluids. A woman's life comes off sounding like some sticky syrup of secretions, as runny as a soft-boiled egg. Man's high and dry rational abstractions are lost in the moist goo of particularities to which a woman's life—and so her mind—are given.

The result is not the fleetness and light of transcendence but body-heavy immanence: absorption in the immediacy of her family and of herself. De Beauvoir has no inclination to wax sentimental over the sacrificing, self-effacing mother. Oh no, that mother is, in living the "life of the species," far more self-absorbed than the ambitious male analogue, pointed outward toward transcendence. "What woman essentially lacks today," she had written in 1949, "for doing great things is forgetfulness of herself; but to forget oneself it is first of all necessary to be firmly assured that now and for the future one has found oneself."

De Beauvoir had peered beneath the housedress—or whatever the French equivalent was, which no doubt was something far more chic and sexy. But even in French the sight was not pretty. The life of woman was viscous, fussy, and small. What was more, I *loved* high and dry abstractions. I was, after all, going to college, and then on to graduate school, to study philosophy.

So, sure, I wanted kids, just so long as they didn't confine me to a life of runny immanence, covered over by a fastidiously ironed housedress. It was important to me to know that I would always be able to step over my threshold into the great wide world beyond, that I would belong to that world as it would belong to me. So though I knew that I was the sort of person who would eventually try to have a baby, I also knew that I couldn't be a mother until I had a firm footing outside. I wasn't going to yield an inch of that world to the "life of the species."

And if I didn't want to have to think about what to wear when I got up in the morning, well, that's why jeans and T-shirts were invented.

I felt inexplicably guiltless about all this, even though there were expert guiltilizers assigned full-time to my difficult case. In particular, my mother and my mother-in-law joined together their considerable forces to convince me that my "insides were going to dry up" if I didn't have a baby, sooner rather than later. I don't know precisely on what they based their medical prognosis, whether the etiology of my gynecological desiccation was, according to them, due to my age (still in my early twenties) or my scholarly inclinations. My professional work was in philosophy of science and—I'll grant those two mothers of mine—it was pretty dry stuff.

I remember a visit to my parents' home for the late-spring holiday of Shavuot when I was twenty-six. I was in the living room, reading, and I could overhear snatches of the conversation that my mother and mother-in-law were having over the kitchen table. My mother-in-law was a widow and so my parents used to invite her to spend the holidays with them.

"So, have you spoken to her again about when she's going to have a baby?" asked my mother-in-law.

"You know how she is, Leah. She's always got her nose in a book. It's very hard to get her attention. If you could get pregnant from reading books, we'd have fifteen grandchildren from her already. "

"She's still on the Pill?"

There was something in the way my mother-in-law said those words "the Pill" that made me think of Lenny Bruce's riff on "Jewish and goyish": "Dig: I'm Jewish. Count Basie is Jewish. Ray Charles is Jewish. Eddie Cantor is goyish. B'nai B'rith is goyish. Hadassah, Jewish. . . . Kool-Aid is goyish. Evaporated milk is goyish even if the Jews invented it. Chocolate is Jewish and fudge is goyish. Fruit salad is Jewish. Lime jello is goyish. Lime soda is *very* goyish. . . ." My mother-in-law had never heard Lenny Bruce and wouldn't have known what to make of him if she had. Nonetheless I think she would have subscribed to some variation along these lines: "Dig: Housedresses are Jewish. Maternity housedresses are very Jewish. Saying you have a headache every night because you already have all the children you want is Jewish. Contraception is goyish. The Pill is *very* goyish."

"On the Pill," repeated my mother in elegiac affirmation. "She's been on the Pill so long who knows whether she can even still have children."

"That's very true. Who knows what that Pill has done to her insides?"

I happened to know, and I smiled conspiratorially at my belly, in which my firstborn, still indistinguishable from a tadpole, was busily gestating.

I held off telling my mother and mother-in-law for as long as possible about my pregnancy. I knew that the older women in my family would feel that they had me once I had a child, that they would assume that I had forgone all my ambitions to make my own way in the greater world. They'd smile at one another in that infuriatingly knowing way, convinced that, at long last, I'd slammed the door shut on any more adventures out there. I hadn't, but I was still insecure enough in my outside footing to feel that their presumptions would make my path even more slippery.

Sure enough, my mother's gift to me on the birth of my daughter was two housedresses, one solid blue, the other yellow with delicate flowers embroidered on its collar. And the smile with which she handed them over was exactly the one that I'd anticipated. At last, her smile suggested,

I understand you through and through. Everything I didn't get about you is now over and done with. I hadn't been mistaken in the semiotics of women's wear. My mother's gift to me confirmed that the housedress stood for all that I'd thought it had, ever since I was a little girl and dreaded the thought of growing up into one.

Of course, I never put my mother's gift to use. I kept the two house-dresses hanging pristine in the back of my closet, rather than donating them immediately to Good Will, just for their ironic value. They hung there, like two disapproving matrons, aggressively unattractive, behind the skirts and slacks I wore to work as an assistant professor of philosophy.

My chair at the department had known of my impending mother-hood well before my mother. I'd very conveniently timed the birth to occur during winter break, but I was hoping to be able to take off the spring semester to do the bonding about which all the baby books spoke so highly. I knew that it would be no hardship to find a temporary replacement for me, since graduate departments were turning out far more PhDs than could be hired in those days of the academic slump that had resulted from the baby boomers hitting the market. Yet my chairperson was rather begrudging about the proposition I presented. Unmarried and childless, she turned out to be a pretty committed guiltilizer herself, subtly suggesting that I would not be as useful a member of the department, much less of the scholarly community, once I was a mother. She seemed to suggest that parturition and its aftermath would cause leakage of my philosophical ability.

"I knew you wanted children," she concluded sternly, "But I didn't think it would be so soon." So *soon?* I felt like answering her (though still well trained to keep demurral demurely hidden). Would you mind telling my mother and mother-in-law how inappropriately *soon* you think it is for me to be having a child?

NONE of these three women ever succeeded in making me feel the slightest bit guilty, however. The either/or dichotomy to which they each subscribed seemed false, at least for me. "Mothers without housedresses" was my fearless motto. "Philosophers with wombs." So I got up every weekday morning, got dressed, and walked across my threshold into the outside world . . . and was overcome, almost to the point of tearful prostration, with scalding lashes of guilt.

Because, of course, where mothers, mothers-in-law, and department chairs couldn't touch me, my infant daughter did. She more than touched me. She grabbed those disputed insides of mine and really worked me over.

I hadn't seen it coming at all, the great forces of evolution that she magisterially summoned forth, long before she learned how to control the movements of her arms and legs. How else could those helpless little creatures survive, unless motherhood brought with it a capacity for feeling guilty that plays havoc with all of one's previous priorities? Those prone to mother-guilt are going to take better care of their infants, who therefore stand a better chance of surviving, the girls among them to live and pass on their own inherited susceptibility to the pitiless pangs of mother-guilt. So it is that mother-guilt, I'm inclined to think, is in our genes, just as mother-worry is, and for much the same evolutionary reason. I'd been decidedly disinclined toward either guilt or worry before I'd had kids, and might never have discovered my truly substantial capacity for both had I not become a mother.

I could never have anticipated the pangs that I would feel when it was time to go back to work full time. During the spring and summer, I had bonded like crazy with that amazing little creature, so that by the time the new semester came around the two of us were as close as, well, mother and child. (For some reason, I seemed to be the only one in the university with a five-day week. I suspect my department might have been punishing me for my audacious frivolity: The very idea of actually using a vestigial organ like the uterus.) Not only did I have to leave my infant daughter every weekday, but I had a pretty substantial commute as well. The thought that I would be two-and-a-half hours away should anything ever happen to my daughter was hyper-agony, a noxious cocktail of guilt and worry.

My daughter, as if intuiting that I had extra-maternal intentions for my future, had always rejected a bottle. Talk about guilt. Not only was I two-and-a-half hours away from the poor child, but so were my breasts, her main source of nourishment. A week before going back to work, trying desperately to get her to take a bottle, I finally got her to sip out of one of those sippy cups, though all she would take in that form was Welch's grape juice. She was eating some solid food by then. So at least she stayed alive while I was off being a philosopher. But needless to say, the moment I could leave my office, I would flee, together with my leaking, swollen chest, back to my daughter, beneath the accusatory stare of my chair, silently espousing her commitment to the irreconcilable contradiction between slovenly maternity and the life of the philosopher.

I began to think that perhaps my chair had a point, for life was undeniably messier, and I was aware that there was some sort of systemic mollification that I'd undergone, though I hoped it hadn't progressed to the softening of my analytic reason. But it was undeniable that I was awash in affect, all sorts of gushy emotions, as I'd never been before. Something that had always remained firm and hard in me had given way in this new attachment to life. I was much more given to being moved, lachrymose . . . Goddamn it, I was downright viscous.

I'd always been able to place myself at a rational distance from life, viewing it from the outside, as it were, abstracting from the identities of the various agents in the situation, even if I were one of them. This sort of extreme objectivity is what the philosophers call the *view sub specie aeternitatis*—under the guise, or the form, of eternity. The view has much to recommend it, but not if you want to be a mother. Just try keeping your baby alive and contentedly gurgling while living sub specie aeternitatis.

In any case, once I gave birth the form of eternity was as remote a possibility as, say, my husband's taking over the nursing now and then. Philosophical distance was simply impossible when it came to my daughter. Every particularity of her gleamed with significance because she was who she was. She was *my* daughter, *my* responsibility, *my* worry, and my most supreme joy.

No doubt about it, it was the life of immanence. Perhaps, as my glaring chair unsubtly suggested, I was a lesser philosopher for having become so very much of a mother, but that didn't make me feel in the slightest bit guilty. That job belonged to my daughter alone.

I felt so guilty about being away from her for so many hours of the day that I went mad lengths to compensate, including continuing to nurse her for an absurdly long time. Even my mother and mother-in-law said it was enough already. I nursed her so long that by the time she was finally weaned, we were able to have an intelligent conversation about it, with her one-upping me, a habit she began early and has cultivated, along with her younger sister, into a fine art.

"There's no more milk here," I told her. "The milk is only in the cup now."

"No milk?" she shot back, giving my breasts the once-over. "Do you have grape juice?"

Ah yes, sweet viscosity.

The immanence may not have helped my philosophical career, but I know that I would never have become a novelist had maternity not slurped me up into the runny immediacy of life. Sub specie aeternitatis is no place to be a mother and it's also no place to write a novel.

Of course, there's nothing like being a novelist mom to make you feel guilty. It's immanence all right, only immanence in some *other* life, powerfully carrying you away from yourself—and from your kids. Writing is the only natural narcotic I know that can compete with the absorption of motherhood itself. (Okay, maybe a really heady love affair is in the running, too.) All of that emotional intensity and attentiveness is diverted from your ever-needy kids. Of course you feel guilty. You ought to feel guilty.

But you learn to live with it, the guilt-provoking foot out the door that is a foot into another reality altogether, the reality of the alternate life you're living in the pages that you're writing. If you're very lucky, as I have been, your children learn to live with it as well, and accept having a mom who is often absent in more ways than one.

Once, my second daughter, then around six, mused aloud after her bath and bedtime story, when I was about to turn off her light and get back to work on either the next day's philosophy lecture or perhaps a few pages of fiction writing, "I sometimes wonder, Mommy, whether I should have kids when I grow up. I can see how much time it takes away from your work." Oh God, I thought, feeling the blistering whip coming down hard. What a rebuke it is for a child to make such a comment. I've betrayed the fact that her existence is an obstacle to my productivity. Poor child, having this poor excuse of a mother. "But then I see," she continued on in her sweetly analytic way, "how much fun you're having being a mother and I think that maybe I should be one, too, even if I won't get as much work done."

Her words conferred absolution as nothing else could have. The lesson she had drawn from watching me, her first role model, was that the life of a mother trying to live in the great wide world was complicated. She'd derived that lesson because, Goddamn it, it *is* complicated. The kid had gotten it right.

But the life looked good to her; it looked as if it were worth it. The important truth that I was having fun, slopping through the complications of immediacy, of immanence and transcendence and everything in between, had gotten through to her. I gave her an extra good night kiss for the gift she had given me, and, for about forty-five minutes at least, I was blissfully free of guilt.

Mercy

*

Gina Nahai

M<small>Y</small> French Catholic grandmother, independent spirit that she was, married a man she barely knew and, in the years between the two World Wars, followed him to Iran as the second of his two wives.

The first wife, a kosher Jew from the city of Kashan, kept the meat and dairy separate, and spoke to her seventeen brothers in a language no one else in the house could understand: the dialect of the Jewish ghetto where they were born. She allowed the Frenchwoman into her house (she was infertile, and my grandfather wanted an heir), but not into her husband's heart. In vain, she tried to impose on her the ways of Eastern wives: obedience, subservience, forbearance.

The Frenchwoman realized she had made a mistake even before she had set foot in the country. In Paris, where he had courted her briefly, my grandfather had seemed gentle, exotic, even amusing. He was importing French cigarettes into Iran; she was the boss's secretary at the cigarette factory. To marry him and leave Paris, she had thought, would be a great adventure—a chance to see the Orient up close. She had already accepted his proposal when he told her he had a wife, and yet she went ahead with the wedding, married him on a rainy autumn day when they stood alone before a civil judge who had been presented a fake passport—one in which there was no trace of the first wife. Her parents, opposed to the marriage, had refused to attend. She went home afterward and packed her things, and said her good-byes for what turned out to be the last time.

It was still raining when they boarded the train that would take them from France to Turkey and then to Tehran. She wore a red dress and red lipstick, silk stockings, a hat. The moment they had crossed the border into Iran, my grandfather reached into a bag and gave his new wife a black scarf.

"Put this on," he said, and his voice was already loaded and stern, "and wipe the paint off your mouth."

THE Frenchwoman asked for a divorce soon after she had arrived—give me a passport and a train ticket—but was told this was impossible. She attempted to find a way to leave on her own, and found there was none: Women in Iran did not—still do not—have a right to a passport. To leave the country, to travel even from one city to another, my grandmother needed written permission from her husband.

She stayed a month, and then another. Bitterly, and against her own judgment, she bore two daughters, then a son. She spent her days fighting her husband and his Iranian wife. She fought their relatives and friends, the servants, the night sentry who stood guard in the alley outside her bedroom. My grandmother had married a Jew but remained fiercely Catholic, let her children be raised Jewish but told me that Jews were Christ killers. She wanted to send her son—my father—to university in America, but her husband would not allow it. My father was married off at an early age and instructed to produce a son; he went on to have three daughters. My grandfather, who had wanted nothing more in the world than for a succession of male heirs to perpetuate the family name, would die bitter and disappointed, convinced he had been shortchanged by God.

AND so we lived, my multicultural family and their many-layered sorrows, seven Jews and one Catholic in a country that was ninety-seven percent Shiite Muslim, at a time when the West cast a shadow nearly as strong as our own history over every Iranian's consciousness. My mother, offspring of a Russian Lubavitcher rabbi and of his Iraqi wife, had internalized the discipline and the sense of duty they had taught their children.

But she was also a freedom-loving soul who dreamt of doing significant things she knew were beyond her reach. She wanted to go to university, but was not allowed to because she was married; wanted to have a career, but had children instead. She was outspoken in a place where women were expected to be silent, restless when she had no choice but to stay put.

By age twenty, my mother had arrived at the conclusion that being a woman was the worst thing that could happen to a person. She said this to my sisters and me, then told us we had a duty to find a way out: We had been born in Iran's golden era, when Jews were liberated from the tyranny of the mullahs and when women were beginning to have rights. We had access to a real education, and, more importantly, permission to believe in possibility. Unlike our mothers before us, we were allowed—within reason—to question authority, to challenge the conventional wisdom that had long ago determined a woman's best option to be a well-placed marriage. My sisters and I were allowed to have expectations: That our parents would value their daughters—not as much as they did their sons, but value them nevertheless; that our husbands would treat us, if not with respect, at least with kindness; that our elders—male and female—would not deny us happiness merely because it had been denied them.

A paltry sum, to be sure—this permission to *want*, without any guarantee that you would *get*—and yet it was so much more than any woman in our history had been allowed, so much more than most of them would have dared imagine. It implied a responsibility that was made clear to us early on and that we are expected to fulfill to this day: To be dutiful and correct as our mothers had been; and to find happiness so great, it will undo all their heartache.

"Study hard," my mother said. "Get a job. Never depend on a man for your livelihood."

"Be patient with your husband," the kosher grandmother whispered. "Give him what he wants. A woman without a man is like a queen without a crown."

"Expect the worst," the French grandmother advised. "Arm yourself against the world and you won't be disappointed."

My sisters and I celebrated every Jewish holiday, went to church with our French grandmother, memorized the text of the Muslim *namaz* for school. We were an odd and solitary bunch, forever caught on the border of things—of faith and culture and personal identity—at once lured and repelled by all the elements that constitute, for most people, the cornerstones of Belief. With the battle forever raging around us, we could not take one side without betraying someone else we loved and so we opted, without knowing it at first, for the neverland of in-betweens.

Hard as we might—and did—try, we would never be able to carry on our grandfather's name, never mend the heart of the Jewish wife who had been denied children and also lost her husband, or release our French grandmother from the adventure that became her prison. We could not compensate our mother for the injury done to her because she was born a woman in a world that was defined and dominated by men, could not please our Jewish relatives who thought us "not Jewish enough" or our Muslim friends who told us we were "different" because we were Jewish.

So we sat in the house, through long summer days when the heat struck the flies dead in the air and melted the silver shell off the life-sized statues of Persian princes that stood guard in every corner of the yard, and listened to our two grandmothers talk about how each had destroyed the other's life. We came home from school in the winter when snow piled knee-deep on the ground and cars skidded like toys on the icebound surface of Tehran's wide boulevards to find our mother looking pale and disappointed, cooking dinner and talking about the day she was told by her high school principal that she couldn't return to get her diploma because she was engaged to be married. We watched the men who oppressed the women, watched the women who were at once our role models and the very examples of what we knew we should not become. We could see that the men were disappointed, that the women were too; that, instead of reaching out to one another, they each stood on a solitary shore surrounded by an ocean that we—the girls of the new generation—were told we could cross.

But to sail from any one shore toward another would mean abandoning the others; to stay would mean squandering the chance we were given to leave; to do nothing would be to bury everyone's dream.

What do you do, mother, when personal happiness is, in itself, a loss?

I think now that it was this same ambivalence, the eternal ticking of this clock that reminds me of my sins against the others—I think it was this torment of the runner who is forever in a race she knows she'll never win that became the driving force in my later life: A sense of profound and unrequited guilt for having failed, even before I had started, at the task for which I had been brought to life.

I studied hard, taught myself to be patient, learned to expect the worst. I aimed to achieve knowing I had already failed, learned to persevere, to distrust.

And I made my peace with guilt.

EARLY in their marriage, my parents had resolved to leave Iran for good. My father could not bear the tyranny of a monarch who ruled by edict and who held the nation at his whim; my mother wanted a fresh start, in a place where the ghosts of heartaches past would not haunt her and her children. Long before the Islamic Revolution sent waves of Iranian immigrants to the West, my parents shipped my older sister and me to boarding school in Europe, then bought a house in America and moved here with my younger sister. I went home to Iran one summer from boarding school and said good-bye, then flew to Los Angeles to go to UCLA. It was the farthest I had ever gone from Iran, the first time I had enough perspective to look back.

I drove to school in the morning when the fog sat low on the hills above Sunset Boulevard and sleep veiled the eyes of my American classmates whose lives were so vastly different from my own—drove to school and walked with books in my arms toward the hollow auditoriums where the echoes of others' voices spilled like rain over the silence and the loneliness that defined me in those early years, watched the young people around me, and wondered what it was that made me so different from them, that made them so much more present, more confident, more able to bet on the future.

I stayed home on weekends and watched my mother cook for the

American neighbors she invited to dinner—older couples with stiff hair and shiny Cadillacs, who arrived on time and left early, sat straight-backed at the table and feigned interest in the conversation only to mask the obvious truth of how little they had in common with their hosts, how little they wanted to know about anything that did not have to do with America.

Through college and graduate school, I reflected on my childhood in Iran, and tried to understand the dynamics that had set our lives spinning as they had. I studied Iran's history and traced the Jews' presence within it, spoke to the Iranians who had come to America to escape Khomeini's mullahs and tried to find the dominant themes among them. I learned about the Jews' suffering under Shiite Islam, the pogroms and persecution, the ghettos and the forced conversions that our grandparents had endured but rarely mentioned—that they had wanted to forget because it was painful, or deny because it shamed them.

And I saw something else as well—something I had thought was particular to me but which I learned was common enough: I saw a hierarchy of pain *within* the Jewish Iranian society itself—generations of women gripped by an eternal sense of loss that transcended class and family, that made real change, even here, in a new country, seem impossible—that trapped even blue-eyed foreigners who rode a train one rainy day in a red dress and silk stockings. I watched these women with awe and astonishment, wondering at the courage they had displayed throughout their lives and at their resilience, but wondering also about this pattern that repeated itself every time, this weight, above and beyond that which was exerted from the outside, that pressed at all their hearts. So many of the Iranian Jewish women I came to know in America, I learned, had suffered at each other's hands back in Iran, been shunned and persecuted by other women for the smallest infractions. So many showed little or no tolerance of anyone who dared question or defy the rules that oppressed them all. So many had been punished for their courage, ambition, honesty. I saw an oppressed people who in turn oppressed each other. I could not tell the victim from the perpetrator, could not be content with having escaped, albeit not unscathed, the fate of the others.

asked questions and pieced together the memories; asked questions and tried to understand; asked questions and began to write.

IT's a strange and inevitable consequence of writing that any story, no matter how alien to the writer at first, will be transformed, through the act of creation, into an experience as personal and intimate as any she has known. Every story we write is about ourselves; every truth we record is our own natural truth. Without it—without the ability to draw on our deepest and most urgent passions—we can mouth the words but not create the sound, tell what happened but not make it resonate with the reader.

The stories I wrote about other Iranians became my own. The women whose lives I had begun to record were replaced by the characters who populated my books—ethereal beings who followed me everywhere I went; relentless creatures whose voices rose from my pages and who told of wasted lives and pointless anguish and the hopelessness of a thousand generations who had lived and died under the same murky sky.

I knew, even as I wrote each tale, that mine wasn't the only truth worth telling, that what I had observed, what any one person can observe, was only a sliver of a greater picture. I knew that my truth would offend as many of my Iranian readers as would relieve it, that it would constitute, to so many, yet another form of betrayal: To portray my people in a light that wasn't always favorable, to show their scars, their shame—not just to themselves but to strangers the world over. I was about to tell the story of a people who had existed for nearly three thousand years in solitude—quiet and self-effacing and able to survive the mullahs' rage only if they became invisible. I was about to present them to Westerners who didn't always understand, to Americans who might rush to judgment, who might hold this knowledge against the new immigrants among them.

Had she known, years ago in the vast living room of our house in Iran, that Friday afternoon when she sat in the green velvet armchair with the wooden handles that were carved in the shape of angry lions—mouths gaping open, teeth ready to tear, tongues scratched and coated with dust—had my French grandmother known that the story she told me then would one day be read by strangers?

All her life, her father had forbidden her to cut her hair short. The day she turned eighteen, she went to the barber and had him chop the hair off at the nape of her neck. Then he brushed the mane and laid it out in a long flower box; she brought it to her father like a dozen roses. Here it is, she said, *You* can have it if you want. I'm my own person now and I don't take orders.

He had kept the box, like a coffin, under his bed. It remained there after she had married my grandfather and left to spend her life fighting other orders.

I did realize—yes—that the very act of speaking would constitute a transgression in many ways; that it would split open, for so many, wounds they had stitched closed; that it would imply that I had, once again, opted for the border. I did not wish to transgress, to hurt, or to betray with my stories. And yet, like the dust that used to settle at the bottom of hundred-year-old wine bottles buried in our basement in Iran, my sense of the importance of ending the silence remained painful and troublesome, but ineluctable.

The sins my two grandmothers had accused each other of, I have tried to say, that they had accused their husband of; the sins my mother had blamed on nature, that women I had grown up with had blamed on men; all those wrongs that my two sisters and I were charged to undo with our own joyful lives, that we were supposed to set right but instead wanted to atone for—those transgressions for which I felt such guilt were not mine alone. They were *ours*, and *theirs*. They sprang from intolerance, from the particular brand of cruelty that is so common among the afflicted, from their desire to protect the community even at the expense of the individual.

I knew a thousand stories of injustice and pain. I could not change the plot or the ending, so I chose the only other option possible: I tried to bear witness.

My Iranian Jewish grandmother came to Los Angeles in the summer before the fall of the Shah, and never went back.

My French grandmother, who had the chance to do the same, refused to move: She had gambled on one adventure and lost; she wasn't about to risk another.

My parents, who had shown enormous courage in leaving their country when they didn't have to, went on to fight, and sometimes to win, even bigger battles. My two sisters have indeed "made something," and then some, of themselves. My fellow Iranians—Jews and Muslims, Christians and Baha'is and Zoroastrians alike—have turned exile into triumph, managed to safeguard, outside Iran, all the precious gifts of a culture that is under attack at home.

And I, who know well the consequences of my words, who carry my guilt still like a shadow, I look through the landscape of events and characters I have painted around myself at their real-life counterparts—at all the women whose lives became my stories, at their children and grandchildren who are scattered now across five continents—I look at them and am only too aware that they remain, for all the witness I might have borne, forever untouched by mercy.

A Grandmother's Biological Clock

*

KATIE ROIPHE

THE other day, standing in the middle of Pottery Barn innocently looking at glass coffee tables, I glanced up at my mother and saw that her
eyes were welling up with tears. "Mom, what's wrong?" I rushed over to
her, alarmed. Suddenly overcome by the symbolism of table lamps and
picture frames, she blurted out, "I just don't want you to spend your
whole life alone."

It's hard for my mother—married at twenty-one, pregnant at twenty-
four, divorced at twenty-seven, married again at thirty—to understand
what she sees as my stubbornly prolonged singleness. Ever since I turned
twenty-five, she's been on a relentless campaign of terror, humor, and
public shame to get me to settle down.

It doesn't seem to matter that I'm just doing what everyone else I
know is doing. Only two of my good friends are married, and their weddings were regarded as something of an eccentricity. The rest of us exist
in an ambiguous state of rented apartments, take-out dinners, and postponed futures. We all want babies, but we want them in the abstract way
that children want to be ballerinas and firemen when they grow up; we
want them "in a few years." The biggest commitment that a surprising
number of people I know have made is to a plant.

On Sundays, my mother studies the wedding pages as if looking
for clues, or at least she did until recently, when she announced, with a
tragic yet resigned air, that she has "given up." It seems to me that a lot
of my friends' mothers are reading the wedding pages, experiencing the
same pangs of bewilderment or envy: Why aren't their successful and

otherwise normal-seeming children settling down now that they are nearing thirty? They don't recognize that the relationships of my generation in their twenties can be like marriages, that we have the equivalent of our parents' first marriages without calling them marriages.

Could it be that lurking inside all the Jewish, feminist mothers of the '70s is a 1950s housewife who values china patterns and baby carriages above the passions of the mind? Lately I've noticed my mother dropping the phrase "old maid" into casual conversation. She refers to me as "the Spinster," even though, in what may be its own kind of sickness, I haven't gone twenty-four hours without a boyfriend since graduating from college. She buys increasingly lavish wedding presents for the children of her friends. "At least someone's procreating the species." She takes me to Tiffany's, where one of her friends' daughters is registered, and shows me the tiny sterling saltshakers and glittering crystal soup tureens as if to say, all of this could be yours.

I look at this beautiful silver-haired woman gazing intently at four different shapes of spoon and have trouble recognizing my bohemian Upper West Side mother, the one who taught me that work was what mattered, that having children and arranging your house beautifully was not the be-all and end-all of female experience. But recently she wrote a column in the *New York Observer* about how it was time for me to get married. It was such an eloquently argued and passionate piece that one couldn't help being persuaded to her side; perfect strangers wondered to themselves on their morning commute, Why is that girl torturing her poor mother?

All of this leads me to think that there must be a biological clock for grandmothers. My mother seems to contemplate every development in my life in terms of how it affects her grandchildren-to-be. When I look for apartments, she worries about where they will go to school. When I mention a man's name more than three times, she thinks about whether or not he would be a good father. I think my mother may be planning for her immortality the way other people plan for their retirements.

My mother's aspirations turn out to be contagious, and the problem of marrying me off has become a familywide sport. Last Thanksgiving, my older sister Emily said, "If you're not careful, you're going to turn into an aging femme fatale with two little Chihuahuas tucked under your arms." And my nine-year-old nephew turned to me over pizza one day and said very seriously, "Katie, maybe if you learned to cook someone would marry you." I'm starting to understand how Jane Austen's heroines feel as they reach their late twenties. I picture a life of solitude, with three cartons of coffee yogurt and a bottle of white wine staring up at me from my refrigerator. I have dreams about having a baby and giving it to my mother to raise.

What makes her pressure even more insidious, of course, is that it is, at bottom, well-intentioned; I know that what she wants is for me to be happy, and that's what makes it all the harder to defend against. Sometimes, though, I do try to argue. I use feminism and United States Census Bureau statistics and all sorts of manipulations of the truth. The truth, of course, is that she's right. All of Western civilization is on her side—Darwin, Freud, Martha Stewart. All I have is a wild impulse, a lingering immaturity, an overwhelming desire to stay up until three in the morning drinking margaritas with my friends or reading nine-hundred-page biographies until the sky is streaked with pink, not worrying about who is going to make breakfast or walk the dog or buy diapers, for just a little bit longer.

FIVE years later, I did finally succumb and give my mother the genetic immortality she so deserved. But the ensuing period of blissful contentment, the pleasant fulfillment of her fondest imaginings, lasted only a little while before a new concern darkened our horizons. Before her beloved granddaughter turned one, she began to sigh about the baby's social possibilities—"she is going to be so lonely if she is an only child!" and "she needs a lot of toys, since she won't have anyone to play with." And about a strange, mutual acquaintance, triumphantly, "he's weird, but what do you expect? He's an only child!" Embedded somewhere in this is a lesson about the infinite voraciousness and inventiveness of Jewish guilt that hadn't occurred to me: The campaign for my happiness would not be thwarted by something so minor, so utterly beside the point, as my being happy.

Being Fruitful

*

BINNIE KIRSHENBAUM

THE thing about saying I don't want children is this: No one believes me. They insist I am just trying to be difficult, shocking, or annoying. Or that I am a woman with parts missing: Either I have no ovaries or I have no heart.

But they are wrong on all counts. All components are in working order. I too have experienced the hormonal urge to reproduce; my genes have cried out for expression. I have carefully considered what it means to be a link in the chain of Jewish history. I readily acknowledge that I have a maternal instinct, and it finds fulfillment in the, albeit limited-to-one-hour, company of my friends' children, whose affection I win with that which is forbidden: candy, nail polish, and plastic vomit.

With my students at Columbia University, I am quite the mother hen, fussing over them, urging the too-thin ones to eat, tsk-tsking at the newest tattoo, listening to their girlfriend woes, and encouraging their futures. I hurt for their hurt and I swell with pride at their accomplishments. But when one of them said to me, "You'd be a great mother; you are so nurturing with us," I reminded her that these are not one and the same. "All of you are over twenty-one," I said. "I see you only once a week, and you are capable of blowing your own noses."

If you're like me, you know that the person most impervious to the claim that you don't want children—the person who will be indefatigable and often ingenious in her efforts to break you—is likely to be your own mother. And if she is a Jewish mother, even one who like mine bore little resemblance to the stereotype, she will pull out all the stops.

As if we were in the middle of a conversation from which I had drifted off, although there was no such conversation in progress, my mother had said to me "Well?"

"Well, what?" I asked, as if I had no idea where we were headed. But I did know. I'd been married now for three years and had been hearing about other people's grandchildren for three times as long.

"Well, have you thought about the fact that I might like to be a grandmother? Because I'd like to be. A grandmother."

"Sorry," I said, sounding like my mother had asked for a stick of gum and I was fresh out. "I can't help you." It was not news to my mother that I didn't want children. Even as a child, I didn't take to baby dolls, fat dolls we bottle-fed with water, which all too realistically came out the other end. Who wanted a doll that peed on you? Barbie I liked; a diaper was not part of Barbie's wardrobe.

At this point in the conversation, such as it was a conversation, my mother pointed out that along with no babies, I'd also contended that I had no desire to get married. I'd been adamant: *no husband, no children.* Yet, here I was with a husband and without regrets. In regards to marriage, I'd changed my mind. That's the thing about marriage: You can be fickle. But there is no divorcing the baby. A baby, a child, changes your life forever, and I liked my life as it was. I still do. I'm happy.

To have a child just so my mother, in a nod to *Bubbe*-hood, could whip out the pictures to show her friends and have the occasional Sunday afternoon at the zoo? I think not.

"I loved being a mother," my mother said. Perhaps, but given that she flew to work the minute my brother and I were old enough to fend for ourselves, maybe my mother didn't love being a mother quite as much as she protested. I did not doubt that my mother loved us, but loving your children is not the same thing as loving motherhood.

Moreover, I suspected that perhaps my mother wasn't quite as keen on being a grandmother as she was on validating herself as a role model. Why wouldn't I want what she had: the ideal, affluent, assimilated Jewish life? Husband, children, dog, cat, and house in the suburbs decorated colonial American. Why wouldn't I want to be all that she was: wife, mother, high school English teacher, and crafts hobbyist?

She believed that because her life made *her* happy, her life should make *me* happy.

When my brother got married, he and his willowy blonde ultra-WASP wife had three children one right after the other. Each of them was saddled with the decidedly non-Jewish trendy name du jour. With the arrival of three grandchildren, I thought my mother would lighten up on me about the baby business. She did not.

That these grandchildren were not being raised as Jews didn't bother my mother. My home was not an observant one, and as a fourth-generation American, my mother had little in common with the mothers of the shtetl. Perhaps due to lack of practice, her attempts to make me feel guilty were infrequent, overblown, and so patently absurd that rarely did she achieve the desired effect.

In a blatant attempt to change my mind to hurry up and have a baby, she told me that she was making out her will and that she would be leaving all family heirlooms—jewelry, silver, photographs—to my sister-in-law. "Because she has children to pass them on to, and I want these things to stay in the family," she said. I didn't bite. Instead, I shrugged and said, "That's your choice to make."

It was her choice to make, but I knew perfectly well she never intended to do any such thing, just as she would never have stayed away from my wedding despite the threat to do just that as well. My wedding was not a wedding, which was the crux of the boycott. My mother wanted to make me a big Jewish princess to-do and there was no way I could cope with that.

"We are going to get married at City Hall. Friday morning," I told her. "I really would like you and Dad to be there. And then after we can go for a nice lunch."

"I don't think I can make it." My mother took her best shot. "I have ceramics class on Friday mornings." Of course she came to City Hall, all dolled up, camera in hand, the beaming mother of the bride.

When the threat of disinheriting me didn't produce the offspring she wanted, my mother floated the most bizarre take of them all: I wasn't having children because I was scared of how much it would hurt.

"You'll forget the pain," she assured me. "Or, if you're really afraid, they can put you under." My mother was accusing me of cowardice, that

I wasn't having children because childbirth hurt. I was a disgrace to my gender, a wimp among women. I was not cut from the same cloth as the stoics who bore up through hours, days, weeks of labor. The women who subsequently wore the agonies and ecstasies of childbirth as a badge of honor, recounting the childbirth the way a soldier speaks of battle, bragging about it as if the longer the labor the more devoted the mother.

My biological urge to mother has found reward with my pets. I am one of *those* people at whom non–pet people roll their eyes. This is one way in which I am decidedly like my own mother. She was an animal lover too, and our cats and dogs (and the occasional iguana) were family members in good standing. Often in better standing than I. On more than one occasion, my mother, while casting a glance my way, waxed ecstatic over the unconditional love of a pet. What was the message there? A dog is loyal forever, but a child will stab you in the heart? Our pets came along on family vacations, at holiday time they got chew toys and catnip; they were fussed over, brushed, scratched, and kissed on the mouth.

At the time when my mother first let me know, unequivocally, that she was ready to be a grandmother, my husband and I had already begun our family. As far as we were concerned, we were parents enough to Newton, our Siamese cat. We kvelled over her every mew and poop, and my husband was fond of claiming, "She has my blue eyes." Lest anyone think my husband is a moron or insane, he knew perfectly well her blue eyes were unrelated to his blue eyes; he just liked the concept.

My mother was hardly the only one who tried to make me feel guilty about my being childfree. Asked by any number of strangers if I had children, I'd nod my head and say, "I have a cat," which inevitably put me on the receiving end of a small and visibly strained smile. But better to be thought a headcase than to endure what was sure to follow.

My decision not to have children makes some people hostile, as if my choice were casting aspersions on them and their babies, as if my choosing from Column B were an inherent criticism of Column A, which it is not. These people tend to lash out at me to let me know, in no uncertain terms, that they consider me to be utterly selfish and unwilling to devote my time, my money, and myself to my genetic off-spring. As far as they are concerned, whatever I do devote my time, my money, and myself to is undoubtedly shallow and without meaning or merit. They go on as if, in an overpopulated world filled with already born children in desperate need of care, having a baby and reproducing yourself is the only path to pure and true selflessness. (Never mind that utter selflessness is the stuff of martyrs, and since when do Jews strive for sainthood?)

The fact is that they have children because they *wanted* children, just as I am without children because I *want* it that way. That we both are, in essence, selfish, is lost on them. These people don't engender guilt as much as they do a kind of anger similar to what I imagine an innocent man condemned must feel.

One woman, who clearly could not fathom that women such as my-self exist, took my hand and with palpable sympathy told me that she knew of a wonderful fertility clinic where they worked miracles. When I said, "Thanks, but no thanks," she said, "But you're not Catholic." Catholics are not supposed to interfere with reproduction in either di-rection, but we Jews have no such papal edict. We are not soldiers in the holy war to protect the fetus and to hell with everyone else. Aren't we the ones who are actually allowed to have sex simply as an expression of love? I thought so, but it often appears as if I was mistaken.

Strangers can be harsh, but friends can be even worse. S., an old friend of mine and a mother of three, periodically asks me, "When are you going to grow up and have a family?" She makes no bones about it: I am just the silliest bit of fluff, and the decision not to have children is the by-product of a prolonged adolescence.

There are those who tell me that I have no idea what I am missing. The experience of having a child is the only experience worth having, and I must hurry and join the club or else regret it for the rest of my days. No doubt, this is a part of life on which I am missing out. A big part of life. But we're all going to miss out on something. No matter what Miss America sees for her future, it's not likely that she will be a kindergarten teacher *and* a celebrity spokeswoman. One or the other has to go.

By the by, I am also to blame for the downfall of our civilization—Jewish and American. As any loony-tunes eugenicist will tell you (as more than one has told me), reading scores are down because intelligent and well-educated women are having fewer and fewer children. Fewer high I.Q. genes are being passed along. Therefore fewer future Mensa members are being born. Ergo, we're rapidly becoming a substandard culture. One of these genetic planners even went so far as to say that when we finally do have children, it is too late; our eggs have begun to turn, and aging eggs produce mediocre minds. So is the message there that brainy teenagers should procreate like chickens? By refusing to reproduce, or reproduce in sufficient quantity, or in a timely fashion, we smarty-pants gals are the sole bearers of responsibility for the decline of Western civilization. The world is getting stupider by the minute, and it's my fault. Well, pass me the fiddle.

As I've never been a fan of human breeding farms for the genetic culling of the species, the condemnations of mad eugenicists are easily brushed off. Not quite as easy to ignore are the charges of my fellow Jews who insist that it is my obligation to compensate in numbers for the Six Million. Algebraically speaking, a plus does cancel out a minus, but birth and death are more than numbers alone. People cannot be replaced. Nothing and no one can make up for the Holocaust. Still, that one gets to me a little bit because what good fortune doesn't come packaged with a sprinkling of guilt? Who among us—those of us who have not suffered—can stroll through the bounty that is ours, bounty such as liberty and freedom and Zabar's, and not feel the tweak of admonishment over the fact that in our world people still starve to death? What American Jew, cozy and comfortable as he or she may be, does not feel that we owe something to those who did, and do, suffer?

Owe something, but what? Must the debt be paid with the contribution of children? What's with the insinuation that the Jews are on the verge of extinction and that that is my fault too? Really, whether I beget or not will have no bearing on the survival of the Jews. I am not Eve.

Okay, if nuclear war happened and I was the last woman left on earth, even if I was the last Jewish woman left on earth, I would do my civic and/or religious duty and have children. But really, this is moot, especially to me, as I walk the streets of New York City, where there is a population explosion among the Hasidic and ultra-Orthodox communities. These women seem to be having babies enough for all of us.

"Exactly the problem," R. (mother of two and a Reform Jew) said to me. "The Hasidim and the ultra-Orthodox are having six, eight, eleven children per family. The Reform, the Reconstructionists, the Humanists, we're having one or two, and worse, like you, none. They're going to take over. We're going to disappear. Jews are going to wind up like the Amish. A community of crazy fanatics, a tourist attraction."

Without going anywhere near that land mine of conflict among the affiliations, I pointed out to R. that perhaps her concern, as well as my observation concerning proliferation, was nothing more than a question of visibility; we can identify on sight the women with their hair covered and their black-hatted husbands, whereas the worldly Jewish families are indistinguishable in the crowd.

"In fact," I said, "last Yom Kippur, I couldn't get a seat in any of the six synagogues I tried. There is no shortage of High Holiday Jews." To that, R. shook her head and said, "You just don't understand what you are missing. Having children changes your whole life." And we were back to that: Yes, I do understand. And I don't *want* my whole life to change.

ALTHOUGH my parents were what my mother called "secular Jews," there are some customs and rituals that we observed and honored. When my mother died six years ago from cancer, we sat shivah, and it was then, as my nieces and nephew swiped cookies from the table, that it hit me: It is highly unlikely that someday a child will be named in my mother's memory.

The grandchildren she had, with their Taylor-Jackson-Emily type names, were not named in memory of great-grandparents or a favorite uncle. With Christmas as their sole nod to faith, I doubt the next generation of my family will even know of the custom, much less adhere to it. This realization saddened me because I consider the keeping of memory to be meaningful, something that matters.

To that end, I light a candle on the anniversary of my mother's death. I dedicated a book to her *in memoriam*. I tell stories about her. I wear things that belonged to her. Sometimes I look at photographs of her, and I have to remind myself that she is dead. I try to remember how much she liked to laugh.

On a cold January night, two winters ago, our beloved cat Newton died. My grief was deep and painful and primal. Say what you will, she was my baby. I got her when she was so small that she could sit in the palm of my hand, and for sixteen years, she slept snuggled in my arms. I loved her.

The balm of time passing did what time's passing does, enough so that eventually my husband and I decided we were ready to get another cat. We came home with a pair of kittens, a boy and a girl. But what to name them? Quark and Brenda, Sid and Vicious, Moe and Sadie? None of these names seemed to fit. Then it came to me. The boy would be named Isaac in memory of Newton, the girl Ferne, my mother's name.

Curiously and coincidentally, or perhaps it is the result of something divine, Isaac is much like Newton: sweet, affectionate, trusting, and a little bit goofy. Ferne, just like my mother, has an outstanding sense of humor and is strikingly beautiful. And just like my mother, she is attracted to shiny objects and far prefers my husband to me.

What was intended to happen did happen. The memories of the deceased are vibrantly alive. I remember my mother all the time now. Not her death, which was slow and painful, not the things about her that annoyed or angered me, but the things that made me smile and laugh and love her.

Still, I wasn't sure that naming a cat in my mother's memory was entirely kosher. It happens that a former student of mine, J., a lovely and wise young man, is now attending rabbinical school. From time to time, he stops by my office and we talk, and so I ran it by him. "Do you think naming the cat for my mother is a sacrilege?"

Never one to shoot from the hip, he thought for a while. Then as Talmudic scholars are wont to do, he answered my question with a question. "Did you do it to be disrespectful or did you do it as a loving act?"

Because we all sometimes hide our true motives from ourselves, I turned over both possibilities before concluding, "It was a loving act."

"And how would your mother have felt about it?" J. asked.

A kitten was not exactly the grandchild she was referring to when she said, "Well?" But it was through my mother that I learned that love can be vast and boundless. And I heard my mother's voice, as sure as if she were standing beside me, agreeing full well that the kitten Ferne is a real charmer. I can so easily picture my mother holding little Ferne to her face, kissing the wet nose and laughing.

I think my mother would have been tickled pink to be remembered this way, but it would not have stopped her from saying, "You know, it's not too late. Plenty of women your age are having children."

Expecting

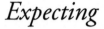

REBECCA WALKER

April 3, 2004

THE mice have eaten the arms and necks off all of my cashmere sweaters and I am just over it. I know they are using the cushy yarns to build nests for their babies, but can't they do that somewhere else and with someone else's cashmere sweaters? Tonight as I brushed my teeth at the kitchen sink, I heard scratching and looked up to see two tiny mice running along the molding over the sofa. When I came up to bed, I found one arm of my black sweater, chewed off as perfectly as a piece cut from a dress pattern, lying on the floor next to the nightstand. I can't take it. We've got to get a cat, or maybe two cats. Or maybe I should call Terminix? I hate the thought of the little beasts gnawing on poison and then crawling somewhere to die, bloated with thirst. But at eight weeks pregnant and counting, I've got my own nest to feather, and mice droppings all over the kitchen counter just won't do.

How Darwinian.

On the way up to this mice-infested paradise, S. and I got into an argument. We were walking into Saul's, the local Jewish deli, and S. said he didn't feel comfortable because there aren't ever any other black people at Saul's and the pictures on the walls remind him of Zionism and all of the horrible things being done to Palestinians in its name. Because I've got a little Jewish in my African-American, or a little African-American in my Jewish, depending on the day, I know what he means. But I feel very at home at Saul's, and I feel this crazy, irrational, out-of-control desire to protect Jews and Judaism from people's negative perceptions, whether they have some basis or not.

I launched into a tirade about how the Israeli government is as far from many of the Israeli people as the Bush government is from many Americans. I pointed out the long, liberal tradition of American Jews. I made analogies to the knee-jerk assumptions people make about African Americans. S. tried to get a word in and have a conversation rather than a debate, but I had already hoisted my ivy-league machine-gun mind onto my shoulder and begun the assault. After a few rounds, my voice was tight and accusatory. S. withdrew from the conversation completely.

Taking a breath, I had a flash of the baby and how arguments like these might frighten him, if they didn't already. I thought about something S. and I have talked a lot about: ceasing arguing in our relationship forever, and prioritizing peace between us over whatever issue our intellects have gotten hooked on. I never want ideology or "being right" to take precedence over loving one another and being a family. There's just too much to lose, S. for starters. My baby's mental health is another important something that comes to mind. He'll never be able to handle being a second generation black, white, and Jewish Buddhist if his parents can't keep it together.

I think that underneath the defensiveness is guilt. I feel guilty about what is happening in the occupied territories. I feel guilty that so many Jews have been able to assimilate and become successful while so many from other marginalized populations have not. I feel guilty that I can sit in a restaurant and feel comfortable while at the same time, someone I love feels awkward and unwelcome.

But I think feeling guilty is just a way out of taking responsibility. As long as I feel guilty I can pretend that I am actually doing something about what is going on—*I am feeling guilty*—when in fact I am doing next to nothing to directly impact the peace process, or to change the culture of Saul's. The guilt-induced tearing at my psyche also makes me feel as if I, too, am suffering alongside the ones being wounded. I, too, am a victim of the whole rotten mess. Which is true, but also puts the responsibility for fixing the whole mess where, exactly?

Before we went to bed last night, we talked about names. I've been calling the baby Milarepa after a Buddhist ascetic who tamed both human beings and animals by singing to them.

I wish we had a cat to tame these mice.

Maybe we should name the cat Milarepa.

June 5, 2004

WENT to my friend Trajal's dance performance downtown tonight, a piece inspired by Bret Easton Ellis's book *Less Than Zero*, all about the deep insecurity that fashion often masks. As someone who has never met a Prada skirt she didn't like, I found it very insightful. Afterward, a bunch of us went to dinner and I asked people to come up with names. The response to Milarepa was lukewarm, but people liked Tenzin, which I've been throwing around for the last few weeks.

"Tenzin Walker," our playwright friend Brooke said. "That's strong." Trajal took to it right away, and started to include Tenzin in all our future plans. "Well, when Tenzin is born, we'll have to have a party," and "I can't wait to go to Paris with Tenzin."

Paris with Tenzin!

Yesterday on the phone, I asked Trajal if he liked his name, or if having to constantly spell it for people drove him crazy. He said he didn't always, but that for most of his life he has loved his name and can't imagine being called anything else. I can't imagine it either. Trajal is so *sui generis,* so unique, that I can't help but credit his name with inspiring at least some of the freedom he's claimed for himself. I don't think he could have been the complex iconoclast that he is if his name was John.

Or maybe he could, and I am just looking for justification to name the baby something that isn't in the Bible. Last week I had lunch with my editor, who has worked on tons of Buddhist books, and she said that the American kids with Tibetan names all want to be named Diane and Michelle. That gave me pause but then I thought, don't all American kids want to be named Diane or Michelle?

Anyway, tonight I felt like the belle of the ball. Even though it was Trajal's night, being pregnant makes every night my night. Not long ago I heard Christiane Northrup speaking about yin wisdom, and how the egg waiting for the sperm is full of it. The egg just calls out to the sperm and then waits, knowing the whole school is going to come calling. I feel like that. For the first time in my life, being is effortless. My job is to sit and glow. All I have to do is wait and the whole world, the whole big life experience, is going to come and land right at my feet.

Tenzin Walker!

September 23, 2004

Last night I told everybody I was thinking about naming the baby Tenzin. My stepmother looked up from her plate and said, "Tenzin? What kind of name is that?" Then my father said that no matter what I named him, he was going to exercise his right as a grandfather to call him whatever he wanted, which was Chaim. I told them that Tenzin is the Dalai Lama's name and that I couldn't think of anyone more inspiring to be named after. And then my stepmother said, "Isn't there anyone in the family you could name him after?" And my father said, "Yeah Rebec, what about Samuel? David? Moishe?"

I felt like Judas.

Before we arrived at the question of what to name the first biological grandchild of our clan, we focused our collective energy on whether or not my sister should take a role on a reality show. My brother and I were vehemently opposed and got so outrageously vocal about the whole thing, with my father chiming in from the sidelines with a "legal perspective" and my stepmother picking at her miso cod and trying not to get involved, that my sister finally had no choice but to accuse us of ruining her life. She stormed out of the room as I yelled, "We are only telling you this because we love you," to which everyone nodded approvingly and my father said, "That's right, Rebec," following which my sister slammed her bedroom door.

It was my first dinner with the fam since being home, the fam being the Jewish half of my family, and home being their apartment on the Upper East Side of Manhattan. My father got a huge kick out of watching me eat two California rolls, one filet mignon Yakitori, a giant salad, an order of Agadashi tofu, two bowls of miso soup, and an entire order of steamed vegetable dumplings. He kept beaming and saying things like, "So you're eating for two, my Rebecca? Eat plenty for my grandson in there, the little *schmutsky*," and asking if I wanted the rest of his chicken lo mein.

September 25, 2004

We went to Ronnie and Tom's to break the fast for Yom Kippur. Jason, Ronnie's black, white, and Jewish son with whom I used to watch *Love Boat* and *Fantasy Island* sprawled on his mom's bed, was there with his new girlfriend. She's Cuban, but has never been to Cuba. Of course this possibility didn't occur to me until after I had talked about how beautiful the island is and how the people are so incredible. The blank look on her face tipped me off. Then I started obsessing about how her family must have lost everything in the Revolution and they probably hate Fidel or at least have serious and legitimate gripes and here I come, a spoiled American, talking about it like just another place I visited and added to my places-I-have-gone-and-now-have-an-opinion-about list. Disgusting.

The whole name thing came up again. Ronnie said, "Tenzin? No, I don't like that so much." Then my stepmother said, "What are the kids at school going to call him?" and my brother said, "Ten." My father threw his hands up and said, "I like Chaim," and I said, "Dad we talked about this," which we had, earlier in the day. I told him that I would not have anyone, including his grandfather, subjecting my child to even the merest hint of identity confusion. I said, "What if Grandma had insisted on calling me Susan?" He paused and said, "You're right, I would have told her that your name was Rebecca. But how is he going to get a job with a name like Tenzin? You know," he said seriously, "there is a group of women with names like Shanequa speaking publicly about how their names have kept them from succeeding in the workplace. They're all changing their names to Mary."

I told him that Tenzin was a perfectly respectable name, and part of a tradition at least 2,500 years old.

Then I asked him how many jobs he thought Chaim would get, and we both burst into laughter.

October 5, 2004

TALKED for a long time last night with S. Seemingly out of nowhere I suggested we name the baby Jonah, or maybe David. S. kind of went through the roof. Um, hello? We're Buddhist and, more than that, we made a decision. Please don't tell me your ambivalence is stirred up again.

But it's not ambivalence, it's guilt. I feel like I am letting the clan down. Even more than that, I worry that if the baby has a name that doesn't resonate with my family's biblical template, they may not bond with him. In this crazy world, my baby is going to need grandparents. Isn't it my responsibility as a mother to make sure the seeds for these important relationships are planted?

I also want him to relate to his Jewish roots, to know what it means to be a part of this crazy tribe of people who mix love and arguing like chocolate syrup and milk, who use Yiddish proverbs as terms of endearment, and who manage to find fabulous YSL sandals in the mountain of lame shoes at the Barney's Warehouse Sale. I want him to know that his grandfather believed in justice the old-fashioned, Jewish lefty way, and that even though he's a Buddhist, he's related to one of the most revered rebbes in Judaism.

Maybe guilt is the mechanism that holds us all together and keeps us from completely spinning out into non-Jewhood. I heard somewhere that human beings, in terms of the way we organize ourselves, most resemble pack animals. As in wolves, dogs, wildebeest. We want everyone in our pack to smell the same. If they don't, we're not sure they're really one of us, and if they're not one of us, how can we trust them?

Biblical name=Smelling the same
Smelling the same=Trust
Trust=Survival

Biblical name=Survival

Sigh.

November 29, 2004

I am starting to think that giving a baby a Tibetan name isn't a betrayal of family as much as it is a sign of maturation.

S. and I were flipping through a magazine, talking about how many people are stunted in their development, hovering in an adolescent state well into their fifties and sixties, even until death. He defined adolescent as being overly concerned with the acceptance of peers, and fearful of rejection or confrontation with the adult world.

Which made me think of George Costanza on *Seinfeld,* the Jewish guy masquerading as Italian who still lives with his parents, and of the stereotypical Jewish man still unhealthily enmeshed with his mother. I think I can safely say that guilt is the mechanism by which he remains ensnared. Who can stand the emotional blowback that comes with breaking away?

If guilt keeps us from moving forward and acting on our beliefs and aspirations, it certainly follows that not acting on our beliefs and aspirations can keep us in a state of arrested development. If we aren't diligent in our efforts to mature, at some point cutting the cord of familial expectation, we become infantilized by it.

That seems pretty clear.

Now every time I feel guilty about the baby's name, I think about George Costanza. Even though he's not Jewish, the image still works.

December 23, 2004

Um, can I ask one small but very relevant question? Why the hell doesn't anyone tell you how much it's going to hurt? Oy f-ing vey. Here I thought I was going to have this natural birth, with my beloved midwife and her fabulous assistant. I thought if the pain got too bad I would hop into the birthing pool, and because I love to swim and take baths, it would somehow relax me and ease the pain.

The only thing that could ease that pain was *an epidural,* and if I do this again, which at the moment I cannot imagine, I will demand one after the first contraction, if not before.

The whole thing was a miracle, but more on that later. At the moment I must document my newfound respect for every human being who has given birth, and I completely retract my judgment of every woman who has had or will have a scheduled C-section. I mean really, maybe I just have a low threshold for pain, but I don't think so. It is *outrageous.* I remember screaming, somewhere in between the toilet, the birthing pool, the bed, and the shower, that I couldn't believe every person on this earth got here this way. It just doesn't seem possible.

But it is and now, 30 hours after it all began, I have this little baby boy who is the most vulnerable, unbelievably precious thing I have ever seen.

I honestly don't know if I can bear it. The joy. The pain. The responsibility.

His name is Tenzin Walker.

III

Babes in Goyland:

*Love, Sex, and Self-Image
in an Unkosher World*

The Monica Metaphor

*

LAUREN GRODSTEIN

In France, they called me Monica—and boy, was that the joke that wouldn't quit. They chuckled "Monica" when I walked down the street, winked "Monica" when I picked up a baguette, sniggered "Monica" when I bought a bottle of wine at the corner store. This was back in 1998, the post-college year I spent loafing in Paris, and here's the weird part: At first I didn't even know what they were talking about. My name was, and is, Lauren.

"*Non, non,* Mon-ee-ka!" exclaimed my pal Eric, making a vulgar gesture with his finger and his cheek. Eric was a balding Parisian who waited tables at the restaurant next door to my apartment, and he was one of my few real French friends. We smoked cigarettes together in the alley between my residence and his workplace, and if I came into the restaurant during the late afternoon, he'd give me free bowlfuls of runny rice pudding, my favorite. His English was worse than my French, but he liked to practice.

"Mon-ee-ka Lee-vin-sky!" Eric said, then looked at me questioningly. "I am saying it right? *Tu comprends?*"

He was saying it right, but I was not "comprending" at all. Did the people on the street, at the *boulangerie*, at the wine shop—did they really think I was Monica Lewinsky? No, that couldn't be it—as far as the world knew, Monica was sequestered somewhere in D.C. with her lawyers. So then they must have thought I looked like her—but I didn't look like Monica any more than I looked like Brigitte Bardot (which is to say, sadly, not at all). So what was it, then, that the French found so

Monica-esque about me? Was it that I wore a beret that one time? That I had puffy hair? Was there something untoward about me, something—slutty? Did I really seem intoxicating enough to topple the American government?

I had done my best, in the few months I'd lived in Paris pre-*scandale Lewinsky*, to disguise my Americanness. I spoke French whenever possible, and when I couldn't, I kept my mouth shut. I wore simple clothing and dark lipstick, chain-smoked Gauloises Blondes, and never asked for directions. On most weeknights I babysat for an American child, the daughter of IBM executives from Texas, but whenever the kid begged to go to McDonald's I dragged her to the corner café instead. Silently, we'd both pout into our pâté sandwiches. What could be more French than that? What could be less Monica?

"I hardly resemble Monica Lewinsky," I informed Eric. "She has long hair. And a teeny little nose. And she's, you know . . ." I tried to make the international gesture for "chubby," tracing the outlines of a round woman's figure in the air with my hands.

"Yes," Eric said thoughtfully. "She does have quite American breasts." Then he turned and faced me, smoke trailing from his nostrils. He looked at me closely, much more closely than usual.

"But of course," he finally said, "she is Jewish, no?"

"Monica?" I blinked. "I guess."

"So then you see." He shrugged one of those awful Gallic shrugs and lit another cigarette. "She is Jewish, you are Jewish." After a second, I realized he would say nothing else; I was just supposed to catch his drift.

"Eric," I said, "not all Jewish women look alike."

He shrugged again.

"Come on. Would you say that all Japanese women look alike? All Arab women look alike? All black women?"

He inhaled his cigarette and made a face that suggested he was thinking hard about the question but really, I knew, he was just trying to remember his English grammar. "With the Japanese women I would say maybe. Arab women, who can tell? They're all covered up, usually. And the blacks . . ." Another shrug. "It is hard to say. But *Lo-rrhonnh* . . . You have that Jewish face, that body. Very, very sexy. Very beautiful. But it is the face and the body of"—here a thoughtful exhale of cigarette smoke— "a Jewess."

When I didn't respond for several moments, Eric's expression shifted from worldly to anxious. He lit a cigarette for me. He patted my knee. When I still didn't say anything, he shook his head, full of disquiet. "I said the wrong thing, heh? The right word is not Jewess? That is a bad word?"

"No," I said. "I guess it's the right word." But frankly, for some reason, it wasn't the word I wanted to hear.

Jewess. I suppose it's not inherently offensive—I mean, it's certainly better than a hundred other derogatory names you could call a Jew. But still it rankles. The word "Jewess" brings to my mind heavy locks of thick black hair, long skirts, clinking bracelets, a musky odor. Something closer to a gypsy dancer than a rabbi's wife, except with the belly covered and without the castanets. A Jewess sounds juicy and slightly dirty, like a lot of other words that end in -ess—mistress, seductress, stewardess. And Jewish women, as far as I can tell, are the only females of a particular religious group to be designated with that voluptuous suffix. You never hear of the Mormoness, the Presbyterianess, the Buddhess. But there she is, the Jewess: exotic and exoticized, heavy-breasted and smoky-voiced. Never mind that most of the Jewish women I know are wildly over-worked, too stressed-out to find the time to be seductive. Never mind that in their current pop-culture depictions, Jewish women tend to be emasculating shopaholics–Jewish American Princesses bearing Daddy's AmEx, not shaking tambourines. And never mind that, as far as clinking bracelets and long skirts go—that ain't the Monica I remember, and it sure as hell isn't me.

But I understand how a person could make a mistake.

INTRIGUED, I did a little digging on the subject and uncovered a major trove of Jewessery. First of all, it was no shock that I came face-to-face with the term in France; the Jewess, or *la Juive* in the native tongue, seemed to be an especially French construction, rife with all the dualities that France shows its own Jewish population. In the French imagination, the Jewess was both saintly and sensual, maternal and singularly erotic. In the literature of Balzac and de Maupassant she was a courtesan, while in de Goncourt she was the buxom model of a Christian painter. Chateaubriand claimed that the Jewess's beauty was compensation to the becursed, humiliated Jewish man; Alexandre Dumas warned that the wily Jewess could, snake-like, loosen the morals of French society. The Jewess even got her own French opera, Fromental Halévy's *La Juive*, in which she played, à la *The Merchant of Venice*, the gorgeous daughter of a tyrannical hook-nosed Jew. *La* poor *Juive* ended up tossed into a cauldron of boiling oil in the final scene; the librettist had two endings in mind, but eventually went with the boiling oil over the triumphant conversion-to-Christianity. Tragedy (boiling oil) or triumph (Christianity)—the choice of the ages, isn't it?

THESE days, the sexy Jewish woman, both in France and elsewhere, is the subject of a different kind of fascination. To some, she's a bronzed lady of leisure, tanning in South Beach or shopping at Saks. To others, she's the whiny, raven-tressed nanny from the sitcom of the same name. And to still others, she remains the Orientalized Other; if you have the misfortune of visiting a skinhead Web site you'll see that the nineteenth-century Jewess stereotype lives on in all its terrible Alexandre Dumas incarnations. But for most people, the platonic form of the sexy Jewish female is "that woman" from Beverly Hills who sucked on Bill Clinton's cigar.

Despite a dramatically different American cultural landscape, six years after the Lewinsky scandal, Monica's impact remains profound. She is the lascivious "portly pepperpot," a lingering late-night television joke. She is hailed by certain ultra-Orthodox Jews as a modern-day Queen Esther. She often appears in the tabloids like the reborn sphynx, boogeying into nightclubs, hawking her handbags. There was a run on the Club Monaco lipstick she wore on her breakthrough Barbara Walters interview. Golda Meir doesn't score a quarter of her name recognition, and Gloria Steinem doesn't get an eighth. For better or worse, she is the Jewess of our age: Monica Lewinsky.

But is Monica really me?

After my discussion with Eric that Parisian afternoon, I went back to my apartment and stared in the bathroom mirror. There was nothing either more or less sexy about me than I'd remembered, nothing that seemed especially suited to flirting at political rallies or fellating presidents. And yet, despite myself, I could see the faintest resemblance between the two of us, if only in the fact that we both—in some obscure but omnipresent way—"look Jewish." Dark hair, light eyes, full mouths, "American" breasts. There was similitude, however faint. Eric knew it, every last person in Paris knew it, and, of course, I knew it.

And I felt ashamed.

Now, the actions of a member of a particular group do not condemn the actions of the entire group. (I remind my grandmother of this fact every time she *plotzes* over a Jewish criminal convicted of a spectacular crime: David Berkowitz, Joel Steinberg, oy, Amy Fisher.) So I knew, consciously, that Monica's indiscretions were not my indiscretions, Monica's sex-for-power exchange was not how *I* would ever dream of achieving my goals.

"But it does say something about us, doesn't it?" This was from an aquaintance of mine, a Jewish woman a few years older than I. We were at a café in Manhattan, a month after I'd returned from Paris, talking about the newly released Starr Report, which had been printed in the *Times* in its full filthy ickiness:

"Ms. Lewinsky," she read, "testified that her physical relationship with the president included oral sex but not sexual intercourse. According to Ms. Lewinsky, she performed oral sex on the president; he never performed oral sex on her."

"It's so typical," my friend said, sipping on her cappuccino, glaring at the newspaper. "Jewish women are such givers. They give and give and give. Even when there's no hope of receiving."

"You know, I'm not sure the Starr report is a testament to the Jewish woman's generosity," I said, shuffling the *Times* to a different section.

"But it is! Look at us! We give to our husbands, to our parents, to our families. To be a good Jewish girl is to never stop giving. After all, we're the ones responsible for creating a Jewish home. We're the ones responsible for passing the religion on to our children. Judaism is matrilineal. It's all on us. We have to give." This from a woman who had no children, who in fact rarely dated.

"But I don't think . . ."

"Did you know," she interrupted, splashing her cappuccino on the café tabletop, "that a woman is exempt from certain commandments because they might interfere with her duties as wife and mother? She's supposed to be so busy taking care of her family that she can't even stop to pray at specific times of day."

"But what's this got to do with Monica?"

"Everything," she said. "It has everything to do with Monica. Monica put her man first. She sacrificed herself. Just like a Jewish woman is supposed to." She grabbed the paper from me and turned it back to the report.

It was tough for me to see Monica as the ur-giver, a karmic representation of the martyred Jewish mother. As far as I was concerned, even if Monica hadn't been repaid in sexual satisfaction, she certainly got some things she very much wanted out of her relationship with the president. And yet I was troubled by my friend's ability to read so much of the Jewish female experience into Monica's experiences. In France, they called me Monica; in America, was I supposed to call *myself* Monica?

I headed home unnerved. When I was in Paris, whatever discomfort I had felt about the whole Monica–Lauren parallel I had attributed in part to the general discomfort of being an expat. If I was exoticized, made to feel different, it was at least in part due to the fact that I *was* different: an American in a sea of French people. But here, back on home turf—New York City, the Jewish capital of the world!—I still couldn't shake that feeling of indictment. Despite myself, I started heading down my grandmother's whole Steinberg/Son of Sam/Amy Fisher spiral. Monica just had to be Jewish, didn't she?

On the subway back uptown, I slumped in a bright orange seat, watching as all the passengers read their papers. It's not that I was a prude, exactly, but I had always been averse to talking about sex in public. And now I felt like the whole world was talking, not just about Monica's sex life, but, by extension, my sex life. All of our sex lives. De Goncourt's Jewess was reclaiming her place on the public stage, crowding out our own ideas of ourselves. Our privacy. Our self-respect. It felt bad.

But just as I was about to start *shraying* into my neighbor's *New York Post,* I noticed an Orthodox woman sitting in the seat across from me. The woman was Jewish, of course, but she was no Monica—nor would anyone be likely to confuse them. While Monica wore low-cut tops and high-cut skirts, this woman was covered from neck to ankle. Her hair was covered by a wig, a *sheitl,* and she wore little makeup or jewelry. She was a picture of modesty, almost invisible in her self-effacing style. But she presented herself like this because, in her community, her innate sexuality was understood to be a thing of overwhelming power. Out of respect for herself and for Orthodox men, she remained as discreet as possible. And whatever my reservations about the politics of her place in the Orthodox world, the truth was she didn't make me nearly as uncomfortable as Monica did.

And there were other, less conspicuous Jewish women on that train, women who acted no more like Monica than they acted, necessarily, like me. Intellectual Columbia students and glam Upper East Siders, downtowners with nose rings and art students with big black portfolios under their arms. Businesswomen in tasteful suits, editors in fashionable shoes, grandmothers in housecoats. Jewish women of every possible variant, living their amazingly diverse lives.

Yet the ones who were my age, the dark-haired twentysomethings with the blue eyes and the wide hips—how many of them had been told that they looked a bit like Monica Lewinsky? That there was something about their hair, maybe, or about their incredible American breasts? That they "looked Jewish" just like Lewinsky did? I wondered, if they had been confronted with the Monica metaphor, whether it mattered much to them. If it didn't, why did it matter so much to me?

Whatever sexiness I put out into the world has always been a sort of intellectual slow burn. I've long depended on my conversation, rather than my appearance, to score boyfriends. Many of my acquaintances, especially my Jewish ones, would say the same thing—that we've been taught to value our brains over our bodies, to think that our rhetorical skills are every bit as attractive as any other assets we might have. Smart, chatty Jewish women like us can *talk* our way into relationships. But Monica had subverted this entire game plan with one little flash of the thong. I suppose a small part of me admired her moxie, but most of me resented being to tied to her with this thick Semitic knot.

A T the end of that summer, the knot tightened. The House Judiciary Committee announced that it would release the tapes of Bill Clinton's X-rated grand jury testimony on September 21, which just happened to be the first day of Rosh Hashanah—the first day of the year 5759. The beginning of the holiest ten days of the Jewish calendar. It was starting to feel like some sadistic preschooler was in charge of this whole thing, using his ferocious magic marker to draw the lines: Whitewater to Clinton to Lewinsky to Judaism. Was this anti-Semitism at its most insidious? Making our New Year a national smutfest? Why couldn't the House Judiciary Committee have waited one more day? September 22 would be a very nice day to humiliate the president, too.

Desperate for someone to gripe with, I called some of my friends, but they were too busy to waste time kvetching. So, two days before the holiday, I called my mother in New Jersey. My mother, a wickedly smart woman, is usually a reliable source of good old-fashioned Jewish liberal indignation. She grew up in western Pennsylvania, where she was forced to begin every schoolday with the Lord's Prayer—even though she attended a public school. She still has a George McGovern pin in her jewelry box, and one of my earliest memories is watching her watch Reagan's inauguration, hissing at the television. So I was expecting some reassuring right-wing-conspiracy, how-they-screw-the-Jews type dialogue. Instead I got a rather mild, "Well, I'm glad I'll be in shul so I don't have to watch."

"But Mom!" I sputtered. "Don't you see! It's like they're waiting for all the Jews to be in temple so they can talk behind their backs about what it's like to fuck one of them!"

"Watch your language," my mother said. "So will you be joining us for *erev* Rosh Hashanah services or what? You need your dad to pick you up at the bus station?"

"Mom!" I said, dismayed at her lack of dismay. "Don't you get it? Monica's a Jew. They're airing the testimony on a high holiday. This is totally *all about the Jews!*"

"Listen to yourself," my mother chuckled. "You sound like one of those people who boycotts the *Times* when they write a good review of an Arab movie. Listen, I'm going to roast a chicken, and I was thinking of making sweet potatoes, but if you could pick up two challahs on your way to the bus station that would be a help."

"But *Mom*." I made one last desperate attempt. "You're not *listening!*"

"Sorry, honey. I've got to go—I'm up to my elbows in chicken livers." With that, she hung up. And, because I had no choice, so did I, letting the phone fall from my hand in bewilderment. Two challahs? That was all she had to say? Of course it *was* Rosh Hashanah. Maybe my mind should be on challah, instead of Monica.

It occurred to me then that if I couldn't turn to my mother, nor any of my Jewish girlfriends for indignation, maybe it was because, in the end, they all had better things to do. The Lewinsky scandal disturbed them, but they did not find it a moment of profound self-definition. Really, who had time for self-definition in the days before Rosh Hashanah? The leaves were changing, the air was cooling, there was poultry to roast and apples to cut up and serve with honey. Kids needed to be picked up from airports and bus stations, and grandparents, aunts, uncles, and cousins were preparing to take their places at the holiday table. This was what mattered. This was what was real.

On the day before Rosh Hashanah, most Jewish women I know go to work, hurry home, order someone to set the table, heat up the soup, pour glasses of Manischewitz, pass bowls of chopped liver and candied nuts, serve and eat a big dinner, put on their good suits, go to synagogue for erev Rosh Hashanah services, and pray. When they get home, they wipe the crumbs off the table, and maybe stay up late, having tea and apple cake with their families. They do not watch television or read the newspaper. They do not contemplate how Monica's blow job defines perceptions of their sexual identity. Their minds are on bigger things.

Two days after talking to my mother I sat by her side at Rosh Hash-anah services. I listened to the rabbi begin his prayers. I listened to the rabbi's son blow the shofar. I knew that it was time to stop my Monica-mania and my paranoia; it was a new year now. After services, I did not read the paper, nor did I turn on the television. Instead, I took a walk to the local creek. Throwing my bread down the river, I let myself off the hook.

Spot the Jew

*

Baz Dreisinger

Is it silly to think that Jews look like, well, *Jews?*

I'm actively snubbing this question as my sister Sarah and I go head-to-head on a round of our favorite mall sport: "Spot the Jew."

"There's one," I say, pointing at a brown-haired, bumpy-nosed, bottle-shaped Gap shopper who's sashaying toward the cash register. She wears an ankle-length denim skirt of the sort that makes Modern Orthodox Yeshivas rejoice.

"Way too easy," Sarah protests. "You get half a point. That's it." She surveys the food court. Having recently graduated from Yeshiva high school, she's better at "Spot the Jew" than I am. "Those two—Jews, for sure. Hair is totally blow-dried." Sarah nods toward a pair of girls chatting volubly while inhaling colossal cups of fat-free frozen yogurt.

"Okay, okay," I reluctantly admit. In our heated rounds of "Spot the Jew" lie paradoxical expressions of Jewish pride: The winner achieves both anthropological distance from Jewishness and—because she knows Jews well enough to pick them out in a crowded mall—complete mastery of it. "Frozen yogurt was the real giveaway. You only get two points."

My sister and I devised unofficial rules and regulations for "Spot the Jew," which we'd consider copyrighting if Lenny Bruce hadn't thought of it first. A sampling: Jewish=frizz; Goyish=the glossy stuff of Pantene commercials. Jewish=long skirt with sneakers; Goyish=Juicy sweat suit. Jewish=breast reduction; Goyish=breast implants. Jewish=bumpy nose;

Goyish=button nose. Jewish=five-foot-seven for men; Goyish=five-foot-seven for women.

Sarah goes out on a limb. "Right there—the blonde." She signals toward a willowy, forty-something woman with brown roots, a radioactive-looking tan, and a cell phone pressed to her ear. Low-rider jeans and a velour hoodie complete the look.

"Hell, no," I declare. "Pure suburban mom."

Sarah is adamant. "You are so wrong," she insists. "Nose job. Bad bleach job. She's trying a little *too* hard to pass." We move within earshot of our subject, and Sarah gives me her favorite "told you so" smirk. Said subject is prattling away on her cell—in Hebrew.

"Israeli!" I sigh. "They throw me off every time."

I HATE to admit it, but sometimes even my own finely honed Jewdar fails me. Especially when it comes to children, since Jewish features often lie dormant during childhood years. Many a straight head of Jewish hair achieves its curly maturation upon adolescence; cute button noses perform Pinocchio routines as the Bar or Bat Mitzvah approaches. Much to the dismay of many an *Ema* and *Abba*, who've spent years marveling at the golden-haired entity that somehow managed to defy Semitic bloodlines, pigtailed Jewish blondes often become brown-haired adults.

I can personally attest to that fact, since once upon a time I was the blonde sheep of the family. A family comprised, to cite Diane Keaton in *Annie Hall*, of what Grammy Hall would call "real Jews": Yiddish-speaking grandparents, two in-house therapists, all of us native New Yorkers bred on farfel and Freud. Every member of my brown- and black-haired clan wondered who the heck I thought I was, emerging from the womb sporting yellow curls. The joke was on me. My father dubbed me "Megan" and told me, day after school day, that I was wearing the wrong uniform and standing at the wrong bus stop: The Irish-Catholic schoolgirls were on the *other* side of the street, next to the lily-white statue of Mother Mary.

Nowadays, I look more like someone bearing the name Dreisinger.

"Megan" and her blonde ringlets took leave in the fifth grade, when I went brown. In high school, my cup size grazed the C mark. And in college, a boyfriend casually asked if I ever felt self-conscious about my nose.

"What nose?" I wondered, before making a mad dash to the nearest mirror. Sure enough, there it was. Small, but plain as the frizz on a humid day: my very own Jewish protuberance. Better late than never, I thought. Then I thought again, and flushed with shame: It had probably been sitting on my face, like a bump on a kosher pickle, for years. How had it eluded all those hours of adolescent self-scrutiny?

The essence of my Jewish identity now lies in my breasts. They were handed down to me from my maternal grandmother, a petite Russian woman who hauled her weight in cleavage. My own load is not quite such a load—molehills beside, say, Pamela Anderson's mountains—but it is distinctly disproportionate to the rest of my small frame. It's also inconvenient. Whenever I try to package my, well, *package* in a cute little halter top, the stubborn twins refuse to be suppressed.

This might be a metaphor for the ineluctable, insuppressible nature of my Jewishness. It's not. I'm being literal: Out-of-proportion breasts are one of those physical features that seem to mark me as a Jew. And before you, flat-chested Jewesses everywhere, start formulating your protests, contemplate something on your body that's a little too, say, globular. Something that maybe sticks out a bit too much, or is too dark, hairy, bulbous, or bulging—something you long ago pinpointed as that which marks you as a Jew (or, for those of you who'd go undetected in "Spot the Jew," some highly inconvenient feature you're vastly relieved you *don't* have).

Then close your eyes and imagine yourself without it. I've done this countless times, mentally conjuring up a shiksa-fied version of me: She never has to hem her jeans, spell her name, or consult the weather report before deciding whether to wash her hair. There are times when I love the imaginary shiksa me, and there are times when I convince myself that she's sorely lacking in that which we like to call "flava." There are times when I think that last thought is just a defense mechanism—a reaction against the oh-so-white beauty standards that we're all sick and tired of hearing about—and there are times when I think *that* last thought is played-out and absurd: Most guys I know would take Beyoncé over Kate Moss any day.

And there are still other times when I'm convinced that there's not such a great gap between shiksa-looking me and Jewish-looking me. Because maybe "looking Jewish" is all relative. It's true that beside my best friend Beth, who's leggy, blonde, and oh-so-shiksa, I might as well have "Jewess" written all over me. But next to, say, my black-haired, olive-skinned friend Esther, who's more African-American than most African-Americans (her mother was born in the Sudan), you might as well call me "Beth"—which, incidentally, is the name I resort to when "Baz" elicits quizzical stares (and "Bathsheba," the English version of my given name, elicits utter bewilderment).

Fact is, when it comes to looking like a member of any particular group, race, or religion, context is everything. Over the years I've developed such a fixation on this fact, on the precise way in which context is everything, that I decided to do a doctorate on it. In American and African-American literature, more precisely, but my specialty became a subject known as "racial passing": Scenarios in which people who belong to one racial group pass themselves off as belonging to another. Most of the time, "passing" refers to light-skinned African Americans passing for white, usually in order to elude prejudice. Nowadays, though, the term is broader than that. There are Jews who pass for Gentile, gays who pass for straight, men who pass for women.

I wrote a dissertation about white people who, from the nineteenth century to the present, passed as black. Yep, that's passing *as black*, usually aided only by context: They married a black person, or they identified with, say, jazz or hip-hop or black power—cultures that were, once upon a time, deemed "un-white."

There were as many Jews in my dissertation as there are in a Brooklyn bagel shop. I ended up with a historical posse of real-life Jews who in one way or another passed out of Jewishness, usually into some form of non-whiteness. There's Mezz Mezzrow: cornet player, disciple of Louis Armstrong, and son of Russian-born Jews. During the '20s, he decided that years of devotion to jazz and jive had physically turned him black. There's Ruth McBride Jordan—nee Ruchel Dwajra Zylska—the larger-than-life heroine of James McBride's stunning memoir *The Color of Water*, a woman who founded a Baptist church and raised a virtual tribe of black children. There's Janet Jagan, onetime president of Guyana: She was Janet Rosenberg before she married a Guyanese man, emigrated to Guyana and, in 1997, became the only Jew to head a South American country.

I know what you're thinking. How did, say, Mezzrow pull it off? Didn't he *look Jewish?* Well, photos indicate that his nose was no button. But the fact of the matter is, it didn't really matter *what* he looked like, because context has a way of trumping all else. After earning my PhD, I spent a year in the African-American Studies department at UCLA, where I gave occasional lectures on race-related issues. By that time I'd also started covering, for publications like *Vibe*, the *New York Times*, and the *Los Angeles Times*, the "urban culture" beat—today's favored euphemism for things young and nonwhite. At the reception following one of my lectures about passing, an African-American audience member approached me, narrowed his eyes, and whispered "are *you* black?"

Never mind that the California sun had brought out the latent blonde in me. I could've said "yes," and—considering my context and my areas of interest—this man probably would've shrugged and moved on. What you "look like" can be as much (and sometimes more) a product of whom or what you associate with as it is a product of your physical features. Part of me, though, wondered how anyone could look at me and not see Jewish. Or maybe he wanted to not see it. Maybe this man did what I do in the mall—what most of us, tribal-minded as we are, tend to do: Read others as being just like ourselves.

Sometimes I'm flattered when I'm not read as Jewish—but not because I'm lusting after a pass into the country club. I'm a dancehall reggae fanatic, so I buy Jamaican newspapers fairly regularly. On one occasion, the cashier took a look at my paper, another look at me, and then asked what part of uptown Kingston I come from. Jamaica's uptown Kingston neighborhood is home to plenty of Jamaicans whose skin tone is as light as, maybe lighter than, that of any Jew. This cashier had derived my race from my reading material. And I played along, mainly because I get a kick out of racial scenarios like these. Scenarios in which seeing is performed by the mind, not the eye. Scenarios in which the body says one thing and means another.

But here's the rub. If the line between Jew and, say, Jamaican—or between black and white, for that matter, or between Middle Eastern and Spanish—is more difficult to draw than we tend to think it is, if so-called racial features can be so varied and so contingent on context, does that invalidate the very notion of "looking Jewish"? After all, Queen Esther hid her Jewishness with ease; not even bad-hair weather gave her away (Persian humidity must have been a killer). The Jewish protagonist of the film *Europa, Europa* avoids the Holocaust by passing as a member of the Hitler youth; evidently the only physical feature capable of "outing" him was a certain man-made modification to an organ that every adolescent boy has trouble keeping in his pants. Most Jews who pass for Gentile don't have physical features that stand in their way.

So who looks Jewish, and what is "looking Jewish"? The fact that someone can take me for Jamaican explains why the Internet is home to many an exercise in "Jewdar." On one Web site, even the Jewishness of Christina Applegate is a subject of debate: The name screams shiksa just a little too loudly, and the hair is almost over-the-top in its platinum blondeness. It's as if the lady—Jewish indeed, concluded most sites—doth protest too much.

Surfing from one Web game of "Spot the Jew" to another, though, I landed smack in the middle of white supremacy territory (which occupies a hefty amount of online real estate). Sadly, that leap is natural. There's a fine line between innocent Jew "outings" and bigoted free-for-alls populated by hawk-nosed, hunched-over Shylock types: grotesque caricatures of those who "look Jewish." In the hands of someone who's not a member of the tribe, my innocent game of "Spot the Jew"—much like the "n" word for African Americans—fast becomes a weapon.

Thanks to Sander Gilman, I learned juicy details about the genesis of this weapon. Gilman is a professor whose books, particularly *The Jew's Body*, explore ways in which Jewish bodies and Jewish looks have been imagined or stereotyped over centuries. He explains, for instance, that there were once distinct pseudoscientific ideas about the markedly different sound of the "Jewish voice" (it came inherently cloaked in what Philip Roth, referencing Charles Dickens, called a "thick, Faginy, Yiddish accent") or the so-called "Jewish foot": Like the cloven-footed devil, with whom they were supposedly in cahoots, Jews were said to have flat, diseased, or otherwise mangled feet that, Gilman writes, rendered them "congenially unable and, therefore, unworthy of being completely integrated into the social fabric of the modern state." In 1891, Francis Galton, father of the eugenics movement, which "studied" the pseudoscience of race, photographed Jewish boys and used multiple exposures in order to concoct an image of the Jew's "essence." A nineteenth-century Jewish doctor insisted that the features of the Jewish face reveal a "melancholy, pained expression," which he dubbed "the 'nebbich' face" (think of it as the look your father gave you when you told him you'd be skipping the seder this year).

Of course, Gilman gives us noses galore. In 1852, the eminent paper "Notes on Noses," its author not a Jew, defined the "Jewish, or Hawk Nose" as "very convex, and preserves its convexity like a bow." Said nose, the paper continued, "indicates considerable shrewdness in worldly matters; a deep insight into character; and facility of turning that insight to profitable account." (And you thought a bump was just a bump!)

Jews quickly internalized the notion that there was such a thing as a Jewish nose. Then they capitalized on it. Modern cosmetic rhinoplasty—better known as the nose job—was invented by a German Jew named Jacques Joseph. Born Jakob Josef, he performed his first successful surgery in fin-de-siècle Berlin and earned a nickname he never managed to shake: Nosef. According to accounts of this surgery—consider it "Extreme Makeover: Nineteenth-Century Edition"—after Nosef had his way with his client's nose, "the depressed attitude of the patient subsided completely."

More than a century later, I laid eyes on a nose job that produced identical results. After a week's absence, Cara, a shy girl at my private Jewish high school, sashayed smugly toward her locker. Her smile was wider than the hallway; her nose, thinner than a rail. I remember being slightly perplexed: Was "fixing" a face that quick and easy?

I recoiled, and insisted to anyone who'd listen that plastic surgery was for the weak and insecure. Looking back now, I see that my high-and-mighty attitude was simply a way of dealing with the beauty standards of Jewish high school—which, I'm told, are as straightforward today as they were back in the '90s. In my high school, the more "un-Jewish" you looked, the more beautiful you were. White was right; Jew was P-U. That meant curly hair was a no; kinky hair, a no-no; and blow-dryers, an absolute necessity. Short or shapely was unflattering; flat and long, stunning. Any girl who had miraculously managed to be blonde—even dirty blonde, even boosted-by-a-bottle blonde—had the whole school at her pseudo-shiksa feet.

Plenty of shiksa-happy Jewish men—the ones who have little interest in me, the ones my uber-shiksa friend Beth practically collects—still employ those beauty standards. I have a theory that it's an Oedipal thing: Countless Jewish men have obsessive love-hate relationships with their mothers, so women whose features suggest Jewishness—and thus Jewish motherness—are too great a strain on the psyche. My Jamaican friend, on the other hand, visits New York and implores me to bring him to the very place that these Jewish men avidly, neurotically avoid—"curly-haired heaven," Jewess goddess territory on Manhattan's Upper West Side.

Jewish men aren't the only ones with an aversion to so-called Jewish looks. My first Jewish boyfriends were as Norman Rockwell as Jewish could get. There was a blonde, dimpled, Polo shirt–wearing cutie from Forest Hills, Queens. And then a blue-eyed stunner, who to this day easily gets away with passing as a *shaygetz*, explaining to sweet young things from Texas—for whom the phrase "Jewish boyfriend" would make daddy reach for the shotgun—that his clunky last name is *European*.

My tastes, though, have changed. As a preteen, I snubbed my nose at curly haired—and thus remotely Jewish-looking—Kirk Cameron. I sent heart-filled fan letters to Ricky Schroeder instead. Nowadays if I had to date an actor, it'd be a toss-up between Adrian Brody, whose colossal nose has miraculously become the stuff of high fashion, and Ben Stiller, who's short, wry, and nebbishy in just the sort of way I find sexy. I look in the mirror differently, too. The very things I secretly wanted to change about

myself in high school—my curls, my breast size, my (lack of) height—
are the features I've come to not just tolerate, but flaunt.

I'm talking about my *Jewish* features, right? Actually, no—more like
features I imagine to be Jewish. Because in the end I have to acknowledge that though I spot them everywhere, "Jewish looks" are nothing but
a long-term illusion. Gilman ultimately argues that pseudoscience about
Jewish bodies fast became prescriptive instead of descriptive. Jews began
buying into bogus claims about our looks—our noses, voices, and feet—
and then we began loathing them. By the late nineteenth century we
didn't need eugenics-minded doctors. Nosefs began cropping up everywhere in order to correct what was essentially an invented reality.

Don't get me wrong—it's a pretty persuasive invented reality (and, for
my little sister and me, an entertaining one). I can't help but look at
Shoshana Lonstein—ex-gal pal of Jerry Seinfeld and creative director of
a clothing line for top-heavy women—and think "Jewish breasts"; I can't
stop ogling Adrian Brody's "Jewish nose." But the point is that I've given
up any and all logical claims about Brody's nose and Lonstein's breasts as
being inherently Jewish, because I realize that such claims are based on
pseudoscientific, haplessly outdated notions about so-called races and
types.

And the real triumph is this: I'm *ogling* Brody's nose—not sending it,
pronto, to Nosef's knife. That ogling is my own little rebellion against
the forces of pseudoscience that have, without my consent, colonized my
brain. If I'm going to disregard logic and see Jewish looks everywhere, I
might as well start liking what I see. At some point in my post-Yeshiva
existence, I began mentally transforming those longtime marks of shame
and derision into badges of pride.

I decided I was something I'd once considered oxymoronic: a Jewish,
Jewish-*looking* babe. I stood as tall as five foot two and a half permits,
stuck out my Russian *bubbe*'s breasts, held my frizzy-haired head high, stuck
my "Jewish" nose in the air for all to see, and shouted forth to the world,
with every bit of self-help-speak I could muster: "I look like a Jew and I
like it, too!" Never mind the biological fact and fiction of the matter.
People heard me, loud and clear. They couldn't help but spot the Jew.

Girl Meets Goy

*

FRANCESCA SEGRÈ

I'VE laid down the law. I will only date Jewish men. I've laid down the law many, many times. I tell myself that if I date a Jewish man, we'll share backgrounds, traditions, and beliefs, and, if we get married, we'll do our duty—we'll procreate. Giving birth to baby Ezra and baby Shulamit will help ensure the continuation of Judaism. To marry another Jew is fundamental to being a good Jew. So then why is it so hard?

One soft look from almond-shaped eyes, or a tender whisper in a Cuban accent, and *bam!* I'm an outlaw. At least I'm not the only offender. Half of American Jews intermarry. Which, I know, is exactly why it's critical to couple with another Jew. So I keep looking.

Looking is easy. Finding is tricky.

In fact, finding another Jew has been complicated for me from the get-go. I was born and raised in Austin, Texas. Not exactly the epicenter of Judaism. My brother and I made up half of the Jewish population in our high school. When it came to dating, my choices were not Mordechai, Moshe, or David. My choices were Trey, Travis, or Clint. Their emblem of individuality was which truck they drove: Blazer or Bronco. Inclusiveness to them meant inviting all the neighborhood boys (geeks too) to go "off-roadin'" in the mud together. They dipped and spit. They called my mom "Ma'am." She winced.

My parents accepted that I'd date Southerners. But they didn't want me to become one of them with "ma'am" and "y'all" speech or Bible Belt beliefs. There would be no Southern twang coming out of their daughter's mouth, and I would know that Christmas and Easter were not my holidays. In the car, on the way to school, my father made me repeat "how now brown cow." I couldn't leave the car until my "hayow nayows" were "how nows." While fending off the Southern speech, my parents gently tried to shape my Jewish identity. They sent me to Hebrew school, but didn't suggest I have a bat mitzvah, and I didn't. They sent me to Jewish day camp, but also sent me to a horseback-riding camp. At home, we observed the Jewish holidays if and when it was convenient.

They also taught us, loud and clear, that other ethnicities were to be respected and embraced. For my fifth birthday, my mom gave me Sasha. Sasha was a foot-high doll with milky brown skin, dark hair, and light eyes. Sasha was Indian. Like from India. I was happy with Sasha and her dark, soft looks. I was happy until I went to my friend Christie's house and saw Barbie.

"I want Barbie!" I insisted the minute my mom came to pick me up. "Barbie!"

I persisted. I whined. I pestered. "Barbie!!"

Eventually, I wore my mom down and she gave me a set of six dolls. Three females, three males. They resembled Barbie in height and style. But none of these dolls had blonde hair. One male–female couple had black skin. Another couple, brown skin. The third couple, white skin. I didn't know what to make of them. My older brother did. The second my mom left the room, he twisted the heads and limbs off the dolls and mixed and matched the parts. I shrieked in horror.

"Make the colors match!" I cried. My brother put a male head on a female doll. One of the transplant victims stared at me through her plastic eyes. I screamed. My mom came running back.

She surveyed the bodies strewn across my bedroom floor. A black torso with white limbs. A white torso with multicolored limbs. She laughed and smiled, relieved.

Now that I'm thirty-one, and have had male limbs of most every color wrapped around me at one point or another, is she still laughing? Maybe she's rethinking those "embrace diversity" messages she preached. She never said outright that I should marry another Jew, it was just understood. My mom led by example. She married my father, another Jew. In fact, only one person in my family ever married outside the faith. But with all these mixed messages about ethnicity and identity, what did she expect? I grew up to identify as the "other" and sought comfort in other "others."

In high school, I found "others." I kissed a black boy. I line danced with cowboys. I was "going" with José for two weeks. My parents supported my multicultural exposure, but also made sure I was *always* chaperoned.

Over dinner, my mom used to grow wide-eyed and animated talking about the ethnically mixed college students she taught in her cross-cultural communications class. With sparkling eyes, she would describe the Haitian-Jewish student or the Chinese-Swede. My brother and I knew a student achieved first-rate exotic status when my father would look up from his food, cock his head, bulge out his eyes and howl "ah-who?"

"Ah-who?" was weird and discordant. The emphasis was on the "who?" In a sound, it said "freak show" with the utmost admiration. The sound was reserved for the ethnically striking person who won the genetic lottery. When she walks by, like a magnet, you whip your neck around for a better look. Where *are* her parents from?

I grew to admire the exalted "ah-who" types of the world, and if you consider an Italian Jew in Texas to be "ah-who," I was one of them too. I watched mixed couples plunge deeper into the melting pot, but preferred to respect it from the brim. I dreamt of growing up to find an*other* more like me. He'd be Jewish from Western Europe or Israel. And of course, handsome, dashing, brilliant, and funny.

Upon high school graduation, I subconsciously launched a Jewish Man Mission. I chose a college where the majority of the students were Jewish. Brandeis University in Waltham, Massachusetts. It isn't a religious place, but it was founded by the Jewish community, and that is evident all over campus: the Middle Eastern study programs, the kosher food in the cafeteria. I majored in sociology (though anthropology would have better prepared me for my multicultural dating future). Sure enough, I had a Russian-Jewish boyfriend all four years. I was on the right track, but it didn't stick. At times, he seemed more committed to the secrecy and exclusivity of his fraternity than he was to me. Yes, we were both Jewish, but, it turned out, that wasn't enough.

Maybe I would have broken up with him sooner, if he hadn't been Jewish.

A few years after college, I got my most profound exposure to Jewish theology. I was living in Connecticut and dating Daniel, an observant Jew. He romanticized religion. He talked to me about *Shalom Bayit*, the Jewish concept of a peaceful home. He went to Manhattan on Monday nights to learn at the Yeshiva. I celebrated Jewish holidays with him and his family—even ones I'd only heard hinted at vaguely before, like *Shmini Atzeret.*

When we moved in together (at my naive insistence), I found that not only was he a conservative, observant Jew, but he had traditional designs for me. He wanted me to stay home at our Brooklyn apartment and make Shabbat dinner every Friday night. He wanted me to go to synagogue on Saturday mornings. His friends were all Jewish.

"Congratulations," I said to Daniel's brother when he announced that he was engaged to a Christian woman. Daniel said sourly, "best of luck." For Daniel, marrying a shiksa was nothing short of apostasy. "Where is his commitment to Judaism? Doesn't he care if our people survive?" Daniel shook his head disapprovingly at his brother's choice.

I didn't want to disappoint Daniel, so I made a constant show of embracing my Jewish culture. His favorite mitzvah was sex on Shabbat. I was happy to oblige. *Tzedakah?* Charity is good. I even cooked a kosher chicken a few times. But I was on edge, constantly expecting him to encourage me to go learn at a yeshiva, so I could become a better Jew. But the more he shoved Judaism down my throat, the more I felt suffocated by it. I resented his rigid and sometimes blind adherence to Jewish law. I mean, come on. No marshmallows in the house, unless they're kosher marshmallows? Eventually I realized he was as stubborn with everything else as he was with religion. I gave up. I moved out.

Perhaps I would have stayed longer, if he hadn't been so Jewish.

After the breakup, and in my mid-twenties, I deliberately moved to Manhattan's Upper West Side. The odds of literally running into a Jewish mate were higher between Central Park West and Riverside Drive than almost any place in the world. It seemed the wandering tribe had collectively pitched tent here. I could greet someone with "Shalom" and no one would bat an eye. The question was not, "is there a kosher restaurant?" but, "which kosher restaurant?" On the UWS, I was not part of the minority. I was back at Brandeis. It was familiar. Too familiar.

"Absolutely," I said when a friend invited me to her thirtieth birthday party in the South of France. I needed something new, something different. And at her party, in a centuries-old villa, I met Different. His name was Khalid. He was from Dubai. Khalid was a sophisticated, globe-trotting young businessman. He regaled me with stories of the pranks they used to play at Harvard Business School. He explained how global economic forces meant his family construction business in the United Arab Emirates was booming. He made me laugh till my stomach hurt. Looking at his dark eyes, I saw his burning ambition. I saw the Semitic roots we shared. We connected immediately. I dreamt of falling in love with him. Rebelling against convention, we would embark on a worldwide crusade to promote Arab-Jewish peace, understanding, and romance. We'd show "them." Being with him, I would not compromise my Jewish identity, I'd enhance it, distinguish myself in relation to him. We would win a Nobel Peace Prize. Arabs and Jews would dance a hora at our wedding.

Reality? I was not ready to move to the heart of the Arab world. I wasn't willing to be a spokesperson for world peace through interfaith relationships. Heck, I could barely read Hebrew. Learn Arabic? Please.

Maybe we'd be married by now, had he been Jewish.

Back in New York, I resumed my Jewish Man Mission with new intensity. My friends and I code-named it JMM. I set out one night on my JMM with laser focus. And I met Manuel from Cuba. At the ultramodern bar, I got sucked into his aura of Latin fun and lightheartedness. Over the throbbing music I found his Cuban accent endearing. I was a sucker for his smooth, coffee-colored skin and strong forearms. And he could dance. I ignored the gold cross hanging on a chain around his neck, except to think that if he's Catholic, we'd probably have guilt in common.

There was no way Manuel could be a long-term relationship, but he'd be a pleasant diversion from my "Jew-Man-Mish." I looked into the bottom of my mojito as he defended elements of communism. What if we did get serious? I envisioned walking on the beach with him on his native island. Our bilingual children chattering away in Spanish and English. Would he want to name them Chris and Maria-Theresa? This was not what I had in mind, but I was tempted. Our family could be, in the words of my father, "ah-who?"

Then one night, after I'd been seeing him for a month, my friend Kathleen asked, "So, are things getting serious?"

"I don't know," I dismissed the question. "Not yet. Why?"

Kathleen pointed to the area below the belt. "You know, you should be prepared. He's probably not snipped." She scissored her second and third fingers together in the air, smiling devilishly.

If he wasn't, I wouldn't, and I didn't want to find out. It was just too unkosher.

Perhaps the relationship would have gone on, had he been Jewish.

Soon after, I met Alistair at brunch. Alistair was an incredibly charming Brit. We hit it off right away. But I knew he was not my type. He wore a thick gold ring with his family crest on it. He had pale skin and blonde hair. He had had tea with the Bishop of London, more than once. I was the first person he'd ever met who went on vacations to Israel. When I declined his invitation for dinner that night, he pressed me for an explanation. I was honest. I told him I wanted to be with a member of the tribe.

"Well, that's rather conventional, isn't it?" he said.

Ouch. How could I prove I wasn't close-minded when my actions showed otherwise? Historically speaking, weren't the Jews the ones always fighting for inclusion in societies like his? In the name of the continuity of my people, I resisted his advances.

But Alistair was irresistibly persistent. Days later, I gave in to his invitation for a picnic at the beach. He served me strawberries and cream and champagne, and I began to think about our future. Would we marry on his family estate in Gloucestershire? Would I go to his annual family hunting event decked out in tweed? I could just see myself in the family portrait, the dark one amid a sea of blonde, pale Brits. I could be the token Jew who could teach the upper crust about the mysteries of Judaism. I would unseat centuries of thinly veiled anti-Semitism with my kindness, charm, and good aim at pheasants. Wouldn't it be a mitzvah for me to spread the good word about the wandering tribe among British aristocracy? As he carried on about his grandfather's role in WWII, I wondered: is Alistair circumcised? Would he allow our sons to be circumcised? The fact that I wondered at all gave me pause. Hadn't I been here before? Hadn't I already learned this lesson? It may just be the tip—but it's likely the tip of the proverbial iceberg.

As it turns out, the question of whether he had a snipped tip became irrelevant. One night, he asked me earnestly, "What's the name of your church?"

I could overlook an unsnipped tip, but this clueless? He had never heard the words synagogue or temple? I couldn't handle it.

Enough of the anthropology experiments. I was done playing special attaché to United Nations dating. I needed to be with a Jewish man. How hard could it be? It'd be like shopping for the perfect pair of black heels. If you know what you're looking for and you look hard enough, eventually you'll find the shoe that fits. Or the Jew that fits. I just needed to be committed to the cause.

I took extreme measures. I went to a Jewish singles party. Surely, even I could not accidentally meet another goy there. In the dark Soho nightclub, the DJ was spinning music that reminded me of Madonna's techno phase. Wasn't she leading Hollywood's latest religious trend—Kabbalah? Even she wanted to be Jewish. Madonna went so far as to give herself a second name, Esther. Madonna Esther. (And I think *I've* got an identity crisis?) I felt better. I was optimistic. I smiled. I met many good Jewish men that night. They were nice. They looked like guys from Brandeis. They looked like they might be the shoe that fit. But none stood out. None sparkled. None clicked.

Surely this was my fault. I needed to try harder. I wouldn't give up. It was too important. I spent the next few months in a blur of set-up dates and synagogue services. I gave it everything I had: laughing, flirting, wearing an artsy Star of David necklace. I was tempted to try JDate, but my friends' horror stories about the men they met online scared me off. Anyway, given my track record, www.anythingbutjewish.com would have been more fruitful for me. Within a few months, I grew to dread the whole process. I resented being on a full-time JMM. I didn't want to meet another David from Jersey. There were plenty of other more interesting activities I preferred. Where was the matchmaker when you really needed her? Couldn't *Adonai* see I was trying and give me a break?

Then, one afternoon, as I tried to squish into a packed subway downtown, a tall man inside the car with big brown eyes, full lips, and a wide warm smile pushed the crowd back half a step to make room for me. The doors slid shut, but the subway didn't move. The edge of my bag was stuck between the doors, holding up the train. Together, we pulled the bag into the car.

"Thank you," I said.

"My pleasure," he said in a deep voice and a foreign accent I couldn't place.

He looked like a member of the tribe, with manners. I was intrigued. I couldn't resist. I had to find out more. After all, I was on a mission, and he was a captive audience.

Turned out he was an Israeli diplomat.

"Your accent doesn't sound Israeli," I said.

"I was born and raised in Italy."

Oh boy.

The first few dates, Enrico proved undeniably charming, accomplished, and intelligent. I was overjoyed. My search had ended. He was "the one." But then he neglected to call—for weeks. When he did call it was on a Saturday, at midnight. Were these the manners they taught him in diplomats' school? A little research and leverage of my Jewish geography connections, and I quickly learned that Enrico was "the one" for two women I knew personally, and a dozen other Jewish women scattered across the globe.

Perhaps the relationship would have worked, had he not been the perfect Jewish man for so many women.

My JMM needed a break. Maybe if I stopped looking, I just might find him. I traveled to Japan. Certainly I wouldn't find my mate there. I wasn't attracted to Asian men. On the way back, I stopped in Los Angeles to visit a Brandeis friend, Shana Cohen. I stayed with her, her husband, Yoshitomo Yamagata, and their newborn daughter, Zelda Yamagata. It was a great break from dating.

One night, Shana's childhood friend, David, invited us all over for dinner. David Chan. He put chopsticks in my hand and served up the best pork pot stickers I'd ever had. "I just cook for fun," he said, flashing a tempting, mischievous smile. "I could teach you."

The next night, I was back at his house. He cooked up an unbelievably sensual shellfish dish. "Pork and shellfish, they're my favorite," he said. "I also make a mean bacon cheeseburger." No, he was not kosher, in any sense of the term. But who cared? He wasn't a contender. I wasn't dating. He was my escape from the JMM, and I enjoyed every second of it. I was at ease.

Over jasmine tea, I learned that his family was all Taiwanese, but he was born and raised in Los Angeles. "Really though, I'm just a kvelling yenta," he said. "Always trying to feed my friends." I looked at him in shock. Where did he get that vocabulary? This was going to be trickier than I thought.

"I have a lot of Jewish friends. Been to a pile of Jewish weddings and bar mitzvahs," he answered before I asked. He hummed *"Hava Nagilah"* as he grabbed real Chinese china from the cupboard. There he was before me, handsome, intelligent, funny. Feeding me.

"Food is my religion," he said, placing a homemade green tea millefeuille dessert in front of me. That was a sentiment any Jew could understand. One bite and suddenly I felt I knew the divine. I looked into his soft, dark, almond-shaped eyes and I saw a foreign face who understood me. What would we name our children? Shulamit Chan? Ezra Chan? How would David and I teach our children about their joint Taiwanese-Jewish identity? There was a name for Japanese-Jews, Jewpanese, but nothing had been invented for Taiwanese Jews. Tai-Jew? Nope, sounds too much like a martial art. Fine. So be it. And what if David decided food *and* Buddhism were his religions? We'd be a family of "Jew-Bus" or "Food-Jew-Bus." "Fujubus." So the kids would look Asian. But they'd be Jewish because I'm Jewish, and that's all the rabbis require: a Jewish mother. I'd be off the hook. I wouldn't betray my people.

Still, all these machinations were disorienting. How could I let myself fall for an Asian man? Our backgrounds were literally worlds apart. I would have more in common with an Arab. Where were my tribal loyalties? My Holocaust-surviving grandparents would've been mystified if they lived to see me marry an Asian man. Committing to him could disappoint my family. It might even disappoint me. But somehow, surprisingly, he really fit. Suddenly a sparkling silver slipper had appeared when I had been seeking black heels my entire life.

Committing to David would mean admitting JMM defeat. It wouldn't be ordinary or easy. And our kids might lose all connection with their strong Taiwanese and Jewish roots, opting instead to be melted Americans. But, then again, they'd know the whole world, East and West. They would know Judaism implicitly. They would be color-blind and color-conscious all at once. An interracial, interreligious family mosaic. Am I on to something, or just being *farchadat?*

In the end, we're all 99.9 percent alike, no? Only commitment to an extraterrestrial or a reptile would be real diversity. So why am I still so torn? Because. Because being Jewish is who I am. It's essential. It's both an obligation and a source of comfort. But maybe it's not everything.

Wearing silver slippers when black shoes were what I had in mind may be awkward at first. But they may lift me gently to a place more magical than I'd ever dreamed of. A whole new world to dance in. I could wear them to Ezra Chan's Bar Mitzvah. Or maybe, years from now, I'll discover that black pumps would have suited me better all along, that I should've worked harder on my JMM.

What to do? What to do? Try it on. Wear it. Does it fit? Aaah. Oooh. Ah-who?

You Sit in the Dark,
I'm Coming Out of the Closet

*

KERA BOLONIK

WHEN I was fifteen, camping out with a bunch of Jewish teenagers in the West Bank seemed far less dangerous than telling my mother that I might be a lesbian. It was 1986, a decade before the Ellens and the k.d. langs would walk out of their closets, and I was living in the conservative Midwestern suburb of River Forest, Illinois. There weren't a lot of Jews in my WASPy little town, and as far as I could tell, almost no Jewish gay people, except for our Cantor's hippie daughter, Tziporah (Obviously, that's a pseudonym. Who but the Ultra Orthodox, *kibbutzniks,* or a sinister writer would saddle a girl with such a name?). The fact of her lesbianism was a subject people whispered about, like cancer—God forbid it should happen to such a nice family—and seemed to earn both her and her supportive parents sympathy from the congregation.

My Mom, and her henchman, Dad, were suffocating me with their suspicions that I had committed some unidentifiable crime. They had no search warrant, but that didn't stop their fishing expeditions, as they snuck through my drawers and closet, imposed an open-door policy on my bedroom, and turned the kitchen into an interrogation room. I decided it would be worth every penny of my bat mitzvah gelt, which my parents strongly suggested I use for a trip to Israel, to flee with United Synagogue Youth and seek refuge in the holy land that very summer. It was genius, really. Mom and Dad thought I was finally yielding to their demands, while really I was busy wedging two continents between the three of us to give me the privacy I needed to work out my Sexual Identity Crisis. So what if I'd be sharing a room with four other girls in youth hostels? My prospective roommates wouldn't notice if I secretly liked this Rebecca or that Rachel—they'd be too distracted as they tried to hook up with some Levite stud named David, Adam, or Seth.

In Israel, I'd finally have the solitude I so desperately craved to sort out this Crisis of mine. I needed to figure out a few things, like: Am I a pervert, a little kinky, or were my increasing number of intense crushes on girls something else entirely? And since I had never traveled by myself, or abroad, or even emerged from my room for much of high school because I was either grounded or stewing in my own miserable juices planning the sound track for my most excellent funeral, it would be a good way to come out of my self-imposed exile.

But a week before my scheduled departure, Mom acted like she smelled a rat when she announced that my trip hinged on our having a little "talk." A sneak attack! Could she really keep me from going? There was no way I was going to risk my life both here at home and in the Middle East! I would keep my lips sealed.

I tried to put off Mom's chat for as long as possible, hoping she'd forget. She didn't. A few days later, she summoned me to a meeting in our mosquito-infested backyard. What could be so urgent? I'd have more clarity, be much more forthcoming, if we could wait until I returned from Israel. But my mistake was in acting evasive; once she sensed that I was holding out on her, she would be determined to shake me down. I panicked and went on the defense.

"My round-trip ticket was purchased with *my* bat mitzvah money. It was specifically was earmarked for this trip!" I said.

"You're not leaving until we clear up a few things," Mom countered. I sank into one of the vinyl chairs on the patio. "Don't forget who here is the parent, and who is the child. *I say* if you're going or not."

Her insistence felt so punitive. All I'd done was to keep to myself. I couldn't remember the last time I'd broken a curfew, or even come home with wine-cooler breath. At the worst, I may have been irritable, because my sleep had become erratic, which made me too listless for my usual screaming-and-clawing matches with my twelve-year-old sister, Shana. I'd been depressed all year, and I suspected the Crisis was the culprit. But I couldn't bear to tell Mom about it. I could barely admit it to myself. I withheld writing about it in my journal, because I didn't want to see those words staring back at me (not to mention the fact that I knew Mom read it). Still, I was pretty sure Mom wasn't onto my secret; she just knew that I had one, and that was enough to vex her.

I certainly hadn't provided her with an opportunity to notice the excruciating blushing fits I suffered in front of the girl I privately called "The Crewcut Beauty." A few weeks into the first semester, I began to notice this girl at school. She was hard to miss, with her vermilion-colored buzz cut and her porcelain-perfect skin. Every time we passed one another in the hallway, I was overcome with nausea, which didn't make sense because she didn't repulse me. On the contrary, I found this Crewcut Beauty absolutely breathtaking. So, why was someone so exquisite making me feel so sick? For months, I convinced myself that the nausea was brought on by awe. The Crewcut Beauty was a senior, and I was a sophomore, and it was a rationale that I could live with. Yeah, maybe I just wanted to be her. By the time Mom sat me down, I was beginning to fear that that wasn't all there was to my feelings.

"You are so damn morose all the time," Mom said. "What's the matter with you?" I shrugged my shoulders. "You have to tell me."

"I can't tell you if I don't know," I said, sneering at her. It was tempting to chalk up my moodiness to the general misfortune of being her daughter, which was partly true, but I decided to hold my tongue. We were gearing up for a long face-off, Mom and I. It was going to take her serious persistence before I so much as hinted at the fact that I was worried about my sexuality, or the fact that I'd been agonizing over The Crewcut Beauty "situation" all year long. If she were just an anomaly, I'd have brushed it off, run with the "awe" theory. Only, I knew that she wasn't. There had been another girl who gave me the "sick" feeling: Pavia Frugoli.

It began a couple of years earlier at Jennifer Steinberg's bat mitzvah. Pavia was that rare middle school classmate who was actually nice to everyone, including me. This was especially notable because I spent the sixth and seventh grades playing the role of the hideous misfit, completely outfitted with a huge bald spot in the middle of my scalp and wire orthodontic headgear, which I had to wear for twelve hours a day.

Mercifully, I began to transform into something resembling normal in time for Jennifer's bat mitzvah. That morning, in the sanctuary at the Oak Park Temple, I was seated in front of Pavia. I turned around to grab a prayer book, briefly nodding hello. Pavia quickly crossed her legs, pulled the short hem of her Gunny Sax dress as far over her knees as it could stretch, and looked down her long Sicilian nose at me, her deep-set, dark blue eyes glaring at me through her wispy, curling iron–fried bangs. I pretended to look at my prayer book, but my face was searing hot, and my eyes were welling up with tears. I wasn't sure what had happened. Was she admonishing me for saying hi in a house of worship? As Jennifer chanted her haftorah portion, I reviewed our exchange over and over in my head. It came to me: In that one brief glance, she must have been reproaching me for leering at her, even though I wasn't sure that I had. I became convinced that she recognized me for the freak that I secretly was.

There was no way I was going to take any chances, even if she *didn't* think I was weird. I had to stay away from her. Pavia's mere presence made me blushingly, shakily, nauseatingly nervous. Except for my infrequent flashes of bravado—when I would change course on my daily bike ride and pedal down her block, or dial her number in the evenings, hanging up before the first ring—I avoided all contact with her.

Nobody in my life would understand these mortifying encounters, so I kept them to myself, where they festered like untended wounds. That meant I alone had to figure out why I would become dumbfounded around Pavia and The Crewcut Beauty. Yet even broaching the subject within the confines of my own mind was as terrifying as grasping my mortality: Was I . . . could I be . . . attracted to these girls? The mere possibility plunged me into the depths of despair—I had to get a grip. If I could preempt these feelings by refusing to identify them, whatever they were, then I could stop these tendencies from evolving. Or so went my thinking.

There was nothing more disgraceful in high school during the 1980s than being a dyke (how handy that it should rhyme with that other epithet for me, favored by the nastier among the country club set). If I were to come out, wouldn't that reduce my entire identity to who I desired, and invite everyone to judge me? Wasn't that opening the door to rejection? Wouldn't admitting such a thing complicate my friendships with female classmates?

Besides, the only women I knew to be lesbians were spiky-haired, whistle-wielding gym teachers. Then there were those we assumed were lesbians: those clingy, needy girls who hugged and cried a lot, and stared too long in the locker room. And then there was Tziporah, the subject of whispering and pathetic sympathy. I did not want to be any of those people. (In college, I would learn the nuances and lexicon of lesbianism, with its full array of butches, femmes, tops, bottoms, lipstick lesbians, riot grrrls—but my adolescent mind was limited to only three equally horrifying possibilities.) I'd hate for The Crewcut Beauty and Pavia to think I had ulterior motives. And yet, I felt guilty for secretly desiring them even though I'd never have the guts, or the know-how, to do anything about it. I mean, who would ever feel comfortable in my company? I didn't even feel comfortable in my company.

"What do you want from me?" I asked my mother in the backyard. I started to cry.

"Anything," Mom said. "You have to shed some light onto this dark, morbid act of yours."

I scowled at her. "It's not an act!"

"Then what is it?"

I shrugged. She wasn't going to get it out of me, not now, not ever. It was better that she thought I was morose than a pervert.

"Let me put it another way: If you don't tell me what is making you so depressed, you're going to Riveredge, not Israel!"

Riveredge was a nearby mental hospital, serving up lobotomizing mood stabilizers and electroshock treatments. My first boyfriend, Henry—an early adolescent attempt at heterosexuality—was sent to Riveredge for a nervous breakdown he suffered when he got wait-listed by M.I.T. At Riveredge, the doctors loaded Henry up on lithium, but he was still raging mad. Within a few weeks of his release from the hospital, he'd call me late at night, demanding an apology because Jews killed

Christ. Sorry, I told him, for not finishing that hand job on our last date before you went into the hospital, but I wasn't around at the time of Christ, so I can't assume responsibility for that. We broke up soon thereafter.

Henry never told me anything about his sojourn at Riveredge, so everything I learned of padded rooms, straitjackets, and shock treatments was culled from Ken Kesey's *One Flew Over the Cuckoo's Nest*. Perhaps Nurse Ratched would be a welcome relief from Mom, but I wasn't willing to hedge my bets. Israel still seemed safer by comparison.

Mom's unwavering stare was boring a hole into my head, and the guilt of my secret, and a swarm of mosquitoes, were conspiring to eat me alive. I wanted to hold my ground and be locked in all-night eye combat with Mom until she broke down. But my skin was burning up, my head was throbbing, and I had to go to the bathroom, desperately. Maybe it wouldn't be so bad to throw Mom a bone. I could offer her a tiny morsel of information, something really vague, but salacious enough to satisfy her. Still, even the prospect of letting some tiny piece of information slip was terrifying. I'd been suppressing my desire for so long—what if I started to talk and everything just spilled from my mouth? How was I going to explain that I was possibly gay to her, when I'd never even said those words to myself?

"I'm waiting," said Mom.

"Give me a second." I took a breath, and then pulled up my legs onto the chair, hugging my knees to shield my face. "Okay, it's like, I think I might sort of have, like, I don't know, maybe some bisexual tendencies." I peeked at Mom through my knees, ducking for cover.

"That's it?"

"What do you mean, 'that's it?' That's major!"

"Not really," said Mom. "Everyone is confused at your age. You're just going through a phase."

What?! Where was her repulsion, her rage, her termination of our mother–daughter relationship? Wasn't I supposed to be scared, humiliated, outraged . . . possibly even a little relieved? Touché, Mom! She managed to belittle years of suicidal ideations by dismissing it all as a "phase." It made me indignant.

"Maybe I'm not saying it right," I said, releasing my knees, allowing my legs to drop to the ground. "It's maybe more than a tendency."

"Have you ever kissed a girl?"

"NO!!"

"Then how would you know?"

"I just know, *okay?!*" I said. "I have these visceral reactions when I'm around certain girls. I get sick to my stomach and all hot in the face."

"You're just confused," said Mom. "I don't think that makes you a lesbian."

"Boys don't make me feel sick to my stomach. Just girls." I couldn't believe I was telling her all of this. I had never articulated these words before. It felt like the verbal equivalent of projectile vomiting. "I just think, I mean, I know I am really a lesb—" I started to say, but the words crept back in my mouth. "Oh forget it!"

Mom looked at me sympathetically.

"You have years to figure it out," she said. "But I really don't think you are."

"How would you know?" I said. "You don't know what goes on in my mind. You don't know how sick I am." I sucked in my breath. "And I don't want you telling Dad. Or anyone!"

"I have to tell your father. But no, we're not going to tell anyone. No one else would understand."

"May I go to Israel?"

Mom considered me for a minute. "Yes. I think it would be good for you to go, actually."

"Am I dismissed now?"

She nodded her head.

As I rose to leave, Mom said, "Being a lesbian, that's a hard life. So much heartbreak." She shook her head. "So. Much. Heartbreak."

I wondered who she thought was destined for so much heartbreak—me or her?

I'M usually been pretty good at warding off Mom's guilt trips—I've read enough Philip Roth and Tillie Olsen to strategize my defense. But self-imposed guilt is another matter entirely: When I returned from Israel that August, I began the slow process of acknowledging (but not yet accepting the fact of) my desire for girls, because it was becoming increasingly clear to me that it wasn't going to go away. Who else was like me, I wondered? What did lesbians look like anyway, and how were we to find one another? In the mid-1980s, I had nothing to go on. Did we look different from other girls? Did I even look like a lesbian?

Some of these questions were unexpectedly answered when an old Hebrew School classmate took me to see The Smiths at the Aragon Ballroom. When we got to the venue, I trembled at the sight of the opening act: a butch woman with a flattop haircut, a flannel shirt, 501 Levi's, and work boots, absentmindedly strumming her acoustic guitar. She introduced herself to the audience as "Phranc, your typical, everyday, all-American Jewish lesbian folksinger."

Nu? Who knew there was such a thing as a typical, everyday, all-American Jewish lesbian? She was nothing like Tziporah. She carried herself with an almost masculine confidence. I liked it. I briefly considered modeling myself after this Phranc person, until she sang a ditty about her unabashed lust for a gym teacher. Ogling the fleece-fancying female wasn't for me. Now I was really in a crisis. Maybe I wasn't attracted to lesbians. Maybe I wasn't a lesbian. But I was attracted to femme-y, bookish, hipster girls—so, what did that make me?

Other than very, very confused, I mean.

I didn't even know until I went to college that lesbian yearning could be met with reciprocal affection and sex. So much of my anguish rested on my belief that I'd be doomed to a life of pining for someone I could never have. I was seventeen before I ever saw two people of the same sex hold hands, walk arm-in-arm, kiss. In high school, my only exposure to gay sex was through stories related to me by a classmate who tricked in public restrooms. I surmised then it was something disjointed and shameful, and always done surreptitiously. When our effeminate American Literature teacher died of AIDS-related meningitis, I worried being gay might also be fatal. But, I also knew I was not going through a phase. I chose a college far from home, came out on the first day of my freshman year, so that I could identify my true friends, and began a string of torturous relationships that satisfied my youthful desire for high drama. My mother made me promise not to tell anyone "back home"—which didn't mean I couldn't tell my *goyishe* friends from high school. It meant: Please Don't Tell Jews We Know. No one from temple, and absolutely no one in our family.

Mom thought that she was making a compromise, like the time she "let me" keep my nose pierced when I was nineteen, demanding only that I take it out before dinner. But she was sitting in the dark if she truly believed I was to straddle the threshold of the closet doorway, or one day give up Sapphic love entirely and settle down with some goatee-sporting, PC househusband.

Faced with the prospect of the double threat of one gay daughter and another who dated only non-Jewish men, my mother became desperate. She told my younger sister Shana and me that she and Dad put a contingency clause in their wills: Whoever married a Jewish man first would get everything. (Not surprisingly, it didn't work. Shana, now married to an Episcopalian man, has Grandma Sedge's silver candlesticks. I live with a lapsed Catholic woman, and have Grandma Chana's candelabra.)

She couldn't bring herself to tell anyone in her life that I was gay. For a few years, I indulged her wish by not telling people "back home." Mom believed Jews—God forbid it should ever happen, throw salt over your shoulder—have kids plagued by Tay-Sachs, not kids plagued by gayness. There must have been some mistake. Gayness was for the goyim.

"Maybe I'm just an anomaly, then," I said to her, "like the cantor's daughter." I was getting tired of her silence and felt enervated by my own dishonest efforts as I pandered to her wishes to be discreet, while Mom attempted to mask her own embarrassment as protective parenting.

"If you don't tell Phyllis, maybe I should," I said.

"Don't you *dare!* She's homophobic." Phyllis, Mom's best friend, was studying Gender Studies at the University of Chicago.

"Ruth, then."

"Her, too." Ruth, another friend, was a shrink.

"Aunt Aylin?"

"A virulent homophobe!" That was fair: Mom told me she voted for Reagan.

"Can I come out to Shana?"

"Absolutely not! She's only a kid. Plus, her classmates at school would make fun of her!"

Shana was a high school junior and had asked about the pink triangle pinned on my backpack. In deference to Mom's request, I told her I wore it in support of gay rights. She thought it was cool.

Four years after I came out, my Mom finally crept out of her closet when one of the four Dorises in her Yiddish club brought her effete son to their kaffe klatsch. He was in town from New York City. "David's an interior designer," Doris #1 announced as she introduced him to everyone.

At their next meeting, Mom asked Doris #1 if David was married.

"Yes," she said. "For five years now."

Doris #3 piped up, "to a lovely man named Barney." Mom looked at Doris #1. She was nodding her head, "It's true. Nice boy."

Doris #4 said, "My Rachel has a great partner, too. You know Leslie."

"Of course," said Mom. There was too much English being spoken at this Yiddish club for her taste.

Doris #2 took a bite of her strudel. "My Joseph doesn't get out enough," she said with her mouth full. "I want that he should find a nice Jewish doctor."

"My Kera isn't a doctor," Mom said. "But she's nice, and very career-minded."

"Oh sorry," said Doris #2. "I meant a male doctor."

Mom let out a sigh. "Well, truth be told, Kera wouldn't want to date your son, anyway. No offense."

"None taken," Doris #2 said before taking another bite.

"Um, does anyone have a daughter available?" Mom asked, growing more nervous when she realized her attempt at a joke was falling flat. "Okay, can someone please tell me when having a gay kid became, you know, a Jewish custom?"

All of the Dorises looked at one another and shrugged their shoulders.

Doris #1 said, "*Nu?* Who knew that it was? Until today, I thought only Doris and I had gay kids." She looked around the room. "Oh, there are four of us here, aren't there?"

Mom called me later that night to report. "Okay, I told people."

"Who is 'people' and what did you tell them?" I asked.

"The Yiddish club. I told them you're, um, you know, a lesbian."

"Why did you tell them of all people? You haven't even told your best friends or your sister! You're convinced they're homophobes! And you're telling these sweet old biddies?"

"They're not biddies," Mom said. "Besides, they all have gay kids. We were bonding."

"So, gayness isn't so *goyishe*, after all, is it?"

Mom let out a sigh of mock defeat into the phone receiver.

If my Mom hadn't tiptoed out of the closet, she would've been forced out a few months later. After she bonded with the Dorises, my name appeared on the cover of the *Wall Street Journal* in a feature on Gay and Lesbian Studies. Mom was incensed—she thought I'd embarrassed her again! But it didn't play out the way she expected.

Aunt Aylin said she'd already figured it out.

Phyllis and Ruth were offended that Mom never told them.

Shana was enraged for being the last to know.

And I no longer felt guilty.

True Confessions of a JDate Addict

*

Amy Klein

Hı! My screen name is AMY (profile no. XXXXXX). I am a 32-year-old female and I am from VENICE, California, UNITED STATES.

My hair is DARK BROWN, my eyes are HAZEL. I am 5'3" (160 cm) tall. My body style is FIRM AND TONED. I am PHYSICALLY ACTIVE. I NEVER SMOKE and I DRINK SOCIALLY. I am SINGLE (NEVER MARRIED) and I have NO CHILDREN.

I am CONSERVATIVE and I go to Synagogue SOMETIMES, and I keep kosher TO SOME DEGREE. I grew up in NEW YORK/ JERUSALEM. I am seeking a LONG-TERM RELATIONSHIP. I'd like to meet someone between the ages of 33 and 38.

I like DOGS.

More About Me:

I post the above information onto JDate.com, the largest Internet dating service for Jewish singles. It's been a year since I ended a two-year relationship I thought was "it," and I guess it's time to try to meet someone else. But where?

I've just moved to Los Angeles, and "deciding" you're ready to date and actually finding someone to date are two different stories. So I'm signing up on this dating site for Jews—because I'm so traditionally, culturally, psychologically, and emotionally Jewish that I never seem to fit with anyone else. Besides, I'm not even sure it would count in my parents' eyes if the guy weren't Jewish.

"Anything interesting lately?" my father, an Orthodox dentist from Brooklyn, asks during our weekly conversations before Shabbat. By "interesting," he means dating-wise, and by "anything," he means future husband material. This succinct line of questioning is a step up from the last lecture I received when I was in New York: I was imprisoned in his dental chair for a free cleaning and had cleaning trays in my mouth.

"You're having fun now, Amy, but as you get older, it's not so easy to find someone," he said as he adjusted the trays. "Especially for women. You get older, your body changes, your face gets wrinkled, and you just don't meet as many people," he said, and removed the trays. I spit, but I wanted to throw up.

I could win the Pulitzer Prize, discover a cure for cancer, fly to the moon, master telepathy, and scale Mount Everest and still my father would ask me, "Anything interesting?" Because for him, his community—and even for the larger non-Orthodox Jewish world in which I circulate—if you're not married, you're not much.

It feels like I've been fighting this way of thinking since I was sixteen. My camp friends actually went ahead and *married* their summer boyfriends, and now they each have two kids. Even as I marched down a million aisles dressed like a taffeta boysenberry, I continued to resist getting married. I've managed to create a vibrant life with terrific friends and a wonderful career, and hopefully, there will be a nice Jewish man in my future, one day.

But, as my father likes to remind me, "one day" might be sooner than I think. The guilt finally gets to me, so at the suggestion of my friend, who swore she's personally known five noncreepy Jewish couples who've met and married on JDate, I decide to throw my hat into the ring.

More About My Ideal Match:

According to the National Jewish Population Survey, there are more single Jewish men than women (thirty percent of the guys are single vs.

twenty-two percent of the women). But usually it doesn't feel that way. Until now.

I log on to my JDate account and displayed before me on my screen are dozens—no, hundreds—of single men. Single, Jewish men in Los Angeles. It's like going shopping. Blonde men, short men, brooding guys, and muscleheads. Who says that all Jews look alike? I go to the JDate home page, do a quick search ("30–35-year-old, L.A., single/divorced, Conservative/Reform/Traditional") and presto! 500 pictures pop up.

Over the next six months, I receive e-mails from more than 250 men, correspond with about sixty, and date about thirty of them. JDating is like a parallel universe, a bustling underground populated by people whose online lives are nearly as demanding as their daily jobs. It requires constant e-mailing, instant messaging, phone calls, meetings, follow-up e-mailing, more meetings, and finally, the messy business of purging failed dates from the system—and getting purged yourself. It quickly becomes an addiction. It's taking up all my time: I can't stop looking at the Web site. If dating is a numbers game, surely this will increase my odds.

I can immediately discount the obvious no-gos: the forty-five-year-old divorcé with three kids, the Orthodox *ba'al teshuva* ("I want a true partner who will raise my children in the service of God"), a man named "Goytoy" ("I like Jewish girls," Chris writes me back when I ask him why he's on this Web site), and a decent looking guy from Kazakhstan ("I don't do long distance," I write).

And then . . . there's Michael. I click on his profile, and as the basic information pops up, I wait for his picture to download. It's the moment of truth, like opening the door on a blind date. Whew! He seems attractive, but it's hard to tell from the thumbnail picture. A thirty-seven-year-old musician, Michael is kind of sitting back, his golden surfer hair boyishly curling up to his white collar.

Michael and I meet on a street corner near my house (you can never be too safe). He does have surfer good looks, but unfortunately, he also likes to surf the streets. He steers me toward a Dumpster, where an old exercise machine awaits pickup. He stops to stare, and then he bends over to pick it up.

"You need an elliptical machine?" I shout over the noise of him lifting it up.

"No, but do you know how much I can get for it on eBay?" he grunts as he dumps it in the back of his truck. When he's done, he's all dusty and I start sneezing because I'm allergic, but it's okay, because we're outside my house so we actually don't have to go out at all. I wish him good luck on eBay, feign a headache, and head home.

My Ideal First Date:

The Michael thing has taken two weeks from my life. At this rate, I see I'll never get through any of my messages, which have increased to about fifty and counting. When I ask around (no one admits upfront that they're on the site, but once you mention it, the floodgates open up), it turns out most people are e-mailing, speaking to, or dating a number of people simultaneously. So I start responding to the overflowing messages in my inbox.

Here are some highlights from my next round of JDates:

✉ DaBrooklynBomber writes: "Hi Amy! I think you're hot, hot hot! We should go slow dancing and cool kissing." I tell him to keep his pants on and his hands to himself.

✉ "I'm a southern gentleman looking for a New York lady," writes Nyles. He's moved to L.A. to become—what else?—a screenwriter. Over dinner at a fast-food Mexican restaurant, he leans in real close, as if a Hollywood exec is listening: "I'd like to work on a screenplay, but I'm looking for an idea," he stage-whispers. Believe it or not, I actually give him one.

✉ I can't put my finger on Joshua, a lawyer who seems so familiar on the phone. Is it because we both love to read? And I'm talking books, not screenplays. When I meet him in person we quickly realize we've gone out pre-JDate but we didn't recognize each other's online photo.

What I Am Looking for in a Man:

Meet Jonathan. He's perfect. He's a Jewish hippie. Underneath his colorful yarmulke, he's got long, dark hair that matches his chocolate-brown eyes. He's nice but sarcastic, creative but ambitious. We click. Oh, by the way, he tells me on our third date, he's moving to Chicago next month and can't start a new relationship right now.

But meeting Jonathan gives me hope—hope that maybe there is a guy for me out there online after all. There's more than one *beshert*, more than one destined person for everyone. If nothing else, JDate proves that there are always multiple options.

Could it be Jason? Jason says the sweetest things to me on the phone, so despite his effeminate voice, he flatters me into meeting him. At Casa Del Mar overlooking Santa Monica beach, the sunset is beautiful, the drinks are smooth, and Jason is a picture from a J. Crew catalog. He's telling me about his workout schedule (talking about workouts in L.A. is the equivalent of talking about your family), when I interrupt: "You take spin class? I thought that's only for women!"

"It's actually a very tough workout," he says, sticking out his lower lip. I just want to reach over and take his hand and say, "Look, you don't have to date women; it's okay to be gay." But I don't, because people can be so damn *tetchy* about sexual orientation.

More weeks go by in a dating haze. Adam? Two Davids? Marcus? I think I'm e-mailing a British doctor, but it's the Persian businessman; I confuse their stories ("Didn't you say you were from Philadelphia?" "You mean you're not an orphan?"). Meanwhile, I plot all my free time around first phone calls, first dates, second dates, e-mailing new people, and trying to keep track of which Dan the Doctor I'm seeing tonight.

I had started out as a little girl in a candy store but now I think I'm getting a stomachache. In the real world of dating, the wide-eyed twenty-two-year-old soon grows into a practical thirty-five-year-old. Online maturation occurs much faster, and cynicism sets in quicker, too. ("He just started JDating," one veteran JDater tells me about a newbie who is meeting two girls in one night and e-mailing six more. "Just wait. He'll calm down in a couple of months.")

What I Learned from My Last Relationship:

Actually, I should be grateful. Besides the obvious petty lying that is rampant on the site, I don't ever have the truly horrible dates I sometimes hear about. There are urban legends of JDates gone bad: There's the one where the guy perpetrated identity theft, or the guy who stopped the car and told the girl to get out because she didn't look like her picture. Then there are the phantoms, the ones who disappear without a trace after a great date.

Judd from Northern California and I talk by phone for a few weeks until he can make it down to visit. I've now met enough locals to understand that I should expand my geographic boundaries. He's an independent music producer and has a deep, sexy baritone. I'm in love with his phone voice, the way he says goodnight like Barry White every night until we meet. And although he doesn't look much like his picture, he's still cute if you don't look too closely at his mossy teeth. Man, do we have fun at the arcade in Santa Monica. Ms. Pacman, air hockey, the Ferris wheel. He even wins a stuffed animal for me. Our date lasts for five hours, and the next morning, he stops by to say good-bye. I guess he really means it, because I never hear from him again.

Judd is not the last JDate to be suddenly MIA. Erez works at a nonprofit and we really, really like each other. I can tell these things from the get-go: The talks till three in the morning, the realization that I'll cancel everything that weekend just to meet. And we drink and drink and then we sober up and the bar closes and still we don't want this night to end—but it does, and *of course* he'll call me tomorrow. Tomorrow comes but the phone call doesn't. I sit by my phone and wait for it to ring.

Suddenly this seems suspiciously like the real world of dating. I'm no longer the confident, brazen woman of profile no. XXXXXX who isn't dependent on one guy because she has twenty guys wanting to go out with her. I'm my old self, not only waiting for the phone to ring, but having to check my e-mail too.

The worst thing about the guys who don't call is that you start to doubt your own judgment. I feel like the court of law in my head is weighing the evidence in the case of Whether He Really Liked Me or Not.

"Isn't it true, your honor, that Erez said they'd go kiting and that he couldn't wait to see her again? Let the record show that Amy did not make that up. If it would please the court, allow me to introduce Erez's request for a second date as evidence."

By dating so many people at once, I thought I'd be inuring myself to rejection. But maybe I'm just making it worse by getting dumped so quickly and so frequently, and by dumping so many others.

"Why is it," my father asks, "that whoever likes you, you don't seem to like, and whoever you like doesn't seem to like you?" I want to launch into a whole explanation about dating and how it's different from when he was growing up, how it's different here in the secular world, different when you're older and set in your ways, and most of all how it's different on the Internet. But who am I kidding? I'm not going to change him. No matter what I say he will continue to think I am just too damn picky.

I don't tell him how else it goes. I don't tell him about sex, and he doesn't ask. We don't come from the kind of world where girls have sex before they are married. But how long is a woman supposed to wait?

What I'd Like in a Sexual Relationship:

About sex and JDating: As in the real world, it happens. Sometimes it happens on the third date, sometimes on the first one. On JDate there are people online only interested in one thing, and they usually type in: "I am looking for A FRIEND." Is there a difference between picking someone up at a bar or hooking up with someone you meet online?

With a Jewish dating site you have a false sense of security that you won't catch a disease or get raped because, after all, this is JDate. But just because someone can spell and went to a Reform temple doesn't mean that you know him or can trust him.

Because you can't. One hangover-y morning I wake up in the bed of . . . Andy? Ari? Alan? And facing me on the opposite wall is a picture of a headless naked woman with her legs spread open. Upon closer examination, I see there are a dozen photographs like this posted around the house, and I see she's not headless, but her head is thrown back.

"Wanna pose naked for me?" A— says, coming up behind me. I jump in surprise at the sight of him, his house. There are dirty dishes piled in the sink, the kind with caked-on food and flies, and suddenly I wonder if I'm in one of those situations that they reenact on reality crime shows. I grab my purse and leave.

Another night, I'm making out with Greg on the beach, and I feel his hands wrapped around my neck. Tightly. *His hands are around my neck,* I think, and I yank them off and pull away.

"Maybe you should ask a girl before you asphyxiate her," I gasp. "Well, you were wearing a choker, so I thought you wanted me to choke you." He shrugs. "Can't blame a guy for trying."

Then I meet Kurt. I like him, and think/hope/pray this could be something special. For him I decide to wait. I don't invite him in until the fourth date. He's kissing me, caressing me, and starts whispering in my ear.

"Bite me, baby. I want you to bite me really hard!" I stop the romance and look at him. "I have diabetes," he confesses. "I lose sensation in my extremities." Kurt wiggles his fingers, his toes and, yes . . . his boxers. "I like it when you bite me," he says. "As hard as you can!" But it turns out I can't. I can't bite him "harder!" like he demands, because while I like him, I'm not sure I want to pick up such bad habits for someone who might not be permanent.

For some, JDate is *all* about sex. My friend went out with a guy who boasted he sleeps with two out of every three women on JDate. Of course, she herself claims to keep four or five guys in the JDate booty-call roster. Others IM at midnight and hook up till the wee hours. I suppose it all beats being alone. Or does it?

"It only takes one," my father likes to remind me during our weekly pep talks. But who? Will it be Jake? He has floppy, sandy hair, cherubic cheeks, and what my grandmother might call *khen*, boyish charm. He's a writer transplanted from New York, and after I've spent a year in Los Angeles, his birthplace alone is enough to make him compelling.

I have given up on anyone looking like his picture, so when a guy walks by the Hollywood café looking exactly like his photo, I'm a bit startled. But I can't tell what he thinks of me. I do this now; internally size up the interaction while it's occurring, like a sportscaster: "And he's looking at his watch, and he says it's time to go! Oh no! But wait—great save! Jake kisses her on the lips and asks her out again!"

The kiss makes me forget the twenty other dates before him. Finally.

We make it to two months. I feel like I deserve a special flag from the Web site, one that says, "Can Sustain a Relationship Past the Third Date!" I'm beginning to suspect that Jake's not The One—he's an atheist with a type-A personality—but I date him anyway. Despite my father's wishes, must I date only for *tachlis*, for marriage purposes? I'm like a roving bird, not necessarily looking for a nest in which to settle down, but perhaps just a comfortable ledge to take a rest.

Alas, Jake is not my respite. He is actually not my anything, because after dating him for two months I don't hear from him for three weeks. Three weeks!

"People are just not accountable on Internet dating," says my best friend in New York, who also dated twenty-five people in three months. Her accountability theory isn't about the people dating online, but the medium itself. "There's nothing holding anyone together," she says. "It's not like a fix-up, where you both know someone, or where you meet at a party and there's some chemistry and some initial conversation."

"But what about someone contacting you online?" I ask. "And the e-mail conversations? Isn't that like meeting at a party?"

"No," she says. "Because they're not talking to you, they're talking to a concept of you based on your picture, and after you meet—if you ever meet—there's no obligation to call, write, or do anything polite, because there was nothing there in the first place." She's not bitter, though; she has another date this afternoon.

After Jake, my success story, it's hard for me to get back in a game I thought I might have been out of. But the cycle begins again, except I feel like I've been here before, because I can glimpse the end at the beginning. When I start to argue with my dates ("What do you mean you voted for Bush?"), I know it is time for me to pull the plug.

Why I Am Leaving This Site—Check All That Apply:

In September, the weather begins to cool and so does my enthusiasm for dating, with all its questions. "How long have you lived in L.A.?" "What do you do for a living?" "How is your experience on JDate?" "Do you want another drink?" My social life is one big dating party, where all the guests start to sound the same.

I'm going to suspend my JDate membership right now. I go to the Manage My Account section at JDate. For the first time in six months, I look over my essays, what everyone's been responding to all these months: "I'm a journalist and a marathon runner," I had written, as if that defined me—and I guess it did six months ago, before I started on this dating adventure.

The girl in the profile comes off as smart, sassy, and independent, like she doesn't have a care in the world, like she doesn't even need a date. Which is probably why so many of the guys who contacted me were commitment-phobic narcissists—athletic and humorous, like I'd requested, but lacking an integrity so crucial for my ideal mate. But they were not responding to me, just something I wrote one late, lonely night.

So I'm not sorry to pull the plug on profile no. XXXXXX. But before I do, maybe I'll just do one last search, just to see who's out there. There's nothing wrong with checking, right? Hey, who is Glenn? He's pictured playing with his dog, pitching a ball, and he has deep laugh lines like he knows a good joke on the world. Glenn is a high school teacher and a poet. What did he learn from his past relationships?

"I've learned some survival techniques, and I've found a little faith;

you love, and love ends. You suffer and somehow you love again. I'm looking forward to one that keeps going."

That could be me! Our love will never end, Glenn. Maybe I'll contact him. This is the last guy. Really. I promise.

PART IV

Guiltily Ever After:
The Chuppah and Beyond

Oy Christmas Tree, Oy Christmas Tree

*

LAURIE GWEN SHAPIRO

MY husband stands directly above me as I slump in the comfortable living room chair. He is forcing me to look up at a steep angle to hear what he has to say, his first words in half an hour.

"You're ready to talk?"

"Maybe."

"Well you bloody well better be because I'm just stumped."

"Threatening is not the way to . . ." I'm trying to sound reasonable, because I am afraid in my heart of hearts there is nothing reasonable about my stance, although I am absolute in my conviction: I refuse to have a Christmas tree in my home. I married a goy boy from Australia, but this is my line in the sand. While I am not observant about nearly any aspect of my Jewish identity, this is one boundary even I cannot cross.

"Look, what's the problem with a tree?" Paul tries to reason with me. "What's so religious about a tree if you don't have an angel or a cross on it? If you want, Violet can hang a Jewish star on top."

Violet is our daughter, who at the time of this argument is nearly a year and a half, and clueless that all the fuss in the living room is over her religious upbringing. Her name is a reflection of the two worlds she was born into. In English, her name is Violet Frances O'Leary, and in Hebrew, in honor of her two Jewish great-grandmothers, she is Tziporah Chaia O'Leary. Violet/Tziporah is, at the moment, too absorbed by a Christmas/Hanukkah pull toy that just arrived from her Australian grandmother to worry about her divided identity.

I sneak another look at her to make sure she is okay. Even though my own grandfather had those impossibly blue eyes, her golden hair has never been seen before on either side of my family. Her nose is a tiny replica of my very Polish Jewish nose, ballish and small. I'm constantly pointing out the lower half of her face, which I think is just like mine. But Violet's coloring throws off passersby. I have dark, dark brown hair and eyes, and have already been asked more than a dozen times if I am her babysitter.

I stare down her father as I gulp my second full glass of water. I am amazed how two strung-together words, "Christmas tree," can have such a polarizing effect on us.

A bright winter sun is glaring in my eyes, and I don't like Paul's position of authority either. I stand and move to another chair. "I never had a tree. It just doesn't feel right for Violet to have one. Not having a tree was the one rule that reminded my brother and me that we were Jewish."

"That's ridiculous. You missed out and you're punishing your daughter for it too?" His question takes me aback for a minute. Have I missed out? It never felt that way exactly. I had admired my fair share of Christmas trees, from the one in Rockefeller Center to the ones in the homes of my separated in-laws. But never one in my own house.

"She can have gelt," I say with the harsh guttural G of a fourth-generation Lower East Side Jew, which I am. My Jewish observance may be lacking elsewhere, but like an Israeli, the place of my birth renders me automatically Jewish, regardless of how much or little I follow the rules.

"Gelt?"

"Chocolate coins." Silence. "And a spinning top." Silence. "And a pile of nuts."

"Like a pile of nuts would get a kid racing to the living room," Paul finally fires.

"Who doesn't like nuts?"

"I thought you loathed religious didacticism. What do you care what she gets or does?" He's got a point. I do loathe the worst of organized religion, but my identity has always been and always will be as a cultural Jew. "A tree is not a sermon. Trees are fun. You get to string popcorn and switch on cool lights," says Paul. "I am not asking you to have our daughter worship Jesus as her savior. I'm not talking about a service here,

I'm talking about a fucking tree. I'm talking about an innocuous tradition, one I want to share with my daughter."

I was a little blindsided by this fight, but not completely. The first time the religious issue waved hello in our relationship was the week after we changed our wedding plans. My mother, once a star fund-raiser and event planner for big Jewish charities like the Federation of Jewish Philanthropies and Israel Bonds, was thrilled to come out of retirement for the event to end all events: the *big* New York ballroom wedding of her only daughter. My extroverted personality didn't mind the idea of dragging Paul into a lively hora circle of everyone I've ever known. The image of the two of us lifted high in the chairs of honor amused me. What a party it would have been! My family alone, even when trimmed of distant cousins, tallies well over a hundred. But late one night after my mother had called with the newest version of the New York Jewish Wedding Extravaganza she was ready to produce, the shy man in my life guiltily confessed that the thought of speaking and dancing in front of all those people terrified him.

"We met in Australia, let's celebrate in Australia," he pitched. Was it his idea or mine to have a smaller blowout at a friend's spectacular garden estate in Mount Macedon, an hour outside of Melbourne? The location was minutes away from the site of our favorite movie, *Picnic at Hanging Rock*. I do remember that after the painfully honest discussion we were deliriously happy to reach such a pleasing compromise. If it wasn't what my mother wanted, it was what we now agreed we wanted: a beautiful, exotic wedding performed by someone who was neither a rabbi nor a priest.

After our friend in Mount Macedon enthusiastically agreed to host the event, I nervously called my parents' retirement condo in Florida. How would they take the switcheroo? Would they catch our enthusiasm for a back-to-nature union?

I explained that the air around the garden estates of Mount Macedon smells different from the rest of eucalyptus-covered Australia. I told them that large oaks and an apple grove grace the periphery of Tanah

Merah, our friend's property. There would also be the lovely scent of wet roses. The wedding party would share the mountain with colorful birds: frogmouths and nightjars, weebills and bowerbirds. Somewhere in the vicinity, if we looked hard, we'd find koalas, feral goats, echidnas and platypuses, sugar gliders and long-nosed bandicoots. And three species of bats. I pitched my mom, hoping to sound irresistibly exotic. I waited. My mother finally spoke.

"The O'Learys will be running around Australia planning a Jewish wedding?"

I sighed inwardly. I tried to explain. I told her that the wedding would not necessarily be strictly Jewish, but it would honor Judaism. We were eschewing a rabbi, but celebrating my family's heritage by using Jewish symbolism elsewhere in the ceremony. This seemed particularly reasonable since Paul had already made it known that he wanted no Christian symbolism. His parents, following their son's lead, had long ago stopped going to church, so there was no fight from them either.

Yes, Mom appreciated that, and how Paul's grandmother in her nineties could attend too, but . . .

"What is it really, Mom?" I said guiltily that day, already knowing the answer: All the action would now unfurl 12,000 miles away from her family and friends eager to celebrate with us. She couldn't even order the herring.

Finally the angry release came: "Doesn't a mother get to plan a wedding day? See how you feel if you have the tablecloth pulled out from under you by your children." She sighed heavily. "Will you at least make sure there is a chuppah?" I was surprised how much Jewish symbolism she pushed for. Whenever the issue of Paul's heritage had come up before, neither of my parents had come after me with a wagging finger. They loved me and they loved him, and they chose to count their blessings in my happiness with a great guy. (And any man who could put up with my messiness was automatically a favored suitor.) But I could tell, despite their best efforts, the actuality of my marrying out of the tribe still rankled a bit.

My father's first words after listening to mother and daughter duking it out: "Who's leading the wine blessing, a bandicoot?"

O N the wedding day our Aussie justice of the peace announced, "In honor of Laurie's ethnic background, we will highlight matriarchal culture. I've asked Laurie's and Paul's mothers to say a few words about their respective children."

Judy, Paul's mother and a former personal assistant to an Australian knight, had her remarks neatly typed out. "Paul is beloved by his family and close friends," she began. "He is a songwriter, a musician, and a poet. Whenever Paul's in town, our family is filled with joy—for we love him most dearly. And Laurie, whom we simply adore, is a cherished addition to the gang." Less than sixty seconds top.

My loquacious, sidelined mother was up next. If she had felt at all left out during the wedding planning, she now had her chance to shine and was going to grab it. I nervously took a breath as she cleared her throat, and began, "Once upon a time a princess named Laurie Gwen was growing up in lower Manhattan. Laurie would examine atlases and maps, and pore over fairy tales that took her far away. She always wanted to travel. Come to think of it, she couldn't go any farther than Australia! Princess Laurie can't wait for anything—she makes things happen. So she took her white jet, Qantas, to Australia . . ."

"Keep it short," my brother David whispered, interrupting her while winding up an imaginary fishing reel.

"Shh, David! I'm talking. There she met her prince, Prince Paul. We welcome him into our family with open arms . . ." She resumed her oratory, speaking for another ten minutes. Finally, the climax. "And may Laurie remember to take a multivitamin every day so she can give us many beautiful, healthy grandchildren."

My mother had spoken long enough that the rain ended and the sun poked out from behind eroding clouds. Our justice of the peace smiled beatifically upward toward the sky. "Laurie and Paul, I will now ask you to face each other," she said, "and read from the vows you have written together."

"That would have been your daughter's idea," my father said to my mother, his New York accent amplifying his already excessive volume.

There's loud and there's my father's level of loud. And so our married life began amid all of its wonderful chaos. Paul may have been from Melbourne, but he was marrying, according to my mother, a real live Jewish American Princess.

As the Christmas tree fight progressed, I couldn't help but think of our wedding. I'd already angered my parents once by removing the hora of their fantasies. I couldn't imagine announcing to them that a Christmas tree was going to be brought up in my elevator. I shuddered slightly.

Paul waited for me to speak. I struggled for diplomacy. "If she's hanging ornaments at your mom's, fine. If you want our daughter to eat her great-grandmother's pudding flaming with brandy, fine. And when she's older she can have fun making popcorn balls at school. I did that when I was little. But not in our house."

"Oh, is that so?" he said, spectacularly angry. It's no mean feat to piss off my loving, affable husband so thoroughly.

"Aren't there two parents here? What about my childhood? Don't I get to pass some nifty traditions along too?"

"Let's just end this argument right now," I said softly and clearly. "No tree. Not here. It really means a lot to me, more than I think it means to you."

"Want to know the truth? I feel betrayed."

"Betrayed?"

"You are not the woman I married. I thought we were a team about religion."

"I'm sorry," I tried. "It's just the tree part that—"

"Who are you kidding? There is a lot more about the subject going on in your head. True?"

"Maybe."

"So just tell me, if you're so adamant about her heritage why did you schlep her all the way uptown to see Santa at Macy's?" I love it when he uses Yiddish words despite himself, although "schlep" may be more American now than Jewish.

"Because that's a Jewish New York tradition. That's how we get out all of our Yuletide longing, and then your mom buys you a half-price coat as soon as the Polaroid develops."

Paul rolled his eyes. "You know, come to think of it, we never fully agreed to anything. Who's to say Violet is Jewish?"

Whoa. He was drawing out the big guns now.

"Her religion is not up for argument," I responded in what I hoped was my best this-is-not-even-negotiable voice.

"Um, am I hearing this correctly?"

"The children of a Jewish-born woman are always Jewish. They can get a passport from Israel on that fact alone."

"What if I threw my little girl into baptismal water?"

"Still a Jew." My knowledge of *Halacha* may be shaky, but on this point I was sure.

"Shaved her little head like Caine in *Kung Fu* and raised her as a Buddhist monk?"

"Jew."

"For Christ's sake. What's come over you? I just saw you eat a shrimp-salad sandwich half an hour ago."

"Look," I said shakily. "This was decided a long time ago. Judaism is constructed in such a way that you don't even have to think about it, you just are. Children of Jewish mothers are always Jews. You don't get a choice about it."

Even I was aware of how silly I sounded. What had come over me?

Was it the new anti-Semitism I read about every day, escalating around the globe? Or was it a delayed reaction to the dusty prayer book with faded copper lettering I had found the previous day with my grandfather's name scribbled in Hebrew on the copyright page? Most likely, it was simply the addition of a child to the mix. No matter how easily I'd thought we'd handle her religious upbringing, a heavy guilt about potentially snapping my ancient family line was slowly seeping through my secular skin.

I imagine my elders reading this will now mutter to themselves: *She should have thought these issues out. This is what happens when you don't think about future children.*

I'd argue that I was too young to think about future children. I was in love, and love conquers all, right? There's no way you don't believe that in your twenties, and there's no way you do believe it in your thirties.

Paul and I met right after I graduated from college. Instead of accepting a TV production job in Manhattan, for which I had fought off classmates, I capriciously bought a one-way ticket Down Under. After scouring the papers, I found what sounded like the ideal landing spot: a Melbourne house-share with three locally known rockers as roommates. I took any menial work I could find, and had the time of my life.

Paul, a dirty-blonde, blue-eyed bassist and a very mellow human being, mistakenly thought the dark-haired dark-eyed girl sleeping late and laughing at corny Aussie sitcoms was a fellow mellow human being. Had he ever met a real live New York Jewish girl before? Apparently not. Since neither of us went to religious services, my deep feelings about my Jewish heritage were never discussed—other than the fact that both of us prefer Woody Allen's later work, not the earlier spoofs so many critics embrace. We dated and it still felt mellow and easy. We never had to fight about where to spend the night. We never fought at all. Then he saw me back in my element, among aspiring New York writers as insufferably competitive as I. Too late. Snagged.

We are that rarest of couplings, the vacation fling that has lasted—much to the disbelief of every one of our friends and family members. We lack matching temperaments, interests, nationalities, and, yes, religions. The two things we *do* have going are an ability to laugh at ourselves and, as treacly as this sounds, love itself.

Don't get me wrong. Before this uncomfortable discussion, our marriage had seen its share of fights, including the silly ongoing battle over the sticks of butter Paul leaves out overnight for "spreadability." The O'Learys of Melbourne have been happily eating rancid butter for years, but I see no reason spoiled churned milk has to be schmeared on my New York toddler's bagel.

Paul's complaints about me include that I don't "offer" opinions, I pound them on the table into thin foils. In addition to my mouthy mouth, he objects to my chronic overuse of the word "rocker" in describing him, especially in print. Still, I know that neither one of us would change our marriage for the world. Since the wedding negotiations, there has been surprisingly little religious discussion between Paul and me until we hit the roadblock of the tree.

Holidays had never been an issue for us before Violet's first year. Some of my observant Jewish friends don't celebrate St. Valentine's Day on account of the saint feted, but if I don't get roses in February, I thwack an Australian head with a newspaper. It's Thanksgiving and Passover with the American Jews, and Christmas with the Australian Christians—if we have the money or the mileage to get there. Hanukkah was a nonissue until the kid came along.

Elders, hear me out: I'm not self-loathing when it comes to my heritage. Or my family. That would be light-years from the truth. My parents have always identified themselves as Jews, proudly pointing to the outstanding secular Jewish minds of the past few centuries the way the observant can rattle off names of great Talmud scholars. My brother and I might not have known who the Rambam was growing up, but we certainly knew that Jonas Salk, a Jew, invented the polio vaccine, and that Curly, Moe, and Shemp were in the tribe too.

My mother is the parent who made sure we went to Hebrew School twice a week. My retired Dad, first a color television engineer, and later in his career a computer programmer, is descended from a line of famous Shapiro/Shapira rabbis. (So I guess both Violet and I are too.) There is no way I would ever be able to consider myself non-Jewish, despite all my flouting of Jewish custom and observance, and it was equally impossible for me to see my daughter as a non-Jew. It may be irrational, it may make no sense, but that's the way it is. I could not, would not, have a Christmas tree in my home.

In the end, I won the Christmas Tree Battle, but it continued all through the night. I yelled. I snuffled. Paul couldn't get over my passion for the fight; he kept staring at me like I was a known pacifist who had attacked him with tear gas. I couldn't get over his stubbornness. The conflict even carried over to the next morning in our building's laundry room.

An older woman, folding her extremely large white underwear into a three-point flag took it all in, silently at first. But like everybody who lives on the Lower East Side, she finally had to weigh in. "Listen to me, kids. My grandson's name is Avi Gonzales. When in doubt, go with the mother's wishes. That's all I'm saying."

"Okay," Paul whispered a minute later with wet eyes. Was he just exhausted? Somehow another opinion had helped. We not only had a plan for the coming holidays, but for decades of holidays. We kissed in the elevator on the way back to our apartment. Violet, riding on top of the shopping cart full of warm clean clothes, smiled at the sight.

Upstairs as our little one napped, we agreed that she would get her exposure to tinsel and Santa Claus outside our house. But since I knew he was compromising more than I, every year that passes I wait with bated breath for Paul to bring up the issue. If he ever does, I suspect the Jewish mother in me will rear up once again, whether I want her to or not.

"So what December holiday are we celebrating this year?" my mother discreetly asks me outside a synagogue in November. We were at a family bar mitzvah in New Jersey and my handicapped father is firmly holding Violet's hand on the pavement as Paul and my brother park the rented minivan. (She's hard to tether in any scenario, but especially when you're confined to a wheelchair.)

"Hanukkah, what else?" I whisper conspiratorially. My mother gives me a quiet high five. Mom leans against a car with her checkbook and a happy smile. I've long suspected the real reason Judaism lives on through the mother is that it is the mother who usually counts bodies in the car and writes out a corresponding check for the bar mitzvah boy or bat mitzvah girl.

According to the Jewish mother rulebook, this amount should always be enough to aid the strapped parents. If the young star of the party is lucky enough to score some of the deposited booty, there is happiness all around. The promise of bar mitzvah booty has lured many a kid back into Hebrew School.

My father calls to me to get my daughter before she flees his grasp.

"Oh, Violet," my mother says when I bring her over to where she is writing out a hefty check. She then kisses her granddaughter's cheek. "Grandma is just going to kvell at your bat mitzvah. We can dance the hora we never had at your mommy's wedding!"

Great, My Daughter Is Marrying a Nazi

*

JENNA KALINSKY

M IDWAY between lick and stick, my father informed me that the tattoo from the Cheerios box was not to grace my forearm.

"Out of respect for those who died in the Holocaust, Jews don't mark their bodies," he'd said with an unfamiliar eloquence, rather than his usual dad-like "no." I was surprised; were the Cheerios people aware of this? Though I failed to grasp exactly how a three-quarter-inch Smurfette would denigrate the memory of the perished, I did as I was told.

This was my first exposure to the notion that certain Jewish issues weren't adaptable. My family had always sedered, *lulaved*, and fasted (at least until lunch), had Hebrew school and bat mitzvahs, and ate chopped liver at funerals. But we also colored Easter eggs, enjoyed shrimp dinners, and as a matter of practicality, Hanukklaus came to our house as a one-shot deal on December twenty-fifth.

While it was fine that the religious observance of most Jews I knew growing up was a Choose-Your-Own-Judaic-Adventure, I soon learned that when it came to two specific, deeply serious issues that threatened the preservation and humanity of our people, there was no deviating whatsoever. First: never have anything to do with Germany, its people, culture, or commerce. Second: marry the one you love—as long as he is Jewish.

Once I was a bit older and learned about the millions murdered during the Holocaust, saw pictures of Nazi parades, the gas chambers, and women screaming for Hitler the way American teens had for the Beatles, this general hatred toward Germany, past and present, began to make sense. Then, every action counting as a protest against the atrocities couldn't be enough. I was proud to know that even my not buying imported German chocolate bars was indeed teaching "those people" a lesson.

If friends or family accidentally visited the verboten zone, say on a layover or prepackaged tour, they usually said, "We loved our trip through Europe. But Germany? Too cold. Didn't like it." The humanitarian in me appreciated that they'd been open-minded enough to see the unseeable for themselves and get their own perspectives. But their immediate dismissal of Germany and all it represented reassured me that they were good people, good Jews, and made it easier to eat over at their houses later on.

As for the marrying of goyim, if you decided to choose outside the chosen, the "you're dead to me" would ricochet throughout the *mishpocha* until you wished you were. Or, you could go for broke by declaring, "Hey, Ma! I'm marrying a nice Aryan boy!"

Unfortunately, this is exactly what I did. I never meant things to turn out this way; my heart had always been in the right place. I just happened to fall in love with one of "those people."

It was then that I discovered that there is indeed one thing on this earth that can render my Jewish mother speechless. I wouldn't have thought it possible. The harangue I expected to ring in my ears when I announced that I was marrying a German was actually a terrible, eerie quiet.

WHEN I was twenty-seven, I moved from Los Angeles to New York. My girlfriends and I were dancing at a party one night when a syrupy Prussian voice caught me from behind, enveloping my flesh in goose bumps. I'd never encountered a German in real life, and with an accent so strong it sounded like a parody. When the voice's owner, with his blonde hair, sea-colored eyes, and precise, fluid moves squeezed in, I got fast confirmation: definitely not one of mine. But we talked; we touched. He smelled good. And just as easily, my shivers abated. He said, "I'll call you tomorrow." He did. (Who does that?) On our first date, on the ice rink in Central Park, we talked in choppy English, making slow loops until the sky grew dark blue. His Germanness became Stefan. It didn't take long. In fact, after his first few sentences, he was just a man.

I'd always imagined that Europeans and Americans couldn't be all that dissimilar, but I soon learned that Stefan and I were culturally alien in almost every way. At first we were intrigued by our differences. But soon we began to devote copious energy to finding what was the same between us. This search was beyond a lark; it was necessity. We'd become a couple. We spoke in future tense.

Yet hovering quietly by was our essential reality: I was a Jew. He was German. He knew as little about my background as I did about his. I was nervous when I finally introduced my Jewishness to him, something I'd never had to do before for anyone, but he was accepting and humble, and handled each etymology and explanation of my faith with the rapt attention usually reserved for holding newborns. I brought him to synagogue for the High Holidays, apologizing afterward for the voraciously swaying daveners. (I hadn't known they'd do that; was it too much for him?) I taught him to play dreidel on his living room floor and cooked him a terrible candlelit Passover seder meal. He also taught me with shy pride about himself and the life he knew and loved back home in Germany.

Still, I marveled at how I could care so deeply for someone who muttered mysterious words in his sleep, a man who deep within his cells held this particular foreign darkness. A man who walked around our shared apartment, without shame, in tiny, European-sized underwear. But our hearts forged ahead, oblivious to border and construct. We took pictures of each other doing ordinary things. We longed for one another and often when we got there, we didn't know what to say. We were as different as night and day. We were the same.

When he accepted a professorship back in Germany and asked me to marry him, I said yes. I didn't want to turn back. We'd come too far and created too much to quit.

The hardest part wasn't that I was leaving my community, my language, my everything; it was that I was experiencing for the first time what it meant to betray. My parents still hadn't met Stefan, so when, upon hearing my plans, my mother blurted out, "Great, my daughter is marrying a Nazi," I understood. When she recovered from her silence and whispered, "I only hope you'll be happy," my heart began to hurt. My father's lips remained sealed. He wasn't stepping in this time.

In Germany, Stefan and I moved into a city sprawling with vineyards, cobbled streets, and Victorian villas. In the row across the way from our own was a double-staircased house with wrought-iron banisters and wooden shutters. Before it stood a monument, a sign inside a bus shelter. This was one of many unexpectedly placed monuments that had been sprinkled throughout the city as part of a WWII historical exhibit. I asked Stefan to translate the sign.

"This house was formerly known as the Judenhaus." While he read, Stefan held me to him with a painful intensity. "The Jews of Wiesbaden were collected and held here prior to deportation to the East." The sign showed three columns: Name, Deported To, Outcome. The list of names was long. All except two read "Perished in Auschwitz." The building was exquisite. It was what we saw out the window when we awoke each day.

Stefan's family made every effort to make me welcome, to make me understand they were good people. During the war, his mother starved and survived bombings. She'd lost her father, "the kindest and most loving of men," she said often. The last photo in the album was of him just hours before he was killed, grinning from a Siberian snow trench, his rifle, *Sieg Heil.* As a teen, Stefan's father had been drafted into the *Wehrmacht* and was imprisoned by the Russians, an experience of which he refused to speak. He did, however, make a point to tell me about the death threats made on his family for trying to listen to the BBC during the war. How he shopped at the Jewish market until the police shut it down. That he believed the Jews were a smart people.

After meeting me, Stefan's mother mentioned to him that I "didn't look Jewish." As it happens, I look *very* Jewish. I am proud that my dark-haired, light-eyed, sturdy-hipped genetics exist as an obvious compilation of my heritage. Had she arrived at her realization with surprise? Relief? His parents also posed copious questions about my religion, background, and beliefs, which made me feel as if I were tiny and squatting in a petri dish. For the first time in my life, my Jewishness was making me feel identified, peculiar, and worse, as though through it all I had to wear a gigantic phony smile.

When our wedding day arrived, my immediates graciously put aside their misgivings and flew over. A pastor presided alone; rabbis in Germany are Orthodox, and none Stefan asked would perform an intermarriage. The beautiful Jewish rituals I'd always imagined—standing beneath the chuppah, chanting in lilting Hebrew, and being thrown into the sky on a chair, dancers circling all around—remained imagined. Still, it was lovely; sunlight glowed through the cathedral's Moroccan stained glass, and Stefan's shaking hand in mine was soft and hopeful. I didn't understand the sermon, but between the organ's final, lasting note, the pastor's smile, and Stefan leaning in for a kiss, I knew we were officially married.

Of the gifts sent from home, ninety-seven percent were Judaica. No one needed to say they were afraid for me. My parents' gift was the most loving of all; they stayed in the country for a vacation. They took a boat tour, bought potholders in Frankfurt, and slept overnight in Stefan's parents' home. "We will be Family," said my father. In his world, Family is capitalized. It is sacred and bonding, and there are no barriers. During the Holocaust, his entire extended family disappeared from their village in Poland. My father, who does not eat sweets, swore that Stefan's mother's apple cake was the best dessert he had ever tasted. I was deeply touched that they'd overcome their own fears for me, learned for themselves what it was they'd rallied their entire lives against. "They have faces now," said my mother. She made a scrapbook of their trip. The whole thing seemed so seamless. I secretly wondered what was wrong with them that they could abandon their beliefs so easily.

In the beginning, Stefan and I had many wonderful times playing married. I learned to feel ownership for our union, glowing with pride at the complex mathematical formulas he doodled, and boasting that he was so smart that he couldn't tie his shoes. He found it hilarious when I sang along to his German songs without knowing the words, and always enthusiastically praised my dinners, no matter how burned or underdone they were.

We adopted the rituals of fresh rolls for breakfast and drinking wine on weekend afternoons in castles. There were abundant outdoor festivals and long walks through forests. We toured the continent, camping by the Mediterranean, biking in France, and vacationing in Italy, Holland, Spain, and even Israel, where Stefan felt nervous, but tried to enjoy it just the same. "They won't kick you out because you're German," I reassured him.

Yet even amid the genteel moments, before long, we began to resemble the embattled. When I came to Germany, I only had a suitcase. Everything else I'd shipped from New York got lost; it was five months before any of it was recovered. Being surrounded by a world of words that meant nothing rendered me mute—spiritually and practically. The few childish sentences in my arsenal weren't enough to ask directions or understand answers. I often got lost. And Stefan—my confidant, guide, and partner in crime—worked. And worked and worked. Promptly after I arrived to join him in our new life together, he evaporated for two weeks to a conference. I stood alone in the shampoo aisle for twenty-five minutes, unable to help myself.

Soon, Stefan and I began suffering rampant misunderstandings that indelibly marked us and our marriage. He tried to comprehend what it was that got me all worked up, but could not. After all, he'd provided for us, he'd watched his bank account dwindle for the rent, the furniture, the car. Leaden silences became normal because it hurt me to talk and because he was hurt that I would not talk. He imagined I was throwing stones, I imagined I'd eaten them. We often slept in separate rooms. Of course I felt uncomfortable in my new home. The war photos of Jewish roundups hanging on the slats of a simulated cattle car in the public square where I bought our fruit had nothing to do with this. Anyone would feel the same, I said over and over, the needle getting stuck.

I tried to grab at anything familiar, anything to take root. On one of my first walks around town, I saw "schmuck" in elegant script on a storefront and laughed my head off. "It means 'jewelry,'" said Stefan, eyeing me as if I'd gone mad. I soon learned that "putz" means "to clean," and "mensch" means "man" or "human," and has nothing to do with one's goodness. A six-pointed star is the popular beer logo that hangs from many pubs, and what look like menorahs are lit in windows at Christmas. At flea markets, grizzled old women sell beautiful jewelry and trinkets for cheap, here and there a Star of David. I always burned to know where they had gotten the stars. I never asked.

It didn't take long before I started to unravel. Every compromise seemed Herculean, each foible or inconsideration became a personal and cultural rejection. I walked too slowly. I'd misestimate my departure time and Stefan would fulminate at the door while I raced about collecting sweaters and shoes. Germans don't exactly understand Jewish Standard Time. Raised by two war survivors, Stefan's frugality and disdain of the material overwhelmed my very American "anything's possible" sensibility. He'd demand we buy the cheap coffee, insist I not bring his mother flowers when he was certain she would cluck at the waste, and resent my suggestions that we improve upon the asylum-chic décor of our apartment. That there were walls at all should have made me happy. After all, I had student debt.

When we did share a bed, when I was vulnerable and wanting, we did so beneath two single duvets wearing mismatching covers on two side-by-side single mattresses with a gap between. In New York, we'd slept as one; now I wasn't allowed to touch Stefan in the night. It kept him awake. So did my new habit of tossing and turning. The divide between us had become too much of a metaphor. All I wanted was to be held.

Until I moved to Germany, I was a person like other people—a composite of attributes worn sure and thoughtless as skin: woman, American, Jewish, five foot seven, ambitious but lazy, crooked from scoliosis, passionate about spicy yellowtail handrolls, peace, and Antonio Banderas (probably not in that order).

But in my new home, my third down on the list—the fact that I was Jewish—was so loaded that when revealed, it wore all the spectacle of a "coming out." Interestingly, the reaction was the opposite of what I'd expected; I was suddenly loved too much, like a bear squeezed until the stuffing leaks out. Once it was in the open, typical Germans my age

flushed through a rainbow of contorted facial expressions and stammer-
ings to express their contrition, to connect. It was awful to watch. In the
end, it was always, "Oh, I know someone who knows someone who works
at the Jewish Museum in Frankfurt. She loves her job!" or, "A woman in
my mother's book club knows someone who is Jewish! You should meet
her!"

Being the target of such shamed, strange deference was nothing compared to finding out that Jews were actually the latest trend. In a beer garden, a young German girl greeted her friend with a cheery, "Shalom!" In
the town square, women swarmed a yarmulke-wearing New Yorker singing
atrocious renditions of Jewish songs as if he were Pavarotti. Teens danced to
klezmer bands and wore stars around their necks. *A schmuck on a shayna
madel,* I smiled to myself since there was nobody to share the joke with.

I was stared at on the street, when I entered the train. Of course I
look Jewish. I was out of context; I felt as though I'd been repainted by
Picasso. My Jewishness had gone from being an easygoing, organic part
of me to being both my dirty secret and my entire glaring identity.

For the first time in my life, I needed tangible, concrete footholds to
remind myself that in my world I made sense; I was normal and whole.
The Nanny dubbed into German was my greatest solace, and I began to
wear my hair like Fran Drescher's without irony. I kept a tiny *chai* charm
around my neck. At the health food store, I discovered matzoh. I towered
over the weeble-sized *Hausfrauen* in line, seething. These women were
old, they'd stood by while my people were killed, let just *one* of them look
at me funny. Come on, *ladies,* you want a piece of this? None of them
seemed even slightly uncomfortable. I stormed out of there, powered up
with a marathoner's endorphins. I'd bought matzoh. I don't even *like* matzoh. Outside, the world going by was easy, people just living their lives. I
was the one with my heart going like a rabbit's. Just me.

On my first Rosh Hashanah in Germany, Stefan and I were arguing. I
decided to run away from home. As if driven by instinct, I headed to the
nearby synagogue. A guard searched my bag and asked questions in English in between greeting regulars by name. There'd been a rise in Arab
anti-Jewish attacks; two Kevlar-vested policemen on a rooftop across the

street kept submachine guns trained on the doorway. Finally, after he took away my camera, scoured my passport, and waved a wand over my every inch, I was wished *"Shana Tova"* and allowed inside.

Upstairs, one woman, frail with gray hair, sat apart, rocking back and forth, crying. The others, mostly Russian refugees, chatted loudly, undeterred by the rabbi's scolding in Hebrew. It was both familiar and entirely foreign. This was not my world. I was getting ready to leave when I heard a woman whispering to her son in English. She was a klezmer singer from Illinois, married to a German. From this we tried to build a friendship. Though she was kind, we had little in common. After our Jewishness failed to keep us together, I didn't stay in touch. Seeing a Jew so happily married to a German was disconcerting.

I had to carry on; I'd made a choice, and I loved my husband. So how did I endure? I discovered living in a winegrowing region had its benefits. I spent whole days composing e-mails and developed a spectacular knot in my stomach. I ground my teeth, and grew a wrinkle in my forehead that was impervious to chemical peels and scrubbing, endless scrubbing. I cried nearly every day for over two years.

Being marked comes in many varieties. Germany is marked by its history. It struggles daily to absolve itself, to move forward and learn from the pocks on its people and story. In my own new story, I also struggled with the past embedded in the present. The company that owned my drugstore had used Jewish slave labor. I taught English at a former Zyclon B industrial plant. People my husband had laughed with, touched, even loved may have taken part in the murder of my people. I fought constant urges to trip the elderly on the sidewalk. Distance had always kept me safe; now I lived in, over, among, beneath. Breath of the murdered whished over my neck at night. I felt cheap and small. I imagined I was building my life above a graveyard; I was dancing on their heads.

Oddly enough, despite the longing and loneliness and incessantly gray skies, at times Germany almost became my home. That I had to work so hard to achieve the simplest things magnified every trial or joy with extraordinary emphasis. The first time I returned a shirt, flirted with the train conductor, and caught the bad jokes on television I felt like flying.

In my best friend from the town across the river, I found one refuge. When I phoned, her Spanish husband would belt out, "Aneeta, your seester is on the phone." My German teacher became a running partner and confidant. After driving two hours to my house for his English lessons, he would shake off his suit jacket and silently lean out the window with me to admire the sunset. German versions of gum, vitamins, and hair goo fast became staples; I learned to cook beets and black root. German directness sometimes even became far preferable to wishy-washy North American politeness, and European produce, breads, and chocolate outshone every international counterpart.

Yet beneath my triumphs, my marriage was disintegrating, rendering the gradual familiarity to all else moot. Stefan did what he could; he unflaggingly gave and gave—coffee in the mornings, flowers, an Alpine ski trip. I thanked him, but by then, we were flanked on all sides by avalanche. The roar, the noise made it impossible for me to say thanks loudly enough, or for him to hear me.

I began carrying myself as if I bore the burden of others. In the beginning, the nearly endless explanation and etymology helped establish unity among our little U.N. of two. But nothing had changed. I was still as foreign an object as I was at the start. Stefan and I spoke in pinched, regretful tones about "misunderstanding four thousand eight hundred and seventy four." When anyone asked how long I'd been in Germany, I answered down to the minute. I whorishly gravitated toward foreigners.

Even after several years, I was still alien to Stefan's family. My mother-in-law asked me to accompany her to the synagogue in her town, reopening from its destruction on *Kristallnacht*. I took her interest as curiosity, but I believe she genuinely wanted to extend herself to me by learning "my" world. I was too worn out to appreciate the benevolence of the gesture. As she followed the sermon with unwavering attention, I couldn't help but wonder, did we all not look Jewish to her?

The next morning, she asked me to read the Hebrew aloud from the prayer book she'd taken as a souvenir. Stefan was off somewhere. She and

Stefan's father leaned in. Their faces looked encouraging, generous. The clock ticked. The backyard fir swooshed in the breeze. The clock ticked. I began. My voice didn't sound like mine. They were reaching out, but I didn't care. I stopped. "It's been a long time," I said. My face burned. I felt a sudden, violent hatred for how utterly other I was.

Eventually, my otherness stole the firma from my terra. Stefan started using verbs such as "handle" and "wrangle" in regards to me. I began crossing lines, no longer caring if the damage was irreparable. I called him a Fascist in an argument. I raised my voice, hoping he would retreat. In his hometown, we visited a "silent monument" dedicated to their deceased Jews.

Little stones, each engraved with the single name of a dead Jew, were set into the ground to make a path up to the great German castle. The stones were turned upside down so that when trod upon, the names ground into the dirt. His mother praised the whole affair and her people for their willingness to repair. She was trying, I knew, but when I went to find company in Stefan, to whisper with him about the wrong of this, I saw his eyes had turned cold. I saw the defeat in them. He'd been attempting to understand me and failing for so long. It made me ache with an indescribable loneliness. I could see he'd stopped. And so had I.

A FTER several years, Stefan was offered a job in Canada. We jumped at the chance to relocate, hoping Germany was our problem. Finally, we faced up to the fact that it was, but only in part. We separated soon after. Stefan's mother wrote me a good-bye letter to wish me well. His sister said good riddance. "I always felt judged," she told Stefan. She was right.

Three countries, two languages, six years, and one failed promise later, we're sitting together in the pub at the Canadian university where we both work.

"Remember how in the beginning we were attracted to the other because we were different?" he asks. "Exotic. And after that wore off, it was so difficult—I had troubles understanding your family and friends, you moved to a place that had ghosts for you; you betrayed yourself to go there. It brought us together, making us more of a team. And it broke us apart, too." He looks at me. "Ironic, isn't it?"

In the end, Stefan never ceased to be German any more than I ceased to be Jewish, American, or a creative speller. We did our best but saw for ourselves why like so often seeks like. There is nothing more gratifying than being able to feel culturally whole. Though I will always be a valley girl from L.A., here in Ontario I have again found myself among the familiar. I don't have to explain that the reason I don't eat meat isn't because all Jews keep kosher, but simply that I don't want to eat meat. My dark, curly hair blends right in. If I am stared at on the street, it is probably because I have spinach in my teeth.

The guilt in my chest, heavy as stone, has been alleviated because I am no longer faced with betraying my people at every turn. But Germany became a part of me, twenty-eight percent at my best estimation. I'm sloppily fluent and can mimic several regional accents, long for steaming *Glühwein* on cold nights, and am quick to point out that Germany is aware and conscious and is making every effort to heal. Here in Canada, I gravitate toward German speakers on the street.

I've learned about keeping the past separate from the present. Not forgetting, not forgiving, but holding the then and the now as mostly separate entities. Life isn't as clear-cut as it once was—I now feel that forswearing German watches, cars, and chocolate is a misplaced effort. If more Jews knew that a German Christmas is nothing without latkes and applesauce, or that the German New Year's greeting *"Guten Rutsch"* comes directly from the Yiddish *"a gut Rosch,"* we'd have some thinking to do about what it means to keep ourselves safe by continually pushing away a culture, or about the benefits of remaining ignorant.

Stefan pushes his Coke toward me. I reach for it with a hand conspicuously absent of a wedding ring. It still fits; I tried it on the other day and marveled at how much my love hasn't abated, at the utterly complicated nature of our relationship. He says, "I would punch anyone in the nose who says something against you or any Jew." He still loves me too. I am pleased; any step forward for humankind of greater cultural understanding, even if it is a punch in the nose, is a good step.

As for me, I have now seen the unseeable, gotten my own perspective. Perhaps discernable in my voice, however, is the thin, underlying sound of apology and confusion. Because honestly, I'm sure if I were to meet me, I would wonder what was wrong with me. A Jew with amicable, even affectionate, views toward Germany? Sure, I would appreciate my open-mindedness. But in truth, even after everything, I wonder if I would eat over at my house.

The New York Times
Divorce Announcement

*

ELISA ALBERT

Jonathan Seth Frankel, 36, and Elisa Tamar Albert, 26, are to be divorced this week after a little over a year of marriage. The decision to separate was made in couples' therapy when it was discovered that Mr. Frankel lacked the commitment and self-awareness necessary to come to the table and attempt to work anything out, and Ms. Albert realized that she was quite frankly "sick of this bullshit" in any case. Dissolution papers will be signed at the midtown law offices of Selman and Oliver.

Ms. Albert kept her name upon entering the marriage, which saves her untold misery in paperwork and small talk now. Mr. Frankel, who, according to his mother, taught himself to read when he was three years old, is very relieved that he no longer has to "deal" with Ms. Albert's incessant harping about his snoring problem, hygiene, and habitual clutter.

Ms. Albert's 95-year-old paternal grandmother, who has said repeatedly that she yearns to live just long enough to see Ms. Albert become a mother, after which she'll be all too "happy to die," has not been told about the split. "I think I'll just pretend everything is fine," Ms. Albert mused. "And maybe I can borrow a friend's baby to bring over to show her."

OH, if only the "Sunday Styles" section could accommodate such an announcement. It's a wee bit glib, sure, but how else is a modern

Jewish girl to inform society of the collapse of all her most fervent, pitched familial hopes?

My *Times wedding* announcement read, as many do, like a smug sigh of relief: Nice privileged overeducated girl marries nice privileged over-educated boy. Accelerated offspring, sound real-estate investment, timely death, and flourishing of Judaism on the planet implicitly forthcoming. Continuity of the Jewish people thusly assured and hopes and dreams of respective families fulfilled, all with a lively hora, some lovely orchids, and top-of-the-line kitchenware to seal the deal.

But less than a year after our triumphant announcement (oh, and the getting married itself), my husband and I separated, and all that pride, joy, and hope inscribed in the paper of record quickly gave way to a tail-spin of failure, reproach, and profound guilt. It wasn't only my life and heart I'd destroyed: I felt I had dashed the hopes of loved ones, wasted an obscene amount of money, and failed to fulfill the needs of my people by not reproducing. I found myself fairly buried under the rubble.

Disaster begets questions. For starters, how do you pick yourself up and dust yourself off when you've colossally messed up in front of every-one you know? What the hell happened, for another? Whose "fault" was it? Did I try hard enough? What does true love look like, if not what I thought I had? Who keeps the gifts? How do I go about the rest of my life trying to forget that box of fabulous wedding-photo proofs buried at the back of my closet? How did something that looked so "right" turn out to be so devastatingly wrong? The answers I felt com-pelled to give—to great-aunts, my mother's friends, my friends' mothers, various dissociated yentas, the lucky red-state bride who won my absurdly out-of-character Vera Wang on eBay—ranged from the practical to the existential. What, in the name of Colin Cowie, had I been thinking?

I wished I could fend off those inevitable, proliferate questions with a *Times* divorce announcement. I had fleetingly grasped the supposed brass ring of my adulthood: a perfect Jewish husband. How could it be over? Unfortunately, the *Times* lacks such a section. And anyway, I have pre-cious few easy answers.

W E met like this: our brothers died. Mine first, excruciatingly, of cancer. His next, a suicide portended by a lifetime of severe depression. Our families were friendly acquaintances, and my mother pushed Jonathan's phone number on me a few days after her shivah call.

"He just moved to New York and doesn't know anyone," she told me. "Call him. You know what he's going through." I remembered Jonathan vaguely from a family dinner long ago: He was an intense, good-looking guy ten years my senior. Curiosity, with a pinch of guilt-laced altruism, overshadowed my annoyance at the possible setup, which, coming as it did on the heels of his cataclysmic tragedy, seemed in wildly poor taste. But I am a good girl, after all, so I did as my mother instructed and I called him. We had coffee, schmoozed about Haruki Murakami and our lost brothers, and fell madly in love.

I had never dated a Jew. And Jonathan was the kind of Jewish guy I hadn't dared to dream existed, had not come across in lonely godforsaken eons of Hebrew school and Camp Ramah and Israel summers and Brandeis University. A six-foot, two-inch vegan, quick-witted, well traveled, well-read, iconoclastic but perversely traditional, unfazed by female body hair, and terrifyingly good at Scrabble. I was beyond smitten.

Everything lined up nicely: our values, worldviews, and tastes in movies, music, and books. Even the pain of the losses we'd experienced in our respective families—death and divorce, specifically—seemed incredibly parallel. Jonathan was my soulmate, period. He would be my partner, and together we would make a new family, end of story. I would not be subjected to the heinous, years-long JDating I saw undertaken by friends. I would not sweat out my twenties fretting about the toll of gravity on my breasts and waiting around nervously for my *beshert*. Jonathan was everything I'd ever wanted. Put a fork in me, I was done.

"We marvel that something so awful can give way to something so positive," I gushed in the *Times*, which featured our delighted photo. And who doesn't love a good out-of-the-ashes tale? If my family of origin had been a Holocaust of sorts, the new family I'd create with Jonathan would be the safe haven of *Eretz Yisrael*. (Little did I realize my true heart would then assume the role of the trampled Palestinians in that metaphor—victimized and destroyed though certainly not blameless—but let's not go there.)

Never mind that the relationship was not quite airtight. Never mind that my intended had an old tattoo that said, *"I don't love anything."* Never mind that he seemed to be on a strict three-year commitment cycle with an illustrious trail of broken engagements and enraged ex-girlfriends in his wake. Never mind that he'd already given me ample reason not to trust him. Never mind that I had some maturity and ambivalence issues of my own. Never mind that I was what my friends anxiously, and quite rightly, referred to as "kind of young to be getting married." None of that mattered.

What did matter was that we were in love. We shared an awful common history and deeply rooted need to refill our familial *nachas* coffers. We bandied about baby names during foreplay, no joke. I doodled hoped-for kids' names the way some women doodle hoped-for married names. I cheerfully announced to a small audience at one of my bridal showers that Jonathan and I were duty-bound to have *at least* six children: one to replace each of us, one to increase the numbers of the Jewish people, one to make up for the Holocaust, and one to replace each of our lost siblings. Six children. Minimum.

"We'll talk after you have one," a hostess laughed nervously, looking about ready to toss her scone. I stared blankly at her.

Six children was a conservative estimate. I had quite a lot to make up for: divorced, aging, heartbroken parents, one lost brother, one surviving brother who seems rather remarkably untroubled by any sense of responsibility to either the living or the dead, and on and on. I believed (and, on bad days, still kind of do) that I, like the heroine of an outlandish science fiction plot, am the last best hope for any real joy in the Albert family, for the creation of a new world, a new family out of the ruins of the old one.

Despite my usual loathing of the trappings of modern wedded bliss—the bank-breaking parties, the love-bling, the blanket use of first-person plural—I managed to take leave of my senses long enough to seize rabidly upon absolutely all of them. I donned my engagement ring with the relish and arrogance of a Tiffany-engulfed sorority skank. I was a cross-

eyed chimp with that ring on; I liked watching it sparkle. It was *pretty*.
I was righting every imaginable wrong via my bejeweled left hand. This
was how a new family would be constructed; this was how death and
genocide and divorce and loneliness and the loss of my own halcyon family
days would be thwarted, definitively. I was pretty proud of this deduc-
tion. This all made great sense to me.

Our gorgeous, enormous wedding (what I remember of it, that is—I
got smashed) was a lot like an extended, multifaceted memorial service. I
carried my long-gone maternal grandmother's inscribed bible. We traded
wedding bands that had belonged to our great-grandparents. Our chuppah was hand sewn by a family friend from the *talitot* of our dead brothers. Our program was a long-winded paean to tradition, bygone times,
and those who could not be with us to celebrate. There were, I seem to
recall, lots and lots of ambiguous, uncomfortable tears (even the *willows*
were weeping). What, exactly, were we all crying about?

A DARK feeling began to catch up to me within the first few months.
Minute to minute I experienced something like emotional prison
bars slamming shut. I had made the classic error of marrying Jonathan,
with all those high hopes and grand plans, without actually imagining
having to *be* married to him; a rookie mistake if ever there was one. He
was so "perfect" for me in so many external ways; he met every last quali-
fication on my checklist. And much about being with him did thrill me
beyond anything I'd ever before experienced in a relationship. But, alas, I
had neglected to focus on some all-important intangibles: empathy, stead-
fastness, and openness, to name a few.

For my part, I was demanding, harsh, depressed, and unsure of myself. Within months we were sleeping separately, prioritizing friends and
family over each other, and, when we did "communicate," doing so in a
manner that prompted our neighbors to write us nasty notes and complain to the landlord. Was this *marriage*? I scoured every self-help tome I
could get my hands on. I'd heard ominous warnings about "the first year,"
but when our couples' therapist shook her head sadly at me one day as we
were leaving her office, I knew that something was acutely not okay.

Even when it had become inescapably clear that it was not going to work, I could not bring myself to walk away. I had *married* him, and that meant I had thrown away the key. Besides, he was Jewish! Tall! A wonderful cook! Lovely in bed! Genuinely kind to strangers and service providers! Expansive and energetic and rebellious! We both wanted kids *yesterday!* Yente the Matchmaker could not herself have done better on the externals. Who was I to turn my back on these recommendations? So what if he could also be distant, petty, and excruciatingly unforgiving? So what if he had markedly little patience for *my* issues, *my* needs, *my* bullshit? Sure, he seemed to care a whole hell of a lot more about the feelings of any given waitress or cab driver or acquaintance than he did about mine, but what kind of idiot expects perfection from a spouse? And what if I really *was* an unwieldy bitch? Who was I to demand more? It was my job, as I learned from a lifetime of singing along with *Fiddler on the Roof* and watching my own family disintegrate into thin air, to *choose* this man, to choose to love him, to choose to live with him, and to *suck it up*, whatever "it" entailed.

I am, after all, the unofficial family archivist, the self-appointed keeper of the pastoral flame, the devoted child who digs up forgotten home movies, has them transferred to DVD, and distributes copies at Hanukkah. There would be no whimpering out of my own commitment; no simple dissatisfaction would make me turn my back on this new family. I would, I believed, rather be unfulfilled within an intact marriage. I had a clear vision of myself at seventy, mobbed by my own grandchildren, wearing a faux-retro T-shirt reading CHILDREN OF DIVORCE DO IT BETTER.

For my own sake, for the sake of my parents and community, for the sake of my cheated-out-of-life brother, for the sake of recapturing some vestige of the vanished world in family photos on my mom's piano, for the sake of the half-dozen unborn children whose being brought into existence would surely set everything right, it was clear to me that I needed to somehow forge a family with Jonathan, this man who seemed to embody everything I wanted, everything I so wanted to want, and exist within it forevermore, no matter what the cost.

And so, as my life began to spin into reverse, I tried desperately to cling to a future with Jonathan. I tried to blur the line between prosaic compromise with a realistic spouse and a life of total misery and desolation with someone who could not give me what I needed, someone unable to see me. I wondered what it would take for me to endure the latter. Could I live with this marriage and seek fulfillment elsewhere? In a blossoming career? With great friends? In a thriving yoga practice, a herd of the most brilliant named-for-the-dead babies imaginable, some ego-boosting affairs? Any foreseeable compromise seemed livable. Leaving behind the dream of a life with Jonathan and watching my carefully constructed survivor's-guilt house of cards collapse? Not so much. If I had to die trying, I figured, I'd at least die married to Jonathan, the Jonathan I dearly loved, as part of a new, whole, intact family, as mother to several of his hardy, athletic little children.

Meanwhile, I can't underestimate the gleefully gossipy schadenfreude characteristic of—but of course not unique to—the Jewish community in which I was reared. Indeed, it was clear almost immediately that the bust-up of this marriage included all and sundry bystanders. Before the ink had dried on my umpteenth tormented should-I-stay-or-should-I-go journal entry, the news was out. Our separation ceased to be about us. It snowballed in a way that felt most intrusive, out of control, and impersonal. Looking back, there's this dreadful worry that perhaps, with only the support and restraint and good advice of those around us, things may not have taken on such a life of their own and evolved into the foregone conclusion that we were simply done for.

I can hardly remember, now, coming to an actual decision, with my husband, that our marriage was over. One day we were fighting and I felt hopeless and things were going dreadfully, and the next his good friend's wife (a rabbi, no less!) ran into a friend of mine at a mall several states away and breezily offered up the news that we were kaput. Then an in-the-dark relative of mine, still more states removed, got a pseudo-sympathetic phone call from said rabbi's sister-in-law. And so on. (Um, an aside, if I may? Perhaps we should collectively be focusing a little less on themed bar mitzvah parties and a little more on philosophical illumination of concepts like *Lashon Ha Ra.* Just a thought.)

It was seriously humiliating to think about everyone I knew (and everyone *they* knew) finding out that I was nothing but an emotional dilettante, that I had so recklessly taken on and discarded something so serious. I had been stupid enough (or so went the projection) to marry someone hopelessly wrong for me, to believe that I could single-handedly plug up all the holes in my family's sinking boat, and now my ridiculously extravagant wedding would be nothing more than a punch line, an admonition to future affianced couples, a judgmental footnote forevermore to passing mention of my name. A deep sense of embarrassment and a desire to avoid this easily imagined torrent of chatter provided me yet another reason to remain in the soul-crushing marriage even as long as I did. Less than a year, a hiccup in the scope of my life (I hope), but an eternity to feel as terrible and mortified as all that.

I feared things were past the point of reconciliation when I finally broke down and admitted the enormity of this misery to my mother. I was in a cab, alone, on my way to the airport for a flight to our months-belated honeymoon. Jonathan and I had gotten into a horrible, pointless fight that morning, and I had set off to Jamaica without him.

"I'm so sorry, Mom," I kept repeating through mounting tears. "I'm so, so sorry." I meant to apologize for, in no particular order, everything lost and mistaken and fucked-up in three generations of our family, and most of all, that it now appeared I was inadequate to the task: I couldn't fix any of it after all.

She was shocked by my feelings of shame, and sad that I had undertaken a marriage on behalf of anyone or anything other than myself and my own fulfillment. She and my father, to whom I sobbed my apologies a few months later, were both confounded by my having felt any such accountability to either of them. They reassured me repeatedly that they wanted nothing more than my health and happiness, in whatever form those may take.

This unforeseen reaction failed to appease me. In fact, it counterintuitively pissed me off. I was stunned to find that the enormous external pressure I'd felt was at least partially invented. Lo and behold, I had staged my own martyrdom! And they had stood by and watched me do it! All these terrible feelings of failure and accountability were coming from *me;* all this smothering guilt was simply my own. So where, pray tell, did I get it? And is there a fallout shelter somewhere where I can be quarantined for this sort of thing so it spreads no further?

IT's pretty clear in hindsight: My starter marriage proves the most ordinary of cautionary tales, your basic sometimes-the-cure-is-worse-than-the-disease. Better that the Jewish people should die out and my dear parents not live to see me with a family of my own (*Kenna hora, poo poo poo*) than that I should try to make a life with the wrong person.

Less than a year after Jonathan and I stood under our dead brothers' prayer shawls and bound our souls together for life, I am living out of a suitcase in a friend's apartment, sifting dazedly through the wreck. In a box I find a stack of wedding thank-you notes, lovely, fresh, and still unused.

My mother and I had rejoiced in the beauty and luxuriousness of this stationery when we'd picked it out together, and now these unused notes are all wrapped up like embalmed recriminations in a filing box. I had refused to simply write them all—I may have gone temporarily bride-insane, but I was not about to start this marriage off as the typical wifely social workhorse, and I insisted that Jonathan write half. He (predictably) wrote only about half of his half, and I (predictably) got annoyed.

"Elisa and Jonathan," they say on the front, beautifully letterpressed in an ashy green chosen to echo our outdoor ceremony and party. I numbly pluck one from the top of the pile and attach an ellipsis to *"Elisa and Jonathan."* On the inside I continue, *". . . have made a terrible mistake and are very sorry for any inconvenience this may have caused you. Elisa is horrified that your high hopes and outpouring of love culminate in this way. Since her beleaguered parents paid for the wedding (yes, weren't those vegan croquettes amazing?), Elisa will most likely be keeping your beautiful [insert gift here], but rest assured you will never have to buy her another. She promises, should she be so lucky as to find another human being on this planet with whom she'd consider partnering, to do it in Vegas next time and leave you out of it."*

I fantasize about writing a few hundred of these, mailing them off, and putting a handy end to discussion about the whole debacle. As with my imagined *New York Times* divorce announcement, this would be a reclamation of sorts: a rejection of the needs and hopes and desires and wishes and projections of everyone else, replete with requisite acknowl-edgment of lingering guilt for refusing to feel guilty. It would also be a fitting send-off down the road toward my new life, in which I'll be reso-lutely on the lookout for a broke, illiterate, infertile, five-foot, one-inch Republican Protestant carnivore who's exceedingly patient and kind and generous and committed, who will adore me and stick by me and wrap his arms around me and cheer me up when I have a lousy day, and with whom I'll be genuinely happy, on my own behalf. If I feel like it maybe I'll send a postcard from the Viva Las Vegas Wedding Chapel, if I feel like it. Or maybe I won't.

* PART *

Feeling *Treyfy*:
Noshing Forbidden Fruit

The Yom Kippur Pedicure

*

DAPHNE MERKIN

How can it be, you might ask, that such a travesty came to pass? How is it, I mean, that a woman like me, born and bred of preening Orthodox German-Jewish stock, came one evening two years ago to usher in Yom Kippur, the Holiest of Holy Days, in the most faithless way imaginable: by having a manicure and pedicure at Iris Nails on the Upper East Side?

You might ask, that is, if this were the beginning of an old-fashioned story by S.Y. Agnon, say, or Sholom Aleichem, one that had never been exposed to those newfangled and profane literary influences that do away with all meaning, much less a divine purpose. The kind of story that always includes a busybody or two—professional meddlers in the detritus of other people's lives—whose ordained narrative purpose is to stand around the town square, alive with the sound of peddlers hawking their wares and chickens squawking, the better to discuss the latest *shanda*, a piece of news that would set your mother's ears on fire. Such sorrows shouldn't happen to a dog—they would undoubtedly cluck if they happened, that is, to get wind of the tale I am about to recount—much less to a family of noble standing such as hers. To fall from such heights to such depths, all in a moment's undoing! Better you should excuse yourself than read on.

My own sordid little history is set in a traffic-ridden twenty-first-century city where anonymity is assured, rather than in a tiny, nineteenth-century shtetl where village gossips hold sway. No one would chance to know of my brazen flouting of basic religious etiquette except for the fact that I feel compelled to reveal it now. Think of it as a form of be-lated penance, disguised as a shameless confessional performance. *S'lach loh-nu, m'chal loh-nu, kahper loh-nu.* Forgive us, pardon us, grant us atonement.

I T was, I suppose, a piece of exquisite, fashionably postmodernist irony waiting to happen, the unforeseen and inconclusive resolution of years of wondering about how, or even whether, I fit into the larger Jewish pic-ture. Such as is left of it, now that the czar has been overthrown and girls walk around with their navels showing.

Then again, you could conclude that my having decided to opt for a set of shiny toenails over the chance to burnish my soul effectively demonstrated just how hopelessly tarnished a soul I was stuck with. Or, even worse, it attested to nothing more profound than my inability to pace myself accurately, to ever be on time for anything—much less Kol Nidre. I mean, it is theoretically possible to see to both the needs of the body and the soul without overlooking either, if one schedules these things accordingly. It's not like every *frume Sarah* wears whiskers on her chin or soiled cuffs on her blouses. But I was always running late, always wildly cramming three plans into two, and why should this night, if I may mix my *yontiv* metaphors and borrow from the Passover *Haggadah*, be different from all other nights? Why, indeed, even if erev Yom Kippur happened to be the Ur-Night of soul-wrestling, the calendrical moment designated for coaxing and flattering and altogether finagling a way into good standing in God's annual ledger?

So there I sat in Iris Nails that Friday evening in September, as the hands on the oversized wall clock moved inexorably forward and the shadows lengthened outside, paging through a month-old copy of *Vogue*, waiting for my toenails—freshly lacquered in some subtle shade with a coy name like Allure or Delicacy, imperceptible variations upon the same basic pale pink theme—to dry.

All around me for the past two hours the salon had been emptying out of its devoutly assimilated Jewish clientele, women with toned bod-ies and cosmetically altered faces who had just minutes earlier been busy discussing their various plans for breaking the forthcoming fast on their cell phones. One coiffed woman was expecting forty for dinner the next night, and worried whether she had enough dessert plates; another described her less-ambitious scheme to order take-out for her family. I had sat there and eavesdropped disapprovingly, a spy in the House of Iris, wondering whether any of these women were real Jews—Jews like me— and knew enough not to wear their designer shoes to shul, or whether they had just jumped onto the newly fashionable ethnic bandwagon.

Did they understand, for instance, that it was crucial to be *on time* for Kol Nidre, that only the religiously ignorant and the hopelessly vainglorious sashayed into synagogue after the service had begun? This lesson had been conveyed to me in my girlhood, and I in turn had repeatedly impressed its importance on my adolescent daughter for the past two days, reminding her to be ready to leave in her sneakers and shul clothes by 6:15. I'm not coming late to Kol Nidre, I warned her. If you're not ready, I'm going without you.

It was ten minutes past six. Twenty blocks away the same *chazzan* who had serenaded me fifteen years earlier as I stood under the chuppah (how was he to know that the marriage was misconceived and would be over in a few years, a minor blot on the golden record of family ceremonies he has continued to officiate at?) was about to commence with *Hallel*, the solemn prayer that announces the start of the twenty-four-hour fast. What was I thinking? Here I had been alerting my daughter to this defining Jewish moment as though it meant something to me and by extension should to her, and now I was keeping her cooling her sneaker-shod heels while I sat in admiring contemplation of my toes.

I had to get out of here fast. I gestured wildly to the shy young woman who had plied her fine-tuned, underpaid skills for the past two hours, trying to communicate some sense of urgency in spite of the fact that I appeared to have all the time in the world. My faith was on the line, but how was she to understand my predicament if I myself couldn't figure out how I had managed to arrange my life in such a fashion that more than four decades of roiling internal conflict about Jewishness had come to a head right here in Iris Nails? On the one side were the hallowed claims of a patriarchal religion presided over by a grim and reclusive (and, needless to say, male) God, who couldn't be expected to understand the significance of socioeconomic factors in the formation of one's approach to shul-going: What did He care if I associated Yom Kippur with the incongruously glamorous, often newly-Judaicized wives of the congregation's multiple tycoons who showed up in the front row of the women's balcony only for the High Holy Days and then disappeared into their brilliantly secular lives? On the other side was my feminine instinct to compete with the buffed and lacquered women in the balcony section of the synagogue from my childhood, which I still frequented, not out of any deep conviction or even a commendable sense of loyalty (I disliked the place as much as an adult as I had as a child) but out of an inability to figure out where else I might convincingly claim a seat.

I may as well admit, for the record, that I didn't make much effort at speeding things up. I had seen customers in a hurry get their freshly-done toes Saran-Wrapped for extra buffering before putting on their shoes, but I wasn't willing to risk messing up the polish. Besides which, even I could figure out that there was no way I could get home, dress, and be at shul all within the next fifteen minutes. And who was He (if He, indeed, existed) to me, when it came right down to it, that I should be rushing myself for Him? Hadn't I tried to find a religious footing for myself all these years, imbued with a degree of good faith that had included my taking private Talmud lessons after I had officially finished with Jewish studies in high school because I hoped I might find some sort of locution for myself in the disputatious language of the Gemorah? I had always warmed to the abstract reasoning of the Talmud over the picturesque tales that we studied in my Chumash classes. The cerebral sparks given off by the various commentators with their differing interpretations of a particular phrase reminded me more of the splitting of semantic hairs that I found so intriguing in the analyses of literary texts than of pious biblical exegeses. But none of this could keep me that night from scrambling around wildly in my head, hurling accusations at myself for failing to provide a role model for my daughter, failing to provide a role model for myself, failing, failing, failing at the Jewish thing.

Iris Nails is a prettier salon than many, mind you, and priced accordingly. It's not one of those fly-by-night affairs that tend to dot the urban landscape, put together with spit and Quick-Dry, one freebie wall calendar with photos of kittens adorning the cheaply painted walls in lieu of interior décor. No, this is a plush oasis of a nail salon, replete with a crystal chandelier. The stations of the manicurists are set luxuriously far apart and there is a sparkling, peach-toned Italianate landscape painted quite convincingly on the walls so that if you half close your eyes and shut your ears to the indecipherable chatter of the Korean staff, you can imagine yourself on a sun-splashed terrazzo.

These incidental details matter, if you are ever to get the setting for this tale of divided loyalties and split identities more or less straight in your mind. If Iris Nails had been a less appealing place, for instance, instead of representing a sanctuary of sorts, a haven in a heartless world, perhaps I would have lingered less among the shy manicurists, the soft lighting, and the trompe l'oeil Mediterranean backdrop. But as it was, I couldn't bring myself to leave this refuge in the midst of the gleamingly impersonal city I had grown up in, a city in which I had always felt spiritually homeless. And so I sat on, in my padded chair with the buttons that enabled you to get a heated back massage while reclining, immobilized by the comforting atmosphere of the salon and by my consuming ambivalence over Judaism—an ambivalence that led me to judge other Jews by my own lapsed Orthodox standards, as though I were a *rebbetzin* in disguise, while I indulged in pork-filled Szechuan dumplings. It drove my daughter mad, the way I kept a foot guiltily in both camps, and tonight's behavior would only further the craziness.

Perhaps, too, if I had ever succeeded in finding a shul that spoke the language of home to me, instead of returning, lemming-like, year after year, to the affluent, snobbish congregation that had made me feel acutely uncomfortable ever since I had first stood in my hand-smocked Shabbos dress and black patent leather Shabbos shoes, gazing down at the men's section where everything worth watching was taking place, things might have worked out differently. I wouldn't have felt the dire need to paint my toenails at just that pre–Kol Nidre moment, for crying out loud, as though I were going to be inspected for trophy wife–level grooming standards before being allowed into the women's section.

PERHAPS, but then again, perhaps not. As you can see, my Jewishness and I are a vexed pair from way back. It's as though we got soldered together when I was still young and impressionable, and now I'm doomed to drag this ancient, sober-minded religion with me through the rest of my life, like a giant ball-and-chain clanking behind me, seconding my every move. Wherever I goeth, my cumbersome Jewish shadow goeth; wherever I departeth, it departeth.

The problem with this kind of tortured relationship, as with all tortured relationships, is that at some point it is no longer possible to conceive of having any choice in the matter. Letting go seems just as self-evident a gesture as holding on. The worst part of it is that I'm caught between a sense of nostalgia for the idyllic, somewhat kitschy shtetl fantasy that I've always harbored—Friday night candles flickering on a snow-white tablecloth, like an image out of *Fiddler on the Roof,* signifying everything that is peaceful and heartfelt about Shabbos, the cozy warming chicken-soupness of it—and an equally strong sense of claustrophobia about the hidebound German-Jewish reality as I experienced it growing up: those Friday night candles once again, suggestive of everything that is repetitive and compulsively ritualized about Shabbos, the enforced glutinous idleness of it.

My Jewishness is further complicated by my blue-chip, Platinum Card credentials—otherwise known as *yichus,* otherwise known as lineage. Although I have never met a Jewish person, of however attenuated an identity, who didn't in some flimsy fashion try to link him or herself up to an ancient towering sage like the Ba'al Shem Tov or Maimonides, I can lay claim to the Jewish equivalent of being able to connect your WASP ancestry directly to the *Mayflower,* to a family history that has produced generations of great scholars and influential community leaders. This foamy bloodline comes to me on my mother's side, which features various founding fathers of modern Orthodox Judaism, including my great-great-grandfather, Samson Raphael Hirsch, who paved the way for the unique approach to living in two competing worlds—the secular German one and the ritualized Jewish one ("*torah im derekh eretz*")—

that characterized German Orthodoxy, as well as Hirsch's grandson, my grandfather, Isaac Breuer, who, alone among his celebrated family, embraced the Zionist ideal when Israel was still only a gleam in the eye of Theodor Herzl.

My mother had been the only one of her immediate family, which included three siblings and their collective seventeen children (the obligation to breed and multiply being one that the entire Breuer clan took to heart) to abandon a life of high principles and scant material comforts for a life of less obvious principles and visible affluence. Meanwhile, her qualms about leaving the fledgling country and modest lifestyle her father had embraced were played out on the vulnerable psyches of her children—with more confusing effects on me and my two sisters, I would guess, than on my three brothers.

And yet I wonder, do one's origins ever explain as much as they obfuscate? It all goes so far back that it would take a team of shrinks working overtime to figure out which complicated antecedent led to which tragicomic outcome. How can I ever get you to see it as it was for me back then, a girl brought up on the de-ethnicized, churchgoing Upper East Side only to take her rightful place in a sleeping bag in the Sinai desert? An unhappy, introspective girl raised on lullabies of hearty *chaluzim,* going up to Israel with pails and shovels like an intrepid toddler in overalls, by a mother who had imbibed her adored father's ideological commitment to the land and passed it on to her children, despite the fact that she herself had chosen to set up her life on Park Avneue, with no sign of a camel or a kibbutznik in sight.

The polar opposite of that benign Zionist image of strong Jews was the darkened one of being caught up in Hitler's net, and it was the other major characterization of Jewishness that colored my childhood. At an age when I was still too young to comprehend the historic evil of Nazism in any but the vaguest terms, I had a clear grasp of the way it had disrupted the natural course of my mother's life, leading to two emigrations, one forced and one voluntary. It was because of the Nazis that in 1937 she had to leave behind her beloved Frankfurt with its famous zoo, which she had regularly visited on Shabbos afternoons, and immigrate to what was then Palestine, together with her family. A decade later, in the wake of her father's death, in her late twenties but not yet married, she left Israel for what was to have been a year abroad in New York to teach at the religious day school that was part of the thriving Washington Heights Orthodox German-Jewish community, established by her uncle Joseph Breuer (as fervent in his anti-Zionism as her father was in his religious Zionism) after he had fled Frankfurt.

Early in her stay, at one of those dinner parties expressly designed for matchmaking purposes that people used to be in the habit of giving, my mother was introduced to my father, an Orthodox bachelor of long-standing and fellow *yekke* (as German Jews were called by the Eastern European Jews they considered themselves superior to). After a stop-and-start courtship befitting a man and woman who had resisted the lure of matrimony until the ripe ages of forty-two and thirty, respectively, they married on the roof of the St. Regis hotel and produced six children in rapid succession. My parents spoke to each other mostly in German, a language that always makes me think of swastikas, and gave off a general air of living where they did only under sufferance since it was all too obvious that America and its silly Orthodox Jews with their casual ways couldn't hold a candle to the old-world restraint and formality of the communities they had known earlier on.

What all this percolated down to was a childhood bombarded with more mixed messages about what it meant to be an authentically Jewish person than you could juggle with three hands. For one thing, I was given the sort of predictably schizophrenic amalgam of social mores and moral guidelines that modern Orthodox Jewish girls are heir to, stemming from the vast and uncrossable gulf between traditional ideals of modesty and purity and imminent wifeliness/helpmateness on the one hand, and the brutal realities of the contemporary dating marketplace and current expectations of female self-definition on the other. To get a sense of the confused atmosphere, you have only to stand outside a Jewish day school like the one I went to on the Upper East Side and watch the girls emerge in clothes that are maximally revealing while being at the same time appropriately unscanty—an aesthetic approach most typically characterized by long, tight denim skirts that are usually slit halfway up the back or side and look difficult to navigate in without resorting to the kind of mincing steps that I imagine Chinese women with bound feet were forced to adopt.

But the messages we received in my immediate family about being properly Jewish went well beyond this in scope, covering every aspect of the way we presented ourselves to a watchful world. This externalized aspect, bewilderingly enough, was all that seemed to count both for my mother and for the shul on the Upper East Side that my father had helped found and presided over through four decades. Although religious conviction was presumably a manifestation of your inner life, Judaism struck me as a resolutely social institution, more about group behavior than private wranglings with God or faith. No one gave a damn whether or not you sinned in your soul, or hated in your heart, or fantasized about group sex in the middle of the rabbi's sermon. Primitive convictions about the transparency of your spiritual failings were fine for Southern born-again types like Jimmy Carter, who confessed in *Playboy* that he had lusted in his heart. Jews—Jews like us—were more sophisticated than that.

Which meant that in my family there was barely any mention of God and none at all regarding vicissitudes of belief. The German approach emphasized rules and more rules—as well as the solemn aesthetic context surrounding their observance, the beautification of ritual that is referred to as *hidur mitzvah.* My mother was particularly proud of this aspect of her upbringing, and it undoubtedly added something to our Friday evenings that your average Friday evening in Great Neck did not have: The table was beautifully set, flowers abounded, and we got dressed in Shabbos clothes, no lounging about in robes or sweatpants as I saw my friends do. But with so much stress on form, I began to lose sight of the priorities—whether it was more important that I look good (which meant WASP good, as in understated, not too much makeup, certainly no red nail polish) or that I pay attention to the davening, or whether the most important thing of all was that I get to shul on time and didn't meander in when *musaf* was already half over.

came home close to seven that evening. My pedicure had dried, Kol Nidre was well under way, and I immediately broke into tears in front of my daughter. She is a wise soul, and I like to think she understood that my abiding sense of conflict spoke to some sort of passion, a connection rather than a severance. How else to explain my perplexing behavior that evening as well as the following day, when I attended shul from late morning until the end of the fast, barely lifting my head from the *machzor* like a person in a trance?

Perhaps it will suffice to note that I am a woman haunted by my past, and that in the present time in which we are all required to live, willy-nilly, ready or not, I have never been able to locate my inner Jew. Nothing in my experience of religious life then or now has clarified for me in what, exactly, the platonic essence of Jewishness—its internal content as opposed to its outer form—resides. And yet I continue to hope it is there, a shimmering and sacrosanct kernel that got lost somewhere between Iris Nails and Yom Kippur.

Big Mouth: Jewish Women and Appetite

*

WENDY SHANKER

"WHY are all Jewish women so fat?"

That was the question the Japanese Reiki practitioner asked me after rolling me around on a hotel bed. "Rolling me around on a hotel bed" ain't a euphemism, either. In my latest foray into alternative health therapies, I'd let this guy spend an hour tossing me back and forth on a mattress in a hotel room. He'd promised to get my "chi," or life energy, moving more effectively through my system.

So I would've expected, "How's your 'chi' flowing now?" or "Can you write me a check?," but certainly not, "Why are all Jewish women so fat?" First of all, there was his implication that I myself was "so fat." Now, I'm perfectly content to describe myself as "fat," but "*so* fat" begins to push it. Not all Jewish women are "so fat" either. I can think of like . . . at least three who aren't. And how did he know I was Jewish anyway? It's not like I have a Jewish name, or stereotypically Jewish features. I wasn't busy moneylending or controlling the media during our Reiki session. I suppose he caught a whiff of my signature scent, "Eau de Noodle Kugel." Or else he should be congratulated on his finely tuned Jewdar.

His question stopped me in my tracks. I believe that by calling all Jewish women fat, this guy wasn't referring only to our size or shape, but to our natures. Fat doesn't just signify too many calories or excess flab; it's a symbol of being too large, taking up too much space, making too much noise, and coloring outside the lines. We ask big questions and demand big answers when it comes to social issues, education, relationships. Jewish women have always represented big bodies, big mouths, and big demands. And too often, we feel guilty for having them. So when we see limits put on the size of our minds, the least we can do is try to control our bodies. Today it seems like there's an unwritten eleventh commandment for Jewish women: "Thou shalt not eat."

But no big theories came to me in the hotel room. The flustered explanation I gave to the Reiki guy was, "All Jewish women are so fat because of . . . the Holocaust." Then I flounced out of the room.

When in doubt on a Jewish question, the answer is always the Holocaust. Which film is going to win Best Documentary Short Subject at the Oscars this year? The one about the Holocaust. Why are the Israelis always right? Because of the Holocaust. Why should I eat this entire honey barbecue chicken while standing at the sink? Because of the Holocaust.

The Holocaust is part of a long history of our central thrust for persevering and procreating: They (the rest of the world) are always trying to kill Us (the Jews). It is the inherent responsibility of Jewish women to bear children, so we can repopulate the numbers that have been slashed, burned, gassed, and turned out by Pharaohs, Crusaders, Russians, Spaniards, country clubs, and most recently and quite successfully, Nazis. So every time They try to destroy Us, we have to head to the factory and make more Jews. We're like Doritos: Kill all you want, we'll make more.

In its perverse way, the Holocaust is a solid excuse to get fat. We starved enough in the past to justify a lifetime intravenous supply of Krispy Kremes in the present. Our very survival as a Jewish people depends on us literally filling our female bellies, whether it be with food or fetuses. Go forth, my fellow Jewesses: Be fruitful, eat fruit, and multiply! Just make sure to work it off if you expect to get yourself a man. And then you'd better bounce back after baby.

There's our paradox. Fat girls get life; thin girls get love. But thinness opposes our very Jewish natures. Look at what we nosh, what typifies the Jewish menu: challah, latkes, knishes, bagels, matzoh . . . even manna from heaven was supposed to be some sort of tapioca-style carbohydrate. To be Jewish is to eat carbs. Which makes you wonder, if none of those Jewish staples are on the approved low-carb eating list, is dieting itself anti-Semitic?

I ate dinner with a non-Jewish family once. It was so strange. They put out *just enough* food. A piece of fish for each of us. Half a baked potato for each of us. Served the salad on the dinner plate rather than put it in a bowl. When we were done eating, all the food was gone. Because there was just enough for each. It was a strange meal. No one snacked off the plates as the mom cleared the table (not that there was anything left to eat). She didn't keep picking as she washed the non-dishwasher pieces in the sink. The guests didn't linger in the kitchen, eyeballing leftovers—we all went back into the living room. Crazy, just crazy, I tell ya!

Judaism is a fat religion. Every life event—a wedding, a bar mitzvah, a funeral—requires endless trays of cold cuts and a buttload of babka. What does a Catholic do at the end of her religious service? She eats a wafer. A tasteless little wafer that represents the body of Christ. For hours Catholics have been sitting there in the pews, looking at this skinny guy stretched out on a cross, a role model for slender suffering. What do we do at the end of our religious services? We sit around and eat cake and complain about the lack of spaces in the synagogue parking lot.

We break in our New Year with apples and honey, celebrate Shabbat by eating challah and chicken and drinking wine. We serve chicken fat (*schmaltz* anyone?) as a condiment on the dinner table. Sure, non-Jews worked it so they could suck down fruitcake (that's the best dessert they could come up with?) on Christmas and a little chocolate bunny on Easter, but that's nothing compared to the Jewish calendar, where every holiday is represented by different, fattening, non-Atkins-friendly foods.

Take Hanukkah, when we celebrate the miracle of light. Except this light isn't so "lite"—it's oil, baby. Crank up the deep fryer, because it's latke time! Oh, to think of the glycemic index on those potatoes. We're supposed to be commemorating the ancient miracle of a dollop of oil that lasted for eight days, but so many of us turn that ritual into a dietary science project using a fat-free zucchini/turnip latke recipe that some lady in our Hadassah chapter found on the Internet.

Forget about Passover. First we remove all the *chametz* (or, what I like to think of as carbohydrates) from our cabinets. We stare forlornly at that seder plate, filled with symbolic foods that are supposed to remind us of suffering. This is after we've spent the whole day in the kitchen cooking, waiting for the moment when we can pass on that stark lamb shank bone and bring on the meal! For eight days it's matzoh meal, matzoh brie, matzoh cake, matzoh lasagna, until our colons feel about as dry as the desert we escaped.

The fiercest food offender of all is Yom Kippur, when we fast. We go without food, because eating is fulfilling and pleasurable, and it's time for deprivation and some serious soul payback. We eat a big old meal the night before, starve for a day, and then gorge on bagels, smoked fish, and kugel. No one eats a nice leafy salad after a Yom Kippur fast.

Between Rosh and Yom, it's time to think about all we did wrong over the past year, time to cast away our sins and start over again. How do we represent this? With a ceremony called *Tashlich*. We tear up little pieces of bread to represent our wrongdoings, then toss them into a body of water. Bread = sin! How more Atkins-y can you get? (P.S. How many of you have noshed on a chunk of that Sin Bread on your way down to the nearby pond? C'mon, I won't tell. And you can always toss in a piece of bread for it next year . . .)

ANOTHER element of our cultural fattitude is good old-fashioned genetics. Many Western and European Jews came from parts of the world where you needed a layer of blubber simply to survive a cold, harsh winter—or a stab wound from a Cossack. Before the twentieth century, fat was a sign of success. After all, a little extra something on your bones meant that a) you had money for food; and b) you weren't working as a physical laborer. For the first few generations of Jews who emigrated to America, fat status held strong. A woman was considered desirable if she was plump under those petticoats. "Zaftig," or juicy, wasn't always the veiled insult it is today. It used to be a compliment. Back in the old country, being called zaftig might well have meant you were the Vamp of Vilna.

The look changed in the 1920s and 1930s when the Gibson Girl arrived on the scene. Trust me, there's a reason she wasn't called the Goldstein Girl. This slender, boyish silhouette (a.k.a. The Super Shiksa) came into vogue, and the full-length mirror entered the hallway. Suddenly flab was not so flattering.

By the 1950s, the *balabuste*, or Jewish homemaker, had lost her value—she got tossed out along with her WASPy alter ego, Donna Reed. Eventually not-so-nice Jewish girl Betty Friedan plumb gave up on her traditional role, and we followed. Now, as modern-day, postfeminist multitaskers, we've disposed with the *balabuste*, her endless superstitions, her patience in the kitchen, her attention to housework, and the soft rolls of fat on her body. But we've carried on her ability to over-love. And with it, her natural Jewish female inclination to overfeed.

I miss that *balabuste*. Today's Jewish *bubbe* is no longer called *"Bubbe"*—she's "Grandma Fill-in-First-Name-Here," thank you very much. She's got an SUV, a membership to Curves, and she's doing pretty well on Match.com. While she may no longer live in South Beach, she's definitely doing the South Beach Diet.

Bubbe "ate her kishkes out" with pride; now we "chew our kishkes out" with anxiety. We struggle to balance tradition and evolution; family and individuality; public life and private dreams. Most of all, contemporary women, Jewish and non-Jewish, fight our bodies as they seem to grow beyond their boundaries, bigger and fatter and curvier no matter how much we diet and exercise and suck in and starve.

In the fight against our natural shape, we forget that women are literally built to feed other humans, and for Jewish women, given our history, this role takes on even greater importance. Our bodies create life, develop a handy storage space for a growing fetus, give it birth, and then supply the necessary food for an infant until it grows enough to eat on its own. We confuse fat and pregnancy. We're shocked, simply shocked when our bodies change and evolve, whether or not we have kids or simply age. We proudly churn out the next generation of Rachels and Joshs, but obsess over fitting into a size six suit at their bat and bar miztvahs.

When all else fails, many of us turn to God to ask for thinness. In Overeaters Anonymous, participants declare themselves powerless over food and give up their power to God. In churches across the country, classrooms are transformed into exercise studios while ministers hand over the pulpit to personal trainers on Sunday afternoons. You can set up a Weight Watchers meeting at your local synagogue. If we don't mix church and state, should we really be mixing church and weight?

A top-selling book is *The Maker's Diet*, encouraging us to dine on "the whole, unprocessed, natural foods our Creator always intended us to eat." In "What Would Jesus Eat? The Ultimate Program for Eating Well, Feeling Great, and Living Longer," the plan consists of Jesus' menu according to the Bible, including fruits and vegetables, fish, kosher meat, olive oil, red wine, and lots of water (I assume you don't walk on it, just drink it). *The Prayer Diet: The Unique Physical, Mental, and Spiritual Approach to Healthy Weight Loss* theorizes that neglecting your spiritual side makes you fat—because you use food to compensate for spiritual starvation. I'm still waiting for *The Jewish Diet*—you hire your own personal Jewish mother to sit and cluck and tsk at you, offering to make you broiled skinless chicken breasts every night for dinner.

Still, it's not just Jewish women who struggle with the battle of the body. We like to think we own the whole "food = love" equation, but that's true of many other ethnic groups, too. Ask a Jewish *bubbe* to throw down against an Italian *nonna* or a Greek *yaya*, and you'll see a major food fight. All of us mark life's big moments—good and bad—with dozens of bagels and Tupperware to take home. We show our families how much we care by tenderly packing tender bag lunches and making them nine-course dinners—or at least ordering in a couple of times a week. We show our community how important our loved ones are to us by throwing lavish weddings and bar mitzvahs where we measure love with hors d'oeuvres by the pound and Viennese dessert tables by the foot.

When we're not feeding others, we're often feeding ourselves. Feeding our joy, our anger, our guilt, our anxiety, our boredom. Trying to replace the dissatisfied space in our heads by filling the empty space in our bellies. It's a very faulty system.

Every day is an opportunity for us to get fatter. Still, everyone we know, fat or thin, is always pushing, pushing for us to lose weight. Sometimes they say it out loud, sometimes they just use those judgmental Jewish eyes, but they all think they have a good reason for it:

Your mother: "God forbid you should have to suffer what I went through with my body."

Your grandmother: "People died so you could not eat this food."

Your father: "How are you ever going to find a nice Jewish husband with that body?"

Your boyfriend: "What are my friends going to think if you look like that?"

Your husband: "How come you look so different than you did at our wedding?"

Your children: "Mom, if you die, how are we going to live?"

Your doctor: "You're going to die."

Your friends: "We're suffering on diets, why shouldn't you?"

Your government: "Obesity is worse than terrorism, an epidemic worse than AIDS."

Dr. Phil: "If you really loved your children, you'd lose the weight."

Oprah: "I'm very happy working out two and a half hours a day."

Big business: "Our food is labeled 'guilt-free'—just for Jews!"

Pass the pastrami.

But don't you dare order that pastrimi sandwich with cheese on it! Our Jewish identity comes complete with biblical dietary laws in the form of kashrut. Keeping kosher might have made perfect sense six thousand years ago, but today it mainly serves as the impetus for intense Big Mac attacks.

You know how to keep kosher: Don't mix milk and meat. Only eat food with a special rabbinical seal of approval on it. Buy an extra set of dishes—not a bad deal for your inner Jewish American Princess. Still, there are ways to cheat—sort of. For example, here's what might be on the menu tonight: a spinach salad covered with Bac-Os (Jews love that fake bacon!), a strip steak marinated in Soy Vey (a staple in every Jewish home), and a nondairy cake baked with hydrogenated oil, topped with a frozen mystery dessert called Tofutti, and Sanka (or Maxwell House, since they do give us those lovely Passover Haggadahs) with non-dairy creamer served on the side. We get to enjoy nonkosher foods and obey God's laws at the same time. But is skirting around the rules what the Big

Kahuna had in mind? Kosher eating runs an ancient parallel to our current dieting dismay, where we engineer fake foods our bodies crave to take the place of the real ones that our bodies need. After all, even reduced-fat Oreos are kosher—and hardly found in nature.

Those who toss the joys of kashrut out of the pantry can enjoy the magic of *treyf*—the foods that are on the kosher "don't" list, like pork and shellfish. Don't forget that it's a Jewish tradition on Christmas to head to the nearest Chinese restaurant for a dinner of wontons and spare ribs before seeing the latest Ben Stiller (only half a Jew, and on the wrong side) holiday movie. The fact that those foods are forbidden just makes us want them more—and makes them taste even more delicious.

We're given subtle messages about forbidden foods and dieting even in our initial forays into our Jewish education.

The first woman we meet in the Bible took a big bite out of life, and we've been paying for it ever since. Remember Genesis? God says to Adam and Eve, "Go ahead, eat whatever you want in this Garden. Just stay away from that one tree over there. I know the fruit hanging from it is attractive, and, oh boy, it's good stuff, but DON'T EAT IT."

It's History's First Diet. Like most diets, I bet ya it started on a Monday.

It's also our initial introduction to the power of deprivation. What makes you want to eat something more than being told not to eat it?

You know the rest of the story: Eve goes ahead and takes a bite of the apple, and the whole world falls apart. An apple. It wasn't even a luscious, wild treat, like tiramisu or really gooey nachos. But that was the game God was playing with us. We eat; so we feel shame. We have to cover up our bodies. No more Paradise; it's Pilates time.

The twist is that the apple wasn't just an apple—the apple was Knowledge. So Eve wasn't punished for eating a fruity snack, but for having curiosity. She hungered not only for food, but for information about good and evil. From that day on, Jewish women have been chastised for pushing past the boundaries, for wanting more than our share, for speaking up and out and over. We pay a price not only for our big asses, but for our big mouths.

That apple keeps showing up, and it keeps getting us in trouble. Sure, it represents the sweetness of the New Year (Rosh Hashanah); the power of the Torah (Simchat Torah); the world's Jewish headquarters, New York, is the Big Apple; and we all know an apple a day will stave off a doctor's visit (where he or she will inevitably tell us to drop a few). But an apple usually means trouble. An "apple" body is worse than a "pear" body. Snow White takes a big bite out of an apple—and look what happens to her. She's poisoned and dropped in a coffin, where she has to wait for Prince Charming to show up and recognize her as his True Love. Isn't that what we're hoping our Prince Charmings will do—look past the limitations of our bodies to see the real Us, the real women under the fat and the stretch marks, understand our hearts and brains and give us a break on our bodies?

I'm so grateful to Eve for digging in. Of course it might be nice to live in blissful ignorance, but aren't you glad to have Knowledge? She introduced us to emotions, to complications, to music, to literature, to taste. We give apples to teachers to signify that Knowledge. The fruit from a tree is also symbolic of the fruit from our wombs, representing our future. That apple is preceded by a blossom, a flower. Isn't knowing—even if it ain't so pretty—so much more interesting and valuable than staying in the beautiful but invisible dark?

No matter how far we've come as women, or how evolved we feel, on some level we're still just nice Jewish girls striving so hard to be good. In traditional terms, goodness means beautiful, obedient, hard-working, and family-making, exactly what our husbands, parents, and communities expect from us. But in our own expectations, it now also means thin. The pressure to keep our big mouths shut is immense, it makes us feel guilty too often, and we need to get over it.

I don't think eating is such a bad thing. I think it's hunger. I think it's appetite. I think it's the same instinct that led Eve to take a bite out of that apple. But we're told that appetite is evil, and we know Jewish girls have appetites. Edible appetite, laughter appetite, sexual appetite. Monica Lewinsky–sized, why-shouldn't-I-shtup-the-President? appetite. We want, we demand, we should go for it. Why not? We deserve it. I am grateful for my thirst for knowledge, my worldly dreams, my big appetite, and yes, even my big mouth. And I have stopped feeling guilty about having them.

Why should we regret for a moment the action of our mouths, possibly the most important parts of our bodies? We use our mouths not only to eat, but to speak, to kiss, to show intimacy. We forget that our female forms are built with two mouths and two sets of lips, echoing each other up front and center, and down below and center. Our mouths are where the action is.

Esther used hers to speak out and save a nation; Deborah used hers to pass solid judgments; Sarah used hers to talk to God and pray for children, the future of Israel. And do you even know—or care—what size clothes she wore?

The Jewish women who rock history, those who become our role models, are remembered for their remarkable words, not their physiques. Can you picture Golda Meir drinking Slim-Fast during lunch at the Knesset? Gertrude Stein writing a poem about the lure of phen-fen? Madeleine Albright missing a Cabinet meeting because she had a session with her personal trainer?

Our collective weight has become more than a survival tactic. It is a revolution, a sign of Jewish women taking up space and growing outside the lines, sending a complex message that we don't want to sit on one side of the room, we don't want to be held back, we don't want to be nice and good and proper anymore. We must open up as big and wide as we can, and the world will just have to deal with it.

Once we accept our big mouths, Jewish women will start to understand that it's okay to take more than our share, whether it's food on the table or physical area in a room. What seems like a private matter—our size—is a part of a larger issue, a message spreading with our Jewish female bodies as we grow. A sign that reads, "There Is Room."

There is room for you. There is room for your ideas and opinions. There is room for you on the bimah. There is room for you at the Wailing Wall. There is room for many of us in the boardroom, and at least one of us in the White House. There is room for your body, there is room for your mind. There is room to grow.

I will make room for your big Jewish ass anywhere it cares to roam.

And that's why all Jewish women, thick, thin, and in between, are so, so fat.

Holidazed and Confused

*

SHERYL ZOHN

BABY Jesus lay faceup on the side of the road, sleeping on an island of wet leaves in the gutter. The Christian Savior had been blown out of the arms of his plastic parents and away from his holiday crèche by strong winds the night before. He looked so peaceful. I wanted to run over him with my mom's station wagon.

You see, by the age of seventeen, I was furious that Christmas had given me a bad case of guilt every single year of my life. And no, I am *not* referring to any kind of pre–Vatican II idea of Jewish guilt relating to Jesus's death. (Even a week trapped in a sensory deprivation tank with Mel Gibson couldn't make me feel that.) I'm talking about a constant feeling of unease; that somehow I had to either enjoy something forbidden, or else risk being completely left out.

Growing up as one of the few Jews in a suburb of Washington, D.C., meant most major religious holidays were awkward for me. It's not that there weren't plenty of Jews living near the nation's capital; it's just that most of them lived on the other side of the Potomac River from us. Somehow, my parents had decided to settle in Virginia, which in addition to being Jew-deficient is also culturally close enough to the South for the non-Jews to observe their holidays zealously. And publicly. Which really wouldn't have been a problem, if it weren't for the fact that their holidays always seemed so darn fun.

Take Easter, for example. Based on information gathered from my elementary school classmates, I concluded that this important Christian holiday was meant to be a meditation on death, rebirth, and high sugar intake. And while the death and rebirth stuff seemed like a drag, the sugar part was something I could get into. The fact that the candy was delivered by an adorable bunny only made Easter more irresistible. In my young mind, munching on chocolate eggs and petting a furry little rabbit while talking to a man nailed to a cross seemed like a wonderful way to spend a Sunday—and this bothered me. After all, I was Jewish. By all rights, supernatural pets and sons of God should have been abhorrent to me. So I hid my Easter lust in shame, and avoided Peeps marshmallow chicks as if they were concocted from radioactive waste.

Meanwhile, Jewish holidays were also fraught with anxiety-producing opportunities. For instance, one Passover my mother decided that her usual custom of locking the *chametz* up in the basement closet would simply not do. Instead, she enlisted my older brother Mark and me to wheel our half-eaten boxes of cereal and three-year-old bags of flour up the street to our Catholic neighbors' house. I'm still not sure if this was due to a sudden religious fervor on my mom's part, or if it was just a sneaky way for her to pry her children out of the TV set's warm embrace and force them to get some exercise. At any rate, my brother and I complied with her request, and left the basket and its high-carb contents under the watchful eye of our neighbor and her suspicious young son Jimmy.

Fast-forward to the end of Passover, and much to our dismay, Mom turned off our fifth *Andy Griffith* rerun and told us we needed to retrieve our bready foodstuffs. This time, as Mark and I began to roll our *chametz* cart back down the hill, Jimmy became indignant, and accused us of being "Indian givers." Although I sensed this was supposed to be an insult, I had no idea what it meant. Sure, my parents were "givers"— they donated to Federation every year. And I had heard of Jews referring to themselves as "Members of the Tribe," but I was pretty sure that did not mean we were Native Americans. Still, Jimmy's accusation left a bad taste in my matzoh-coated mouth.

Being a Jewish student in the Virginia public school system also made me a reluctant participant in the annual "Explaining To My Teacher/ Coach/Bus Driver Why I Will Need To Be Excused From My Math Class/Band Practice/Bus Ride In Order To Observe The Hebraic Holy Days." While school authorities were mostly understanding, Paul, the head of the trumpet section in my high school marching band, was less so. Paul was certain that my absence from the trumpet section was the only reason our Dionne Warwick medley/marching extravaganza fell from number one in the AAA class to number two.

Without a doubt, however, the most trying time to be Jewish in Virginia is that endless period between Thanksgiving and New Year's, when the joys of Christmas seem to be everywhere. It all started in kindergarten with those holiday-symbol-shaped butter cookies the other kids brought to school. Long before I even knew what a calorie was, let alone how to calculate the inches it would add to my hips, I sensed that I should feel bad about eating anything in the shape of a Christmas tree. After all, we didn't have a Christmas tree at home, but now I was putting one in my stomach—complete with green sprinkles—and that cookie was delicious. It was almost as if I were ingesting Christmas itself. Gingerbread men were no less problematic. Sure, they weren't technically Christian symbols, but I knew that when they weren't being eaten, they were being hung on Christmas trees, right next to the three wise men. So I'd ease my guilt by maiming the gingerbread people as I ate them, tearing off their legs and biting off their candy button eyes. They were yummy, but they suffered.

As a little girl who was quite naive about the ways of fashion, I also experienced extreme Christmas clothes envy. Why couldn't I wear socks with little reindeer running up the ankles? Or one of those heavy knit sweaters with an adorable elf on the front? Or a pair of panties with Santa Claus all over them? My mother wisely discouraged this particular sartorial interest, pointing out that as Jews we didn't wear symbols of the Christian holiday—especially if they combined a bearded old man and her daughter's underpants. Instead, Mom tried to entice me with a pair of blue-and-white dreidel gloves. Feeling resentful, I turned her down. It was Santa on my panties or no dice.

Fortunately, in first grade I got my first taste of Christmas revenge. One day in early December, our teacher made an announcement to the class: "Today, we are going to write letters to Santa and mail them to the North Pole."

The other kids excitedly began pulling out construction paper and crayons. I, however, was perturbed by our assignment—not just because we could barely write our names, let alone a foreign mailing address—but because our teacher had proposed corresponding with a man my parents had told me was fictional.

I waved my hand in the air. "Excuse me, Mrs. Simons . . ."

Mrs. Simons clearly sensed trouble ahead. She answered, "Shhhh. We are all writing our letters quietly."

"But Mrs. Simons, I'm Jewish."

"Well, you can still write a letter to Santa. You want presents, don't you?"

"But my parents say there's no such thing as Santa Claus."

Suddenly, twenty small heads perked up.

"Fine, Sheryl. You can just write a letter to your parents. Everyone else, back to work."

Across the room, Brent's hand shot up into the air. "But Mrs. Simons," Brent protested, "if there's no such thing as Santa Claus, who eats the cookies I leave out on Christmas Eve?"

Two seats away from me, Elizabeth furrowed her brow and asked, "Can I just write to my parents, too?" Mrs. Simons suddenly had a code red emergency on her hands.

"Class, that's enough. Finish your letters, and no talking."

But the genie was out of the bottle. My classmates kept furtively comparing their "Santa request lists" to my "parent request list," which looked remarkably similar. There was no doubt I had planted the idea of Santa's nonexistence in their minds. To this day, they are probably cursing me repeatedly to their therapists—a thought that brings me some real Christmas cheer.

Then there was the issue of Christmas presents. Throughout elementary school, teachers, classmates, and total strangers were constantly asking me the supposedly innocent question, "What do *you* want for Christmas?" The various checkout girls, hairdressers, and flight attendants had no idea what a weighted inquiry this was. Sometimes, I tried to explain that my family didn't celebrate Christmas, which left the questioner feeling either embarrassed or puzzled. Other times, I just gave an answer, pretending that we were like all the other families in town, enjoying our delightful dead Messiah–based holiday.

Unfortunately, when I got specific with my answers, I probably caused even more confusion. You see, for my parents Hanukkah was not a big gift-giving holiday. They always gave us sweets, money, and useful things. Most folks probably thought I was pulling their leg when I said Santa would bring me eight pairs of socks, eight bags of chocolate coins, a box of dripless candles, and—if I were very lucky—a graphing calculator.

And there was *no* way I could ever explain the "imaginary presents" I usually started to receive around the fifth night of Hanukkah, when Mom ran out of steam. We would light the candles, and then she would announce, "Tonight's present is from your Great-aunt Esther."

"But I don't see any present," I'd protest, scanning the table again in case I had missed something.

"Take it up with Esther," my mother would answer with a grin.

Eventually, I got the joke, even if I didn't like it. But I was pretty sure my Christian neighbors would just think it was weird.

The worst holiday moments for me were the first bus rides back to school after the holiday break, when everyone compared notes on presents. One January, Christine—the most popular girl in sixth grade—had received the ultimate cool toy for that year: a Rubik's Cube. I envied her as she twisted and turned the colorful plastic puzzle (though I must point out that she never actually solved it). I begged her to give me a turn, but Christine ignored me. Finally, in frustration I cried out, "Oh yeah? Well, you can't use my graphing calculator!" I sure showed her.

Even my friend the television set turned on me. As a TV-obsessed kid, I was always tempted by those amazing Christmas specials. Every year, I would watch Charlie Brown decorate his pathetic little Christmas tree, and Rudolph use his nasal condition to help the other reindeer. I was absolutely transfixed by the residents of Whoville, even if none of them were little Jewish girls. One year, as an experiment, I tried rooting for the Grinch. But even that cranky green bastard learns to love Christmas at the end. I didn't stand a chance.

Then, there were those "very special holiday episodes" of my favorite sitcoms. You know the type: One of the characters starts out feeling cranky about the holidays, but then gets tricked into dressing up as Santa Claus, decides to take in a homeless man, and ends up snowed in with his family, only to discover the true meaning of Christmas. It seems so comforting. And get this: That "true meaning" always involves a family meal where—unlike in certain families that shall remain nameless—the mom doesn't passive-aggressively criticize everyone's eating habits, the brother doesn't silently resent the dad's disapproval of his science fiction hobby, and the dad doesn't lecture everyone on why a second Holocaust is just around the corner.

When I finally reached junior high, the shopping mall had become my Christmas guilt breeding ground. Even though my friends and I spent every other weekend at the mall between January and November, once those wreaths, red ribbons, and candy canes covered every inch of the place, I felt like I needed a passport to enter. But did that keep me away? Oh no. I mean, if the mall insisted that I save thirty percent on that cute pair of red suede sneakers I'd wanted for months, who was I to stop them?

The mall also featured wall-to-wall Christmas music. Now Christmas has inspired some fantastic songs, but for me, along with the hummable tunes and memorable lyrics come weightier issues. I first noticed the problem in seventh grade, when I had to sing in the school choir's annual holiday concert.

Of course, everyone knew what "holiday" really meant. To balance out the endless renditions of "Silent Night" and "Drummer Boy," our music teacher would always stick in the obligatory Hanukkah song. But inevitably she would choose something crappy like "I Have a Little Dreidel." All the other kids would complain. My only consolation was that the Kwanzaa song sucked even more.

In high school, I solved the school choir problem by prematurely ending my singing career and joining the aforementioned trumpet section of the band. If I concentrated hard enough, I could pretend the instrumental music was about anything I wanted it to be about. To this day, when I hear "Sleigh Ride," I have vivid mental pictures of the Jamaican bobsledding team.

By college, my biggest Christmas temptation was eggnog. That spicy dairy treat was so delicious I could down an entire quart-sized carton in one sitting. Several years later, Starbucks managed to turn eggnog into a latte flavor sold only during the holidays. I love the eggnog latte, but I always shudder when the baristas loudly repeat my order for the entire world to hear. They might as well be announcing, "Venti half-caf Blood of Christ for the Jew."

After I finished college, I knew I needed to find a more permanent solution to my annual holiday dilemmas. That's why I decided to move to someplace much more Jewish: Los Angeles. Or as I like to call it, the Land of Soy Milk and Organic Honey. I was convinced that by surrounding myself with Jews—albeit very tan Jews, many of whom have had extensive plastic surgery—I would never again have an awkward holiday experience.

But I was still wary, since years of Christmas celebrations in Virginia had left me scarred. As I stepped off the airplane and into LAX airport shortly after Thanksgiving, I cringed, expecting the worst. Would there be "Rudolph the Red Nosed Reindeer" Muzak playing in the terminal? Airport security personnel dressed in red fuzzy elf hats? An entire plastic Jesus family hanging out with their goats at Gate 16A?

Lo and behold, the airport looked normal—crowded, dirty, and completely wreath-free. I wasn't in Virginia anymore. Encouraged, I headed to a nearby shopping mall, where there was nary an elf in sight. This was simply incredible. As it got closer and closer to December twenty-fifth, I noticed that even the few houses with Christmas lights didn't seem to turn them on. Sure, California was in the middle of an energy crisis. But who cared? Clearly in this part of the world, Christmas was not the powerful force it was back in Virginia. It looked like I had finally gotten rid of my holiday guilt once and for all.

Nine months later, the High Holidays rolled around. I was working on a TV show where the executive producer was Jewish, the writer was Jewish, the editor was Jewish, the accountant was Jewish—I think even the office intern was Jewish. Rosh Hashanah fell on a Tuesday that year, and I thought surely this would be my easiest explanation of "Why I Will Need To Be Excused From Work In Order To Observe The Hebraic Holy Days" ever.

But then something strange happened: None of the other Jews asked for the day off. Even odder, they actually couldn't believe I would take the day off myself—as they kept reminding me.

It seemed that by moving to Los Angeles, all I had done was trade in one source of holiday guilt for another. Which made me realize—if I can't please everyone during the holidays, maybe I should just try to please myself. In fact, I think I'll start now. So where are those small Christian children? I want to tell them Santa doesn't exist.

Shtreimel Envy

*

PEARL GLUCK

I have shtreimel envy. Those voluptuous fur hats that Hasidic men earn just for getting married have held a certain fascination for me my whole life. Just by perching those thirteen tails that make up a perfect circle of fur atop their heads, Hasidic men become part of a two-hundred-year-old tradition and gain an intimate connection with the world of our grandparents.

How could I not envy them their shtreimels? As a woman in the Hasidic world, there's no equilvalent for me, and now that I've left the fold, I've forsaken my only chance to even get near one legitimately by marrying a Hasidic man. So instead, I covet. I've replaced traditional Jewish guilt with green envy.

In the meantime, I appease my longing for the world I've left behind by wearing the rest of the Hasidic male outfit (the three-quarter-length black jackets, the black pants, the loafers). I guess my clothing could easily be seen as an abomination analogous to the way I treat my Hasidic heritage, but I don't see it that way. Why can't I turn the patriarchal clothes and role of the rebbe, the leader of the Hasidic communities, into my own adapted form of matriarchy? In some way, what I wear symbolizes my struggle. I live between two worlds, and constantly try to find the place I can be true to myself and true to my heritage. I am as much an artist and filmmaker who is inspired by feminism and modernity as I am the daughter of a Hasidic Jew who is utterly bewildered by the life his only daughter leads.

On this particular spring morning, out of respect, I wear a long skirt and keep my blouse buttoned above the collarbone. I am sitting in the back of a bus filled with Hasidic men, including my father, speeding over the highways of Eastern and Central Europe in search of rebbes' graves. We are on a pilgrimage to find the gravesites of the founding fathers of Hasidism.

Hasidism was born out of the need for a passionate approach to Judaism, one that wasn't entirely based on scholarship and study. Hasidim are known for accepting singing and dancing as a form of prayer. In its early years, some Hasidic rebbes disappeared into the woods for days to show their devotion through contemplation and respect for nature. Two hundred years later, Hasidim are considered the "old school" of Ultraorthodox Jews, known for their fundamental observance of Jewish law. They are divided into sects, and each one is based on the town from the *alte heym*, the "old home" of their founder, the rebbe. The sect I grew up in stems from Satmar, hails from a town in Transylvania. Three generations later, long after the Holocaust drove so many of our families to America, pilgrims still return to visit the remnants of what their grandparents left behind.

How I came to be on the back of this bus is a study in compromise. The deal was that I would be welcome to join on this pilgrimage, to fulfill my undisputed passion for the rebbes and visit the graves of my folk heroes, but only if I took the goal of prayer more seriously and asked for a husband at the rebbes' graves. I agreed to forgo my usual lifestyle of trousers and late-night bars, and my father agreed to bend the rules and let me come along.

I feel a little like a Jewish Rosa Parks as we swerve along the highway. The women (well, both of us) have been allotted the back row of seats on the bus as we are not allowed to mix with the men. I expected this, but what I did not plan for is that the food would be stored in the front of the bus. We have to wait to be offered sustenance before we can eat, lest we shamefully mix with the men and defy the deliberate segregation.

Our tour guide, Shimon Feld, announces in Yiddish that we will need to include prayers for the children who have left the Hasidic world. "They are slippery souls and fall from the nicest homes," he says over the bus microphone as we continue north. Back in Brooklyn, where he (and everyone else on the bus) lives, his job is to take care of the boys who slip from Orthodoxy, while his wife takes care of the girls.

"Their mothers have wet pillows because they cry from having lost their kids—we must pray for them at this next grave," Feld says, pulling out the list so we know these kids by name. "Please add these names to your *kvitlekh*." Like the little slips of paper tucked into the stones at the Western Wall, we are to write the names down and tuck the *kvitl* under a rock at the graves of our forefathers as a means of requesting a special word with God.

Out the window, the tree trunks along the highway are painted white, and they flash as they catch the headlights of our bus. The cemeteries stream by like toothless grins, some aged with a few stones still standing, others rotted with barely a trace of the lives that were once buried and remembered there. We are now in Romania, and I wonder if my name is on a *kvitl* tucked into a rebbe's grave. At least I know my mother isn't crying in her pillow for me—she's a ballroom dancer already deeply intermingled with the outside word since her divorce from my father twenty years ago. With her Sophia Loren eyes and her Cyd Charisse legs, her story is a novel unwritten. My father, the parent who is more likely to cry over the state of my unmarried, pants-wearing soul, is sitting in the front of the bus near the driver drinking a nice glass of kosher slivovitz.

My father has brought me on this trip because he sees me as one of those "slippery souls." While sometimes I try it tries to find my way back, but it's never quite in the way he hopes for—namely, giving up my current lifestyle and coming back into the fold. Still, I have always been devoted to the legacy and intricacies of the rabbinic families of the Hasidic world. If I had been a boy this obsession would have been embraced, though I doubt it would have affected my decision to leave the kingdom of Borough Park, Brooklyn. As a girl it was met with an amused curiosity. As it is, the legacy of the rebbes and my fascination with them remains a glimmering, delicate thread by which I am still connected to my father.

IN our Hasidic world, we avoided all deliberate contact with American pop culture. We were considered the "insiders," and everyone else was "outsiders." Although I was born in the '70s in New York City, as a child, I had no idea who John Lennon was, nor my accidental namesake Janis Joplin, who also went by Pearl. In Borough Park, we had other superstars. Instead of Peter Pan and Cinderella, my fairy tales were about the Ba'al Shem Tov, the founding father of Hasidism and the first Hasidic rebbe. He was the rebbe who who created magic, found love, cured diseases, and celebrated good deeds by the common man with miracles.

As a girl I went to school with gusto. I was devout. I believed in the Torah wholeheartedly. I even believed that our very own rebbe was as holy a man as the Ba'al Shem Tov and that he could perform miracles and grant blessings in the name of God. What's more, because we were related to a rebbe, I believed that our family was special, sacred, part of the inner circle. I felt deep pity for those in the outside world who didn't have the benefits of the spiritual elite I was born into. Hasidim are royalty. We have the official clothes, customs, cuisine, and lineage. We were the chosen of the chosen people.

Until I was ten, I prayed every morning, and stood the longest during the *shemoneh ésreh*, a series of blessings thanking God for making us who we are, even if we're not perfect and can still use divine guidance. My fantasy was to marry a Torah scholar and have ten kids. I had it all figured out. As soon as I was done with high school, I would get started.

How was I to know that one day I would turn fifteen, try on my school uniform in the seamstress's basement, and the room would start to spin? The basement suddenly turned into a trap, the uniform followed suit, and there I was stuck in a basement in Brooklyn. I wanted out. I could no longer believe that all people who weren't Jewish, all the people I saw eating *treyf*, all the women wearing pants, and couples walking hand in hand were heathens. I became uncomfortable with the idea that all of the rules of my daily life were God-given: the color of my stockings, my hemline, the type of texts I was allowed to read. The "outside world," as we called it, couldn't possibly just be a conglomerate of peripheral garbage. There had to be some redeeming qualities.

From that day on, I had a dirty little secret. I began to think about life on the outside. I'd make up stories and create fantasies of having my own apartment, going to a place called college, and discovering a world I wasn't sure existed.

By ninth grade, I was sneaking into the principal's office to find the science textbooks before the school ripped out the chapters named Reproduction and Evolution. The information was astounding, a sacrilege. Unsatiated, I went to the library wondering what else I wasn't being taught. I read *Our Bodies, Ourselves*, someone named Darwin, and the ever-popular *Sweet Valley High*.

I cut school and escaped to the movies. I went from *Ferris Bueller's Day Off* to the sizzling on-screen romance of *Rocky II*. The Torah scholar of my childhood dreams dissipated into the fine ether of Sylvester Stallone. But when I saw Barbra Streisand in *The Way We Were*, I finally saw a glimmer of myself. Like Barbra, I wanted to be out there changing the world. But college wasn't approved of for girls. And I was only fifteen.

The world beyond my street gently expanded. I found a companion on my slippery decline, a friend who also had unanswered questions. One of us heard of a basketball game at a mixed school gym in Flatbush. Mixed! Boys and girls together! Hallelujah! We had to go. As far as we knew, the "outside world" was squeezed into stretch jeans and painted in bordello-red lipstick, and since we had neither of those two on hand for the evening, we had lots of preparation to do. I was in charge of the makeup and jewelry, she would take care of the denim jackets and miniskirts (we didn't have the chutzpah to go as far as wearing the forbidden pants).

That night, we got on the B11 bus out of Borough Park heading to Flatbush. We were a mix between Superman in the phone booth and Wonder Woman with her twirly magic, as we transformed ourselves at the back of the bus from our demure blue school uniforms into little Joyce Leslie harlots.

The bus pulled up to the school. We walked into the gym, done up like Cyndi Lauper and found, to our shock, that we were totally inappropriate. The boys and girls at the gym stared at us in their frumpy sweatsuits. Their ordinariness was sudden and horrifying. We spun on our pumpy heels and left the room with only a trace of our cheap perfume and exposed legs left behind. In that instant, the "outside world" lost its glamour and mystery and gained a whole new terrible reputation of disappointment. We knew for sure that we'd never really know it, nor would we ever fit in.

That was the year my parents divorced. I moved out of Borough Park with my mother; my three brothers remained Hasidic and stayed with my father. I transferred to a liberal Jewish school, a school my father would never approve of. Though the school was Orthodox, it was miles—if not movements—away from the life he had hoped I would create for myself and my unborn kids. It was the first of many disappointments for my father. I began what would become a litany of betrayals.

I didn't turn into Barbra Streisand, but I did manage to go to college and turn into the heathen of my father's worst nightmare. My intentions were pure. I even went to Brandeis, the mecca of Jewish universities. But Brandeis may as well have been Christ College to my dad as my exposure to secular poison took full blossom. I imagined my pursuit of education to be a comfortable fit into the Talmudic tradition of study. On the other hand, as a woman who wore sleeveless shirts, joined a feminist collective, and chose to write a full-blown thesis on autoeroticism in women's texts, I was also turning that tradition inside out.

During my second year of college, my phone rang. It was my father. He wondered if I was okay, and wouldn't it be nice to get back in touch. There could be nothing nicer, I thought, and relished the idea of a rediscovered relationship. The conversations continued periodically and included topics such as religious devotion, updates on the rebbes, and queries into when I was going to get serious about getting married. I was eighteen years old.

After I graduated, we celebrated in Brooklyn over a fancy kosher fish meal. The fact that I *still* wasn't married at twenty-two hovered over the cooked carrots, the flaky pastry of dessert, and the long good-bye before my blemished soul and I finally got into a cab to Manhattan.

In my adult life, I'm still considered safe within the conventional bounds of being deemed a "good Jewish girl." I'm not intermarried, not converted, not tattooed, and not pierced below or between my ears. But I am no longer the kind of "good" that grows in Borough Park. When I'm around my father's table, all goes well until my four-year-old niece asks me if I'm married yet, and then my ninety-year-old great-aunt recites the Hungarian poem about building castles in the sky instead of walking on earth. They are implying, not so subtly, that my life as a filmmaker is a waste of time and that I am ignoring all the obligations to which I should be bound—such as moving back to Borough Park and raising a family within the community. But instead of defending my choices, I slide back into the quagmire of my self-imposed exile and have another slice of kugel.

I'm sandwiched between the two worlds. Just because I strayed from one world and could never live in it again doesn't mean I feel its presence any less. Even at moments when I am surrounded by Bulgarian sailors at a late-night joint, the little Hasidic rebbe inside of me seems to pop out and sit staring at me across the bar. Or, when I'm eating, he perches himself *on* my table to watch me enjoy my Cajun shrimp. The world of sin I've created bubbles just outside the boundaries of my old neighborhood like a volcano. I am not married, not Orthodox, not with child, and not living in Brooklyn. I am not "good."

Why have I given up a life of Hasidic bliss and domesticity? The crisp white tablecloths for the Sabbath, the ease with which one knows one's life trajectory like one foot in front of the other, the clarity of faith and belief, the comfort of belonging. My great-aunt would say I've turned into the Hungarian poem's dreamer—secular, and overeducated. I would say I'm more like Lot's wife, turning back to the world I come from, but refusing to turn into a pillar of salt. I insist on finding a footbridge that connects both worlds.

Because the truth is, I am still connected: I collect the rebbe cards, baseball cards filled with facts about the sages, like the best of the boys do. I know what each of the rebbes is known for, and I can tell most of their stories. I teach in Jewish schools. I make documentary films that include the teachings of my rebbes. In Pirkeh Arot, it is written *"Godol hamaaseh yoseh min ha'oseh"*—the person who causes someone to do good is greater than the one who performs the deed himself. I teach this lesson. That's my defense, and I cling to it like a rope keeping me from slipping entirely into the abyss. The defense works for a while, until my father says that I should practice what I preach and *act* like a Hasidic rebbe, not just dress like one!

I tried many a spiritual placebo prior to this trip. I sat in a circle around the bonfire and threw blackened sesame seeds into the mouth of Buddha, hit pillows with tennis rackets to revive pre-nascent anger, and took vows of silence for three whole days to get in touch with the joy of an inner child. But the little Hasidic rebbe inside would never seem to join me at these events. Even my slippery soul is too Jewish.

When the idea for this pilgrimage came up, this trip to the rebbe's graves, I could feel the delicate, knotted thread of connection to my Hasidism and my father pulling. Though I was meant to pray for a husband, I approached it as perhaps the only opportunity I'd have in my life to make both my father and myself happy simultaneously.

And so here I sit, in the back of the bus, and much to my surprise it is a refuge. I can sing (though only quietly) with my companions, I can finish (though only to myself) some of the stories the leader begins on the microphone. Here among the pilgrims, more than anywhere else, I am at home.

On the brink of the sixth day, at four in the morning, we arrive at the grave site of the holy Ba'al Shem Tov, the hero of so many of my childhood stories. A makeshift market emerges out of nowhere, and there it is. Sitting among the mamushka dolls, Ukrainian wooden puppets, and vodka flasks is a shtreimel: The proper hat, the married man's chapeau, the hat my husband would have worn if I'd followed my intended path. Here, on the soil of the founder's grave, I can finally live out my wildest dreams of Hasidic devotion on my own terms. I pay the woman and take the rabbit fur in my own hands.

We pile back on the bus and I take my seat in the back, holding my shtreimel. Somewhere deep inside the underbelly of the bus, with the muffler and the spare tire, is reality. This trip will not bring me a husband, nor will it cause my father to finally give me his approval. It might, however, bring the two worlds I will always be living between—my father's and my own—one step closer. And that, for now, would have to be enough.

As I get off the bus one last time to board the plane back home, Shimon Feld says to me, "May you get what you prayed for." And I reply, "Amen."

Quitting Guilt

*

SUSAN SHAPIRO

'VE spent the last two years saying no.

I have declined invitations for breakfast, brunch, lunch, dinner, drinks, and coffee dates. I vetoed anniversary soirees, charity benefits, graduations, consecrations, and the bar and bat mitzvahs of my friends' children. I steered clear of kiddie birthday parties for my nieces, nephews, and cousins. I turned down assignments from clients I used to chase, rejected free business trips I was offered, and refused to read manuscripts that aspiring scribes sent me unsolicited. I chose not to join my in-laws for Thanksgiving dinner or Passover seders, or to break fast on Yom Kippur. I ended a writing workshop with twenty-five members where I'd been the literary den mother for almost two decades. Additionally I said goodbye to the guilt that goes along with giving up roles one has outgrown.

In that same time frame, I also nixed a twenty-seven-year two-pack-a-day cigarette habit, quit alcohol, dope, gum, and bread—and dropped seventeen pounds. I sold three nonfiction books, enhanced my second career as a writing teacher, greatly increased my income, made my first real estate investment, and fell madly in love with my husband, Aaron, again.

Was there a correlation between RSVPing "Sorry I will not attend" to the daily requests of my relatives, pals, protégés, and playmates to getting exactly what I wanted? You betcha. In fact, I accomplished such major feats only because I stopped pleasing others. Instead—horror of horrors for a nice Jewish girl who grew up in my milieu—I was taking care of myself first.

I pulled the plug on my modern martyrdom in October 2001, when I started addiction therapy to stop smoking. Dr. Winters slowly weaned me from cigarettes, then insisted I give up several other self-destructive substances, analyzing the secrets behind my bad habits. He showed me how my impatient need to cut corners and soothe myself with substances to avoid pain had actually been causing more pain—by keeping me from getting everything that I wanted. Instead of smoking, toking, drinking, and eating away my discomfort, he taught me how to suffer better, allowing bad feelings to unravel and tell their own stories.

Kicking long-term crutches necessitated extreme measures. Everything landed in two categories: You were either part of the problem or part of the solution. I was ruthless. As a recovering addict, I also needed to recover from nice-Jewish-girl-itis. I had to become less nice to stay sober, spice up my marriage, and make it in the Manhattan literary scene. Especially since for six years I had tried and failed to sell a book. During this period, while smoking and drinking, I wasn't fulfilled in love or work. Instead I was constantly fixing up singles, busy hosting the workshop, and running a reading series, helping an amazing number of fellow writers get published. I finally focused inward, stopped assisting everyone else, and harvested my hours to get what I wanted.

I was lucky to be able to simultaneously spurn and burn so many social settings. As a forty-three-year-old childless big-city journalist, who first wed at thirty-five (to a chorus of crazy Jewish *mishpocha* shouting "Hallelujah!"), I'd already established my dual career and feminist credentials. If I'd embarked on a traditional union at twenty-three and had toddlers to take care of, I might not have been able to toil past midnight, crooning along to Bob Dylan's "Blood on the Tracks," guzzling caffeine-free Diet Cokes, preoccupied with passionate literary projects.

I was fortunate that my mother and father were in good health and that my brothers provided five gorgeous grandkids for my parents to kvell over, taking the proverbial "get me grandchildren" pressure off me. If I were the only child of ailing parents, or the mother of drooling munchkins who needed feeding and diaper changes, dropping out would have been more difficult.

Still—even without children, adult dependents, or a full-time office job—I needed a lot of aid. Along with two weekly visits to Dr. Winters, I relied on my literary agent, book editor, housekeeper, and former students toiling as my assistants, along with my understanding husband. I learned to help him help me by expressing *exactly* what I needed. Some days it was "Pick up an extra ream of paper at Staples on your way home." Other days it was a long hug, a foot massage, or for him to visit his mother on Hanukkah solo so I could have six more hours to complete the chapter I was in the middle of.

Not everyone was so understanding. My mother's confidante Betty sent me an invitation for a fancy seventieth birthday party she was throwing my mother in Michigan last June. When I said I couldn't make it, a few ladies in my mom's inner circle left messages implying that a good daughter wouldn't miss such an historic occasion.

My mom meant the world to me. Yet I'd already made reservations for my annual Midwest visit in August, when my work crunch was over. I was horribly conflicted. Until I realized that Betty had planned the party six weeks after my mom's actual birthday—when it was convenient for Betty's schedule and didn't conflict with Betty's summer travel schedule. If it was so essential that I be there, Betty could have called me in advance or made the soiree when I was in the Midwest. Meanwhile I asked my parents, who said it wasn't a problem and they'd actually prefer my husband and I meet them in Florida for their fiftieth anniversary celebration in February, which we did fly in for.

My relief at escaping obligations is tinged with mixed emotions. When my old college roommate Dana asked me to be a bridesmaid at her California weekend wedding extravaganza last spring, I was delighted that Dana was marrying a cute mensch under a chuppah. I was also under pressure to hand in a book and complete a heavy term of teaching. Thus I felt no compulsion to trek to the West Coast to say "Mazel Tov" in person. Besides, I was too old to wear a horrible pink dress and had always hated out-of-town weekend wedding extravaganzas. When I told her that I couldn't be in, or at, her big day, Dana was upset and got off the phone quickly.

I felt like hell. What a lazy, harried, horrible comrade I'd turned out to be! I put myself on a major head trip. Until—miraculously—all that expensive therapy kicked in. I recalled #1) Dana did not fly east for my blessed union eight years ago, #2) I'd been very supportive of Dana's high-powered career and six-figure salary for two decades while my first real book advance just paid off my debts, and #3) It wasn't my job to jump on a plane whenever I was summoned to celebrate landmarks in other people's lives.

Once in a while I felt miserable missing the important milestones of those I loved. More often it was liberating to break the cycle of giant ex-pectations for ongoing generosity. My father and two of my brothers are doctors. Growing up they took care of whoever was ailing in the neigh-borhood while my mother offered TLC, brisket, chicken soup, and potato latkes, to her own four kids, sick relatives, the neighbors, and all the neighborhood children. I memorized Sylvia Plath's "Ariel," eating alone in my pink room. I didn't mind cleaning up after myself, but I didn't want to clear my father's, brothers' and next-door neighbors' plates from the table. "Let them bring their own dirty dishes to the sink!" I once yelled. My mother called me "selfish." I called her "selfless."

Yet what was so wrong with being selfish and devoting yourself to your own work and welfare? That described myriad writers, artists, and entertainers I admired, including Picasso, Gloria Steinem, Bob Dylan, Philip Roth, David Sedaris, Ellen DeGeneres, George Clooney, Maureen Dowd, Annie Leibovitz, and Oprah. Their single-mindedness had won them fame and fortune. I would rather aim for their talent and income bracket and fail than stay home all day, cooking, cleaning, and/or chang-ing diapers.

Not that my mother remained a housewife. After her offspring went to college, this domestic dynamo ran a popular party-planning company. One day, on her way to deliver a blue balloon-and-candy basket for a boy's birthday, I asked why there was also a pink basket next to it. She said "How can I give the boy a present and not bring something for his little sister?" She became famous locally; her phone rang constantly. But needless to say, the kind red-headed Robin Hood of West Bloomfield did not become a billionaire.

I couldn't compete with my mother's maternal prowess, but I could court material success. I turned off the sound of my phone, leaving the answering machine on so I could concentrate. I didn't buy a cell phone because I didn't want to be bothered by anybody else's emergencies. For the first time ever I did not return calls promptly—or at all. I wondered why I'd always felt obliged to get back to everyone who had left a message, including old employers, freelancers seeking the names of my editors, relatives I barely knew. If I didn't return their calls they might think I wasn't nice (God forbid). Or that I was an arrogant businesswoman too preoccupied with her life to be on call to help others. (What a *shanda!*)

My mother used to encourage charitable acts, whispering her rule, "A mitzvah always comes back to you. But that's not why you do it." I tried to be a good person, but I no longer aspired to be a walking mitzvah machine. I was tired of editing dozens of essays by former students daily, as if a professional author's duty was to endlessly serve every wannabe scribe in the country for free.

I once attended the baby shower of a former boss's wife, a woman I barely knew, while I was going through infertility, knowing in advance that it would ruin my Saturday. Another night I attempted to be supportive by catching a playwright pal's sixth Off-Off-Broadway production though I couldn't stand her last five shows. Now I saw that making a few self-mitzvahs wasn't magic. There was a fast formula: fewer minutes for you, more minutes for me. It was crass and calculated, but how freeing to no longer feel the compulsion to placate other artists, friends of friends, and virtual strangers.

Growing up, anybody we knew could stop by, ring our bell, and my mother dropped everything to put out coffee and pound cake. She'd yell, "Susie, come say hi to Lanie and David." I'd drop the book I was reading or turn off the TV show I was enjoying, and rush down the stairs to overeat and be charming on command, like a dancing monkey.

Now I told friends *never* to stop by without calling first because I would not entertain uninvited visitors. When my former writing group colleague Natalie dropped by anyway, I said, "Sorry, it's not a good time.

I'm working. Next time call first." She mumbled that I was "a control freak," as if that was a major insult. "Who should I let control my day? You?" I asked. Not surprisingly Natalie was unhappy and broke, and hadn't been able to publish her own book. Had she merely e-mailed first, I might have met up with her later—and maybe even offered to edit her damn four-hundred-page manuscript. If she needed my advice and expertise, you'd think she could at least adhere to my agenda.

As a one-time cheerleader, straight "A" student, and hungry free-lancer, I used to aim to be a helpful social butterfly. I'd agree to multiple pitch meetings I wasn't paid for. I would lecture at seminars, journalism classes, and panels, flattered I was popular, without asking for a speaking fee, or even a car service so I could avoid taking two buses and a subway to do somebody I'd just met a good deed. I'd allow gangs of comrades to crash on my couch, eat my food, call me in the middle of the night. I bought popcorn, cookies, beer, and wine to have the writing workshop at my place every Tuesday night. I never knew that my husband resented having to go out weekly, that it bothered him when I'd move his coats and jackets to make room in the hall closet, that I was too tired cleaning up at eleven o'clock to hear about his day.

I currently vow to be a miserly misanthropic hermit who does not make room for anybody else, or at least hardly ever. When somebody asks to get together, I say "I'll have to check with Aaron, let me get back to you." It's not that I need my husband's permission. I need to debate whether it's in my best interest. Will it interrupt my afternoon? Will I feel exhausted and resentful later? Will guests get drunk and blow smoke in my face? Will there be too much food that will ruin my low-carb diet? More importantly, does the requester have toxic energy that will eat up my internal amity? If so, no go. I'm saving my strength for me.

It took creativity to come up with excuses to worm my way out of guest lists. Did I lie? You're damn right! Every chance I got. In fairness, I told little white lies, such as "Sorry. I can't. I'm on deadline," rather than hurt a parent by confessing, "I would rather have root canal than drive three hours at nine in the morning to New Jersey for your thirteen-year-old's bat mitzvah service when I've only met your kid once, don't have kids, and have avoided going to temple since I was her age."

In the last twenty-four months I have alienated many acquaintances, like Natalie, who no longer speaks to me. Truthfully it's the unhappy, draining drones who've blown me off, which leads me to believe they're doing me a favor. Other connections were worth fighting for. When I called Dana to apologize for missing her sacred ceremony, she shot back, "I guess this is your payback since I couldn't come to your wedding eight years ago." I reminded her that my career was as important as hers, that I wasn't going to break my book stride when she had two hundred other guests glad to attend. Plus, unlike her, it was the first year since we'd graduated that I was out of debt. I was over being broke and feeling like a failure.

"Oh come on, you've always been a success," she yelled at me. "You were working for the *New Yorker* and writing for the *New York Times* in your twenties."

"I did not feel successful making thirteen thousand dollars a year and not being able to pay my rent without my father's help," I yelled back. "The way you—or anyone else—perceived me has no meaning compared to how I felt!"

Okay, I can see that my sudden shifts were strange to friends who were used to my amiable company and compliance. With cigarettes as a smoke screen, it was easier to spend holidays with my clan and attend fancy functions that made me crazy. I was basically anesthetizing myself to withstand the agony. By middle age I chose to be jagged and erratic, rather than smooth and self-medicating. I did not care what "they" thought. I cared what I thought.

While becoming a workaholic addicted to my laptop, I tried to over-compensate for my new no-show status. I sent more extravagant gifts. (I had seventy long-stemmed red roses delivered to my mother on her real birthday, and despite our conflict, sent Dana and her mate $200 gift coins from Tiffany's.) I spoke on the phone more often, snail-mailed cards and heartfelt letters, e-mailed congratulations, and hosted events on nights and locations that suited me. My worry that I'd lost my standing amid the urban literati turned out to be unfounded. Five hundred people showed up to my book party, more than I'd invited. I should have anticipated the irony: Becoming reclusive made everyone desperately request my presence. Being unavailable was the perfect aphrodisiac. The more I said "Sorry, too busy," the more the world wanted me.

I had been using substances to cope with complex emotions since I was a teenager. So when it came to clean and sober interactions, I had to start over. Instead of going to bars and Italian bistros, I picked readings and literary evenings at bookstores (where nobody smokes, drinks, or overeats). I chatted with cronies while taking long walks or getting manicures, pedicures, and massages. If the ally I invited couldn't afford it, I could now sometimes afford to treat.

Do friends find it odd when I recite such extreme dicta as "I don't do restaurants," "I'm not traveling anywhere this year," "I'm booked solid until September," and "I can only meet for lunch at two o'clock in my neighborhood on Thursday"? Yes. They call me eccentric, inflexible, closed off, kooky, obstinate. Then they ask me for the name of my agent, editor, housekeeper, and/or addiction specialist, and/or wonder if my great husband knows any single guys just like him.

Lately Aaron and I have been much closer. We've gone from making love once a month to rendezvousing several times weekly. So instead of hobnobbing with acquaintances at banal uptown bashes, I'm enmeshed in true intimacy with my partner. I call my parents and brothers often, assuring them of my deep affection and gratitude. Dr. Winters likes me better now, he says, because I'm more real and honest (albeit more rigid and overreactive). Those nearest and dearest to me admire my resolve. My good cheer is so infectious that half of the students in my classes last term had their assignments see print or won internships. I'm more compassionate to underlings, volunteer added hours, and donate more money to the homeless people at the soup kitchen where I teach writing. In fact, I recently edited and sold an anthology of their poems and stories, where all royalties will go back to feed the hungry.

It may always be a struggle to say no to those less needy. Just yesterday, Peter, an important mentor, asked if I'd edit his new manuscript. Panic swept through me. I took deep breaths, waited to return his message. I pulled out my journal and scrawled down the subtext of my annoyance. Peter had published fourteen books, while I was only on my third volume. He had a highbrow editor, well-known agent, many other critics to ask, and lots of cash to offer a ghost editor. Though he'd thanked me in one of his acknowledgment pages, he'd left me out of the last one, even though I'd spent hours helping him. Interesting that he didn't forget to thank those who were paid to enhance his prose. I e-mailed back, "Sorry. I'm on deadline for my new book. But congrats on all your great news."

His response was nice, "No problem. Good luck with all your projects." The "no problem" made me laugh. Little did he know the potential traumas lurking, how hard it was to once again dodge the bullet, or even that he'd fired the weapon. But if there was no harm in asking for help, there was no harm in answering, "Can't do it."

Every time I get my mail and messages, I am a bit rueful noting the favors and festivities I'm planning to avoid like the plague. These days I am more apt to be called an "odd duck" than the most popular person on the planet. Still, losing that title is a small price to pay for sobriety, career fulfillment, marital bliss, and immense happiness.

When Dana thanked me for her lovely Tiffany present, she mentioned an upcoming business trip to Manhattan. She asked if I wanted to spend a July Friday with her. I rarely took off a whole day from work. But, looking at the calendar, I saw that I was giving my agent the new draft of my book that Thursday. Thus the timing was ideal. So was the geography, as Dana was staying at a hotel six blocks from my apartment. We went out to a long lunch and shopping in Soho, catching up on a few years. I won't exaggerate and say it was blissful; it was complicated and chaotic.

She was forty-five minutes late, and wore the wrong shoes for a long downtown stroll in my carless city. We argued about me never visiting L.A. anymore. We debated the unfinished business of my past feelings of inadequacy over my former low salary. She contended that I was always successful. I contended that it was easy for a high-salaried vice president to say so, and that she didn't make a big enough fuss over my recent hardcover.

Though we didn't see eye to eye on everything, it was cleansing to have it out and express anger. It was certainly better than smoking, drinking, or shoving food in my mouth to repress any bubbling hurt that had been brewing. It was fun showing her my apartment and neighborhood, in jeans (not high heels and bridesmaid outfit), convenient for both of us this trip. All in all, it made me remember how smart and strong Dana was, the reasons I'd always liked her, and how fine it felt to really be present, heart and soul, on the rare, right occasions when I did say yes.

Selected Glossary

Abba—Hebrew word for father

Adonai—Hebrew word for God

Am Yisrael—People of Israel

Ashkenazi, Ashkenazic—Jews of European origin

Ba'al Teshuva—A Jew who turns to a religiously observant life

Balabuste—Yiddish term for Jewish housewife

Bar or Bat Mitzvah—Rite of passage in which a Jewish child is called to the Torah and given adult status in the community

Beit Din—Rabbinical court, usually consisting of three rabbis

Beshert—Soulmate; meant to be

Bimah—Platform for public speaking in a Jewish synagogue

Bubbe—Yiddish word for grandmother

Chai—Hebrew word for life

Chuppah—Jewish wedding canopy

Chutzpah—Nerve

Cossack—Peasant in Czarist Russia who sometimes participated in pogroms

Daven, Davened, Davening—Jewish praying

Dayenu—Song sung on Passover, meaning "enough"

Ema—Hebrew word for mother

Eretz Yisrael—Land of Israel

Farchadat—Yiddish word meaning confused, mixed up

Goy, Goyim, Goyish, *Goyishe*—Non-Jews, or something not Jewish

Haggadah—Book containing liturgy for the Passover seder

Halutz, Halutznik—Jewish pioneer in Israel

Hanukkah—Jewish festival of lights

Hasid, Hasidic—Sect of Judaism founded in Poland in the eighteenth
century by Israel Ba'al Shem Tov

Hava Nagilah—Jewish song danced to at weddings and other celebrations

Hekhsher—Marked with a Kosher symbol

Hora—Raucous dancing at happy Jewish occasions, such as weddings

Kenna Hora—Expression for warding off the evil eye

Keppe—Yiddish word for head

Kippah—Jewish head covering

Klezmer—Yiddish-influenced folk music style

Knesset—Israeli Parliament

Kosher—Following Jewish dietary laws; slang for something being Jewish

Kvell, Kvelling—Yiddish term for being full of pride and joy

Kvetch—Complain

Kvitle, Kvitlekh—Small notes with prayers on them

Lashon Ha Ra—Idle gossip

Levite—Member of the tribe of Levi

Lulav—Ritual object used during the holiday of Sukkot

Mazel Tov—Congratulations

Mensch—Yiddish word denoting a good person

Meshugenah—Yiddish word for crazy

Mishna—Oral Jewish law

Mishpocha—Hebrew word for family

Mitzvah—A good deed; commandment

Mizrahi—Sephardic Jew of Middle Eastern origin

Modeh Ani—Jewish prayer recited upon waking

Moshav—Form of communal living in Israel

Musaf—Additional prayer service recited on Shabbat and holidays

Nachas—Familial pride and joy

Ostjuden—Eastern European Jews

Oy, *Oy Vey*—Yiddish phrase of exasperation

Pogrom—Organized massacre of a minority group, especially of Jews

Rabbi, Rebbe—Jewish religious leader

Rebbitzen—The rabbi's wife

Rosh Hashanah—Jewish new year

Satmar—Hasidic sect

Schlep, Schlepper—To carry something burdensome, someone who isn't totally together

Schmaltz—Animal fat; sentimentality

Seder—Ritual meal during Passover

Sephardic, Shephardim—Jews of African, Spanish, and Middle Eastern origin

Shabbat, Shabbos—Jewish Sabbath and day of rest

Shalom—Hebrew word for peace; used to say hello and goodbye

Shalom Bayit—A peaceful home

Shana Tova—A Jewish greeting of Happy New Year used at Rosh Hashanah

Shanda—Scandal

Shaygetz—Non-Jewish man

Shayna Madel—Yiddish term for a pretty girl

Sheitl—A wig worn by traditional Jewish women

Shema—Hebrew word "hear," shorthand for the central prayer in the Jewish liturgy, "Hear O Israel" or *Shema Yisrael*

Shiksa—Non-Jewish woman

Shivah—Jewish mourning period

Shmini Atzeret—Jewish holiday celebrated after the seven days of Sukkot

Shmoneh Esrai—A prayer that is the central component of the thrice-daily prayer service in the Jewish liturgy

Shoah—The Holocaust

Shtetl—Small Jewish village, typically in Eastern Europe

Shtreimel—Fur hat worn by some Hasidic Jews

Shul—Yiddish word for synagogue

Sukkot, Sukkoth—Jewish festival of the harvest and temporary shelter constructed for the holiday

Tachlis—Yiddish word for practicality; getting down to business

Tallis—Jewish prayer shawl

Talmud—Collection of Jewish law and tradition

Tashlich—Ritual performed on Rosh Hashana where bread is cast into water as sins from the past year

Torah—The Hebrew Bible; Hebrew word for the Five Books of Moses: Genesis, Exodus, Leviticus, Numbers, and Deuteronomy

Treyf—Nonkosher food

Tzedakah—Charity

Tzitzit—Ritual fringes worn on undergarments

Yarmulke—Jewish head covering

Yekkes—German Jews

Yenta—A gossip maven

Yeshiva—Jewish religious school

Yichus—Familial lineage

Yom Kippur—Jewish Day of Atonement

Acknowledgments

M Y deepest appreciation goes to the writers who have contributed to and, in essence, constructed this book. It has been a privilege to work with so many smart, funny, honest, and insightful Jewish women. I thank them for the time and effort they put into this anthology, and admire them for their wonderful writing.

Julie Doughty, editor and friend, was my partner through thick and thin on this book. Bright, kind, and blessed with a wicked sense of humor, Julie lovingly guided this project to fruition, and maybe—just maybe—after all the work she's done on Jewish guilt, she'll consider joining the tribe. My thanks also go to the talented people at Dutton and Plume: Brian Tart, Jean Anne Rose, Robert Kempe, Susan Schwartz, Joseph Mills, Trena Keating, Julie Saltman, Neil Gordon, and Erika Kahn.

Betsy Amster, my very nice agent, offered sage counsel and valuable editorial insight. The folks at the Los Angeles bureau of *People* magazine were tolerant of my absences and extremely supportive while I was working on this book, especially Marisa Laudadio, Cecilia Matsumoto, Elizabeth Leonard, Tom Fields-Meyer, and Todd Gold.

The following people offered critical help and advice at various stages of production for this book, for which I am in their debt: Aryeh Cohen, Harron Ellenson, Cathi Hanauer, Emily Hodos, Carolyn Hessel of the National Jewish Book Council, Andrea Grossman of Writer's Bloc, Rob Kutner, Ellen Miller, Elliott Rabin of Makor, Judith Rosenbaum, Daniel Schifrin of the National Foundation for Jewish Culture, Yermiyahu Ahron Taub, Paul Zakrzewski, and Daniella Zax.

I am also indebted to the many friends and family, especially my wonderful parents and siblings, who offered support, encouragement, opinions, and welcome distractions as I edited this book. They are not listed because I know I will inevitably forget someone of critical importance and I can't live with the guilt, but please know how much your help has meant to me.

My husband, Robert, held my hand and cheered me on throughout this endeavor. As always, I am grateful for his great mind and even greater heart. He eases my guilt considerably and enriches my life immeasureably.

Contributors

Elisa Albert received an MFA from Columbia University. Her fiction and nonfiction have appeared in *Washington Square, Response, Pindeldyboz,* and *Body Outlaws: Re-writing the Rules of Body Image and Identity* (Seal Press, 2004). She teaches creative writing in New York City, and is at work on a collection of stories and a novel.

Aimee Bender is the author of *The Girl in the Flammable Skirt* (Doubleday, 1998) and *An Invisible Sign of My Own* (Doubleday, 2000), as well as a new collection of stories, *Willful Creatures* (Doubleday, 2005). Her short fiction has been published in *Granta, GQ, The Paris Review, Harper's, Tin House,* and more, as well as heard on NPR's *This American Life.* She lives in Los Angeles and teaches at USC.

Jennifer Bleyer founded *Heeb* magazine in 2000, and was its editor and publisher until 2003. A journalist who lives in Brooklyn, she has written for the *New York Times, Spin, Salon,* and the *Progressive.* She contributed to the anthologies *Yentl's Revenge* (Seal Press, 2000) and *The Fire This Time* (Anchor, 2004).

Kera Bolonik, a native Chicagoan, has been living in Brooklyn, New York, for more than a decade, and still she speaks with those flat Midwestern "A's." Her writing has appeared in *New York,* the *New York Times, Glamour, Salon, The Nation, Nerve, Slate, Forward, Advocate, Tin House,* and *Bookforum* magazine, among other publications. She is the coauthor of *Frugal Indulgents: How to Cultivate Decadence When Your Age and Salary Are Under 30* (Henry Holt/Owl, 1997).

Rabbi Sharon Brous is the founder and spiritual leader of IKAR, a vibrant, exciting new Jewish spiritual community in Los Angeles that is both traditional and progressive—dedicated to serious study, soulful encounter, and passionate engagement with the world. While studying for the rabbinate, Rabbi Brous studied Conflict Resolution and International Human Rights at Columbia University, and has written numerous articles on the issues of religion, human rights, and human dignity. In 2004, the *Forward* named Rabbi Brous as one of the 50 most influential Jews in the United States, an assertion that truly made her parents kvell.

Baz Dreisinger is a writer and adjunct professor of English and American studies at Queens College, City University of New York. She has written about pop culture and race-related issues for the *New York Times Magazine*, the *Los Angeles Times*, the *New York Observer*, *The Nation*, *Blender*, *Vibe*, and the *Village Voice*. She loves Caribbean culture and noodle kugel, and she holds a PhD in English from Columbia University.

Pearl Gluck went from Borough Park to Brandeis to Budapest and back in search of her great-grandfather's divan, the namesake of her first documentary film, *Divan* (2004; Hungary/USA/Ukraine). *Divan* was developed with the assistance of the Sundance Institute and the support of foundations such as the New York State Council on the Arts and the National Foundation for Jewish Culture. Her award-winning short film, *Great Balls of Fire* (2002; USA), which is a homeless man's response to September 11th, was played and installed worldwide. Gluck received a Fulbright to study Yiddish in Hungary and was an artist in residence at the Paideia Institute in Stockholm. Her work is available and continues to be created through Palinka Pictures, a production company she started for documentary to inspire art and art to inspire community.

Rebecca Goldstein is the author of five novels, including *The Mind-Body Problem* (Random House, 1983), *Mazel* (Viking, 1995), and *Proper-*

ties of Light (Houghton Mifflin, 2000), as well as a book of short stories, *Strange Attractors* (Viking, 1993). She is most recently the author of *Incompleteness: The Proof and Paradox of Kurt Gödel*, which is part of the Norton Series on Great Scientific Discoveries (Norton, 2005). The winner of numerous awards for her fiction and scholarship, including two National Jewish Book Awards and two Whiting awards, one for fiction and one for philosophy, in 1995 she was named a MacArthur Fellow.

Lori Gottlieb is the author of the best-selling memoir *Stick Figure: A Diary of My Former Self* (Simon and Schuster, 2000), an American Library Association "Best Books 2001" selection. A commentator for NPR's *All Things Considered* and singles columnist for the *Jewish Journal of Los Angeles*, her work has appeared in the *New York Times*, the *Los Angeles Times*, *Time*, *People*, *Elle*, *Glamour*, *Redbook*, *Slate*, and *Salon*, among many others. Her personal essays also appear in the anthologies *Scoot Over, Skinny* (Harvest, 2005), and *This Side of Doctoring* (Oxford, 2003). Her next book, a collection of humor essays about dating, will be published by St. Martin's Press. She lives in Los Angeles, where she also writes for television. Her Web site is LoriGottlieb.com.

Lauren Grodstein is the author of the short story collection *The Best of Animals* (Persea, 2002) and the novel *Reproduction is the Flaw of Love* (Dial, 2004.) Her essays, stories, and reviews have appeared in various publications, including *Virgin Fiction 2* (Robweisbach, 1999), *Before and After: Stories from New York* (Norton, 2002), and *The Ontario Review*. A graduate of Columbia's MFA program, Lauren teaches creative writing at Cooper Union. She lives in Brooklyn.

Dara Horn was born in New Jersey in 1977. She is currently a doctoral candidate at Harvard University in comparative literature, focusing on Hebrew and Yiddish, and a visiting professor at Sarah Lawrence College, teaching courses in Jewish literature. Her first novel, *In the Image* (Norton, 2002), received a National Jewish Book Award, the Reform Judaism Prize for Fiction, and the Edward Lewis Wallant Award. Her second novel, *The World to Come,* will be published by Norton in January 2006. She lives with her husband in New York City.

Molly Jong-Fast is the twenty-six-year-old author of *Normal Girl* (Villard, 2001) and *The Sex Doctors in the Basement* (Villard, 2005). She has written for the *New York Times,* the *Times of London, Cosmo, Mademoiselle, Marie Claire,* British *Elle,* and many other newspapers and magazines. She has an MFA from Bennington College. She recently chronicled her wedding for *Modern Bride Magazine.* She lives in New York City with her husband, her child, their cocker spaniel Godzuki, and Pete, the world's fattest cat. Her mother wrote *Fear of Flying,* her grandpa wrote *Spartacus,* and her great-great grandfather was a herring merchant.

Rachel Kadish is the author of the novel *From a Sealed Room* (Putnam, 1998). Her short fiction and essays have appeared in *Story, Zoetrope, Prairie Schooner, Tin House,* and *Bomb,* and have been anthologized in the Pushcart Prize collection and elsewhere. She has won fellowships from the NEA, the Bunting Institute, and the Massachusetts Cultural Council, and was the 2004 Koret Foundation Writer in Residence at Stanford University. Her new novel, titled *Love [sic],* is forthcoming from Houghton Mifflin in 2006. She lives outside Boston.

Jenna Kalinsky earned her MFA at Columbia University in New York, lived for several years in Germany and now lives in Canada, where she teaches writing at the University of Western Ontario, coordinates a community creative writing program and acts as an associate editor for the online magazine *Drunken Boat.* She is a two-time Breadloaf Writers' Conference scholarship recipient and an Eden Mills Literary Festival (in Ontario) poetry prizewinner. She has published fiction, poetry, and nonfiction in *EM Literary,* the *Oklahoma Review, Eleven Bulls, NYC BigCityLit, 12 Magazine,* and *So To Speak.* She is working on a novel and a collection of poetry.

Cynthia Kaplan is the author of a collection of autobiographical essays, *Why I'm Like This: True Stories* (Morrow, 2002), and her work has been published in numerous newspapers, magazines, journals, and anthologies. She has also appeared in many plays, some movies, and a few commercials, but has never been on *Law & Order*. She lives in New York City with her husband and children, and should be handing in her second book any year now.

Binnie Kirshenbaum is the author of two story collections and five novels, including *A Disturbance in One Place* (Fromm, 1994) and *An Almost Perfect Moment* (Ecco, 2004). She is a professor at Columbia University's Graduate School of the Arts, and lives in New York City.

Amy Klein has worked as a reporter, editor, and writer for the last ten years at the *Jerusalem Post*, the *Forward*, and the *Jewish Journal of Los Angeles*, where she is currently the Managing Editor. She is an MFA candidate at Antioch University in Los Angeles.

Daphne Merkin is the author of *Enchantment* (Harcourt, 1986), which won the Edward Lewis Wallant award in 1986 for the best new work of fiction based on a Jewish theme, and *Dreaming of Hitler: Passions & Provocations* (Crown, 1997), a collection of essays that includes the wide-ranging writing she has done for the *New Yorker*, the *New York Times Book Review*, and various other publications. Ms. Merkin lives in New York City with her daughter, Zoë.

Tova Mirvis is the author of two novels, *The Ladies Auxiliary* (Norton, 1999) and *The Outside World* (Knopf, 2004). She has an MFA from the Columbia University School of the Arts. She lives in Boston with her husband and two young children. Her website is TovaMirvis.com.

Gina Nahai is a best-selling novelist and a professor of creative writing at the University of Southern California. Her novels include *Cry of the Peacock* (Crown, 1991), *Moonlight on the Avenue of Faith* (Harcourt, 1999), and *Sunday's Silence* (Harcourt, 2001). She's currently at work on *Dreams of a Caspian Rain*. She is a former consultant for the RAND Corporation, and has researched the politics of pre- and postrevolutionary

Iran for the United States Department of Defense. Gina's novels have been translated into twenty-six languages, and are taught at a number of universities in the United States and abroad. She holds a BA and a Master's degree in International Relations from UCLA, and an MFA in Creative Writing from USC. She has written for the *Los Angeles Times*, the *Chicago Tribune*, the *San Francisco Chronicle*, *Los Angeles* magazine, and the *Jewish Journal of Los Angeles*.

Katie Roiphe is the author of *Still She Haunts Me* (Dial, 2001) and *The Morning After* (Back Bay Book, 1994). Her articles have appeared in the *New York Times*, the *Washington Post*, the *Los Angeles Times*, *Vogue*, *Harper's*, *Esquire*, and *Tin House*, among other places.

Francesca Segrè is the author of the novel *Daughter of the Bride* (Berkley Books, 2006). The novel is based on her personal essay, *Bride and Joy: Walking Mom Down the Aisle,* which was published in the *Washington Post*. The book and the article explore the role-reversal she experienced while acting as the mother of the bride to her own mother. MGM optioned the article for a movie in which Goldie Hawn is to play the mother. Segrè, who has been a TV reporter for ten years, works and lives in Los Angeles. She was born and raised in Austin, Texas.

Wendy Shanker is the author of *The Fat Girl's Guide to Life* (Bloomsbury, 2004). She grew up in Detroit, Michigan, wore velvet knickers to her bat mitzvah, was big into B'nai B'rith Girls in high school, and currently lives in New York City. Wendy is one of *Us Weekly*'s Fashion Police, and has appeared on *The View*, CNN, VH1, and *The Ricki Lake Show*, and hosted a style and shopping show on the Oxygen network. She has also written for *Glamour*, *Shape*, *Cosmopolitan*, *Marie Claire*, *Seventeen*, and MTV. Find out more about Wendy at WendyShanker.com.

Laurie Gwen Shapiro is the author of three adult novels, *The Unexpected Salami* (Algonquin, 1998), *The Matzo Ball Heiress* (Red Dress Ink, 2004), and *The Anglophile* (Red Dress Ink, 2005), and is a new writer for the young adult market. With her brother David Shapiro, she co-directed and co-produced the IFC documentary *Keep the River on Your Right: A Modern Cannibal Tale,* recipient of an Independent Spirit Award. With Sergeant Conor McCourt, she co-produced two HBO/Cinemax documentaries about the illustrious McCourts of Limerick. She lives on the Lower East Side of Manhattan with her husband and daughter. Visit her Web site at LaurieGwenShapiro.com.

Susan Shapiro is the author of *Lighting Up: How I Stopped Smoking, Drinking and Everything Else I Loved in Life Except Sex* (Delacorte, 2004) and *Five Men Who Broke My Heart* (Delta, 2005)—provocative memoirs her mother hates—and editor of *Food for the Soul* (Seabury, 2004). Her work has appeared in the *New York Times, Washington Post, Los Angeles Times, Salon.com, People, Glamour,* and *Jane.* She lives with her (long-suffering) husband in Greenwich Village, where she tells her NYU, New School, and Mediabistro writing students "the first piece you write that your family hates means you've found your voice." Susanshapiro.net is her Web site.

Ayelet Waldman is the author of *Daughter's Keeper* (Sourcebooks, 2003), *The Mommy-Track Mysteries* series (Berkley), and the forthcoming *Love and Other Impossible Pursuits* (Doubleday, 2006). She lives in Berkeley with her husband, Michael Chabon, and their four children. She can be visited on the Web at AyeletWaldman.com.

Rebecca Walker is the author of the international bestseller *Black, White and Jewish: Autobiography of a Shifting Self* (Riverhead Books, 2001), and the editor of *What Makes a Man: 22 Writers Imagine the Future* (Riverhead Books, 2004) and *To Be Real: Telling the Truth and Changing the Face of Feminism* (Anchor/Doubleday, 1995). Her work has appeared in *Harper's, Salon.com, Interview, Essence, SPIN, Glamour,* and *Buddhadharma,* among others, and her essays are widely anthologized. Since giving birth to her son Tenzin, she divides what is left of her time between Berkeley and New York City, and can be visited on the web at RebeccaWalker.com.

Sheryl Zohn has written for a variety of TV shows, including Showtime's *Penn & Teller: Bullshit!*, CNBC's *Dennis Miller*, and Comedy Central's *Straight Plan for the Gay Man*. She also co-wrote the movie musical *'Til Birth Do Us Part* with her favorite collaborator—and favorite husband—Rob Kutner.

About the Editor

Ruth Andrew Ellenson was born in Jerusalem and raised in New York and Los Angeles. She received her MFA from Columbia University, and her writing has appeared in the *Los Angeles Times*, *People*, *Forward*, and *Heeb*. She lives with her husband in California, where she is at work on a novel.